In Cobb's Shadow

IN COBB'S SHADOW

*The Hall of Fame Careers of
Sam Crawford, Harry Heilmann
and Heinie Manush*

Dan D'Addona

McFarland & Company, Inc., Publishers
Jefferson, North Carolina

LIBRARY OF CONGRESS CATALOGUING-IN-PUBLICATION DATA

D'Addona, Dan, 1981–
In Cobb's shadow : the Hall of Fame careers of Sam Crawford,
Harry Heilmann and Heinie Manush / Dan D'Addona.
p.   cm.
Includes bibliographical references and index.

ISBN 978-0-7864-9716-4 (softcover : acid free paper) ∞
ISBN 978-1-4766-2048-0 (ebook)

1. Crawford, Sam, 1880–1968.   2. Heilmann, Harry, 1894–1951.
3. Manush, Heinie, 1901–1971.   4. Baseball players—United States—
Biography.   5. Detroit Tigers (Baseball team)—History.   I. Title.

GV865.A1D24 2015   796.3570922—dc23   [B]   2015030335

BRITISH LIBRARY CATALOGUING DATA ARE AVAILABLE

Front cover: (left to right) Harry Heilmann,
Heinie Manush and Sam Crawford (Library of Congress)

Printed in the United States of America

*McFarland & Company, Inc., Publishers
Box 611, Jefferson, North Carolina 28640
www.mcfarlandpub.com*

For my grandparents.
Their love of the game, the Tigers
and history inspired this book.

TABLE OF CONTENTS

ACKNOWLEDGMENTS

The first big thank you goes out to the families of the players. Without them, I could not have put this together. So a special thanks to Norma Manush, Frank Manush, Sue McCaw, Mark Manush, Dan Heilmann, Harry Heilmann III, and Marguerite Heilmann.

Christine Abma and the entire Herrick District Library staff in Holland, Michigan, for all the help with microfilms every week for two years. The entire staff at the Wahoo Public Library in Nebraska.

A big thank you to Gabriel Schechter, John Horne, Jim Gates, Cassidy Lent and the library and photo staff at the National Baseball Hall of Fame and Museum, as well as Tim Wiles, Jeff Idelson, Bruce Markusen and Brad Horn for their help and support over the years. And a huge thank you to Peggy Steele for giving me a chance to work at the National Baseball Library as a part of the Frank and Peggy Steele internship program.

Thank you to the Wally Pipp, Detroit, Toledo and Don Lund chapters of the Society for American Baseball Research, especially Gary Gillette, Peter Morris, Rich Newhouse, David Fleitz, Brian Borowski, Marc Okkonen, Ron Haas, Jim Lannen, Don Peterson, Rod Nelson and Steve Weingarden, for their excitement and help with the project.

Other SABR members from across the country gave me guidance, research and support, especially Jan Finkel, Rockne Skybyrg, Lyle Spatz, Steve Krevisky, Gary Sarnoff, Dr. Trey Stricker, Leslie Heaphy, Mark Armour and John Thorn.

I would like to thank author Tom Stanton for his support to an up-and-coming writer.

A special thank you to late Hall of Famers Ernie Harwell and George Kell. Both took the time late in their lives to talk with me specifically about Harry Heilmann, the broadcaster.

I would not have been able even to start this project without the loving support of my family. Mom and Dad, thanks for always believing in me. Dave and Matt, thanks for your support and insight. Grandma and Grandpa Hoff and Gramma D, thanks for your inspiration and unwavering support. My daughters, Lena and Mara, you are the wonderful reasons this project took as long as it did, but I would make that trade every time. My cousins, aka Circle of Strength, and the rest of my family, thanks for standing by me. And lastly, to my wife Corene, you endured the ups, the downs, the edits, the frustrations, the revises, the overwhelming times and the final draft. I cannot thank you enough for believing I could do this and supporting me through the entire process. You mean more to me than I can put into words.

PREFACE

Ty Cobb was one of the greatest and most controversial athletes the world has ever known. He was the most dominant hitter ever to play baseball, but is remembered today as a violent player with a dark history of rage and racism. However, during his prime, journalism wasn't the same as it is today, and many of his infamous deeds were swept under the rug. Fans during the Dead Ball Era (1900–1920) knew Cobb as the greatest of all time, and today's fans still regard him as one of the elite but also one of baseball's black marks. With his outstanding play on the field and his intense personality, Cobb cast a pretty big shadow over his teammates, and even the game itself, during his playing days. His shadow left many other stars of his era, especially on his own team, forgotten.

In Cobb's Shadow examines the careers of the three players most overshadowed by playing on the Detroit Tigers with Cobb—"Wahoo" Sam Crawford, Harry Heilmann and Heinie Manush. All three had careers strong enough to reach the Baseball Hall of Fame, but few fans—even Tigers fans—remember much about the trio of outfielders. Fans just know that their last names are on the brick wall in the right-center field bleachers of Comerica Park as Detroit Hall of Famers. The Tigers honored them by putting their names up in right field, but a century later, Ty Cobb still casts a shadow with his statue located prominently in the park. Cobb and five others (Al Kaline, Hal Newhouser, Hank Greenberg, Charlie Gehringer, and Willie Horton) have large plaques explaining their accomplishments. However, the players whose names appear on the wall in right field: Crawford, Heilmann, and Manush, along with Mickey Cochrane, Hughie Jennings and George Kell, have their memories left to the imagination of most fans. With the exception of Kell, each was a teammate of Cobb at one point, and each player was overshadowed by him. But as far as lasting legacies, Crawford, Heilmann and Manush stand most in the shadow.

Crawford was the biggest slugger in the history of the game until Babe Ruth showed up. While home runs were rare in his day, real power was measured by doubles and triples. Some parks didn't have outfield fences, so the farther batters hit the ball, the more bases they would accumulate. Crawford was so dominant, he still holds the record for most triples in a career with 309. Home runs get sluggers remembered, but since Crawford played before home runs were prevalent, he is forgotten whenever power hitters are talked about. Historian and statistician Bill James calculated in his *Historical Baseball Abstract* that if Crawford had played in Ruth's era, he would have hit 494 home runs (he had 97) and knocked in 1,931 runs (he had 1,525). Those marks would have put Crawford second only to Ruth at the time of his retirement. Basically, if home runs were part of the game during his career, Crawford may have been the first ever to reach 500. When that possible total is added to his .309 career batting average, he would have been remembered with the greats of all time. Instead, he was even left off the top 100 players of the century when Major League Baseball released its All-Century Team in 1999.

Crawford is also the all-time leader in inside-the-park home runs, which attests to his foot speed and distance hitting.

Heilmann was Cobb's teammate during the second decade of Cobb's career and was one of the best right-handed hitters in baseball history, finishing his career with a .342 average. He won four batting titles and eclipsed the .400 mark in 1923. Older Tigers fans may remember him as a broadcaster, but mostly his deeds on the field are forgotten. He made the All-Century Team's top 100 players, fortunately, considering his average is still tenth-best all-time and second-best among right-handed hitters.

Manush played with both Cobb and Heilmann in the same outfield for a few seasons and was doubly overshadowed. He finished his career with a .330 average and won the batting title in 1924. Manush played his first five seasons with the Tigers, then bounced around to five more teams during his career, mostly the St. Louis Browns and Washington Senators—two teams that are no longer around and therefore have no fan base. Manush entered the Hall of Fame as a Tiger, but most Detroit fans have never heard of him.

The intention with this book is to remind people how great this trio of Hall of Famers was. Sam Crawford, Harry Heilmann and Heinie Manush deserve to be remembered as baseball legends, but played with a legend so big that they could never escape Cobb's shadow.

❖ *Part I: Sam Crawford* ❖

1. WAHOO

Wahoo, Nebraska, is a quaint little town of fewer than 4,000 about 30 miles outside Omaha. Though it has kept up with the times, Wahoo isn't much different than it was when it produced one of the greatest sluggers in the history of baseball.

Samuel Earl Crawford was born on April 18, 1880, as Earl Lee Crawford, according to his birth certificate. He was born at his family's home, 959 Orange Street in Wahoo, Nebraska, to Stephen Orlando Crawford and Ellen "Nellie" (Blanchard) Crawford. Stephen was born in Vermont and was a Civil War veteran who owned a general store in town. Stephen was of Scottish descent and Ellen, born in Iowa, was Irish. Crawford had six siblings, though one brother died as an infant. Sam had three brothers, Stephen, Willie and Neil, and two sisters, Tracy and Zadia. Sam's grandparents, David and Margaret Crawford, emigrated from Scotland around 1858.[1]

Crawford, who ended his schooling after seventh grade, began playing baseball at an early age. He tried other sports and was a part of two state champion football teams, but baseball was always his passion.

"Well, I played ball all the time as a kid, you know," Crawford said. "I always loved it. I grew up in Wahoo, Nebraska. 'Wahoo Sam.' I insisted they put that on my plaque at the Hall of Fame. That's my home town, and I'm proud of it. That was a long time ago. My dad ran a general store, just a little country store where they sold everything."[2]

When Sam wasn't helping at the store, he was playing baseball.

In those days baseball was a big thing in those little towns. The kids would be playing ball all the time. Nowadays basketball and football seem to be as popular among kids as baseball, maybe more so, but not then. And we didn't have radio, you know, or television, or automobiles. I guess, when you come to think of it, we spent most of our childhood playing ball. Heck, we used to make our own baseballs. All the kids would gather string and yarn and we'd get hold of a little rubber ball for the center. Then we'd get our mothers to sew a cover on the ball to hold it all together. We didn't use tape to tape up the outside, like kids did ten or 20 years later. We didn't see much tape in those days, about 1890 or so. Of course, they had tape then, electrical tape, but not much.[3]

Of course, as much as Crawford might have wanted to, he couldn't play baseball around the clock. But he found ways to keep himself busy. Wahoo barber Sam Killian took an interest in Crawford. He had caught Sam smoking as a teen and offered to buy him a new suit if he quit smoking. "[I] accepted his offer and never smoked again for fifty years,"[4] Crawford told the *Lincoln Sunday Journal and Star*. Killian also let Crawford run the shoeshine stand in the barber shop. That is where Wahoo Sam learned the barber trade, something he might have done for a living had he not been so good at baseball. Working in town led to a lot of interesting sights for Sam. "I can remember very well the first electric lights in Wahoo, on the street corner. Just one loop of wire, kind of reddish. We used to go down to the corner and watch this light go on. That was a big deal. Then we'd go over to the powerhouse, where the dynamos were, and see where they made the electricity. After that came the arc lights, with the carbons coming together. That was the next step. But the first ones were just one loop of wire in the bulb, and they gave kind of a reddish glow."[5]

Little did Sam know that despite seeing the first electrical bulbs in town, he would be around until 1968, living through two world wars. He saw the Model-T become a sports car, the start of the highway system, the rise of the telephone and television. But none of that was around in Wahoo then, just baseball. But a ball was hard to find. It was all about having fun, yet the competition was there. As Crawford and his classmates got older, they hoped to make the town team.

> Of course, there were regular baseballs made back then. We'd call them league balls. But we couldn't afford to buy them, not us kids. That was for the men to play with. For bats we'd find some broken bat and nail it up, or sometimes even make our own. Every town had its own team in those days. I remember when I made my first baseball trip. A bunch of us from around Wahoo, all between sixteen and eighteen years old, made a trip overland in a wagon drawn by a team of horses. One of the boys got his father to let us take the wagon. It was a lumber wagon, with four wheels, the kind they used to haul the grain to the elevator, and was pulled by a team of two horses. It had room to seat all of us—I think there were 11 or 12 of us—and we just started out and went from town to town, playing their teams.
>
> One of the boys was a cornet player, and when we'd come to a town he'd whip out that cornet and sound off. People would all come out to see what was going on, and we'd announce that we were the Wahoo team and were ready for a ball game. Every little town out there on the prairie had its own ball team and ball grounds, and we challenged them all. We didn't have any uniforms or anything, just baseball shoes maybe, but we had a manager. I pitched and played the outfield both.
>
> It wasn't easy to win those games, as you can imagine. Each of those towns had its own umpire, so you really had to go some to win. We played Freemont, and Dodge, and West Point, and lots of others in and around Nebraska. Challenged them all. Did pretty well, too.
>
> We were gone three or four weeks. Lived on bread and beefsteak the whole time. We'd take up a collection at the games—pass the hat, you know—and that paid our expenses. Or some of them, anyway. One of the boys was the cook, but all he could cook was round steak. We'd get 12 pounds for a dollar and have a feast. We'd drive along the country roads, and if we came to a stream, we'd go swimming; if we came to an apple orchard, we'd fill up on apples. We'd sleep anywhere. Sometimes in a tent, lots of times on the ground, out in the open. If we were near some fairgrounds, we'd sleep in there. If we were near a barn, well....
>
> That tour led to my getting started in professional baseball. We beat the West Point team, and after the tour was over I got a letter from the manager at West Point, Nebraska, asking if I wanted to play with them. He said they'll pay me, or at least get me a job. I was apprenticing to be a barber at the time. So I went up there, and there I met a fellow from Omaha who had been with Chatham in the Canadian League. His name was Johnny McElvaine. He was going back the next season and wanted me to go along with him. So Johnny wrote the manager of the Chatham team and told him about me, and they sent back transportation money for both of us. That was in 1899. I was only nineteen at the time.[6]

Writer F. C. Lane wrote an article about Crawford's start in professional baseball in *Baseball Magazine*:

Sam, be it understood, had been associated with the town team of his native burg for some time and while considered a great slugger by his fellow-citizens, had never given special thought to the prospects of a career on the diamond. In short he had never even played a game of semi-pro ball for money until, in the season of 1897, he started in as a pitcher and outfielder with West Point, Nebraska. Sam had tremendous throwing speed and enormous strength. From his muscular build it might have been conjectured that he would shine in the pitcher's box. But fate ordained that the more humble role of outfielder, which he played merely to fill in when he was not officiating in the box, should be the role that he was to assume in the activities of later life. And whatever he might have become as a pitcher—which is, of course, but pure conjecture—there is no doubt of the talents which he has revealed as an outfielder, for he has for years been rated as one of the three or four best outer gardeners in the whole range of major league talent.

Sam's initial performance in 1897 was not encouraging from a monetary standpoint.... Sam Crawford is willing to pastime in a uniform for a daily wage of $1.17—yes, indeed.

Sam's season, while not a particularly brilliant one from the financial standpoint, had produced one result. It had made him dissatisfied with the labors of the barber shop and aroused in his mind the determination to proceed with his baseball career. He continued in the barber shop through the winter of 1897, but the following summer he said good bye to the swivel chair for good. That is to say, of course, that any subsequent acquaintance he may have had with the chair was solely in the capacity of customer.

1898 might have been supposed to be a better year for the budding ball player than his previous experience, but it wasn't. He was unfortunate in becoming involved with a failing venture. He joined the club at Wymore, Nebraska, but the club found the sledding a little too difficult and disbanded early in the season. A mid-season shift from club to club is about as undesirable as changing from one lifeboat to another in mid-ocean. For a time no job offered on the horizon, but at length he secured a berth with another miniature team, this time with the town of Superior.[7]

On May 10, 1899, Crawford, now 6 feet tall, made his professional debut with Chatham, Ontario, of the Canadian League. He started his career off, fittingly, with a triple off a pitcher named Bradford of the Hamilton team. It wasn't the only triple of his career. In fact, Crawford would become synonymous with the triple. In Chatham, he also showed his youth, making an error in the first game, and Chatham lost, 3–2. After 43 games and a .370 average—including 12 triples—he was called up to Grand Rapids, Michigan, of the Western League. It was looking more and more like baseball was going to be a career for the young slugger, something he wasn't always so sure about.

Yeah, I was going to be a barber, but then baseball came along, and I never went back to barbering. I was learning the trade the hard way, there in Wahoo. And I do mean the hard way. Cleaning cuspidors, and washing windows, and mopping the floor. Then sometimes they'd let me lather somebody and get them ready for the real barber. And sometimes a tramp would come through and want a haircut, and I could practice on him. That's the way we learned in those days. That was a tough way to make a living. Stand on your feet from seven in the morning to ten or eleven o'clock on a Saturday night. Saturday was the big haircutting day. All the farmers would come in then, hay in their hair and all. We used to give a haircut and a shave and a shampoo for thirty-five cents. Ten cents for a shave, twenty-five for a haircut, and they'd throw in the shampoo. Now a haircut alone costs two dollars. Looks like the same old quarter haircut to me. So when I got this chance to play professional ball, I didn't think twice about it. At Chatham I got $65 a month, plus board. That was pretty good. A dollar was a dollar in those days, you know. That Canadian League was just a little six-club league. Folded up about July. From there I was sold to Grand Rapids in the Western League, where I played with Rube Waddell, and in September they sold me to Cincinnati in the National League. All three leagues in one year, and I hit over .300 in all of them. So there I was, in 1898 touring Nebraska with the Wahoo team in a wagon, and in 1899 playing in the Big Leagues with the Cincinnati Reds.[8]

Crawford made his debut in Grand Rapids, Michigan, on July 8, 1899, and went 1-for-4 for the Prodigals. He took off from there, hitting .334, including 21 multi-hit games. He contributed a lot to the team, scoring 37 runs in the final 48 games of the season. His best game was July 29 against Kansas City where he was 4-for-6 with a double, a triple and two runs scored.

It was an adventure playing with star pitcher Rube Waddell, who was a volunteer fire-fighter, as the major leagues would find out soon. "Baseball was truly a game to Rube, nothing more. Putting out a fire was serious business. Baseball was just fun. He would turn cartwheels, walk on his hands, chat and joke with the fans, make odd noises. He would still run into the stands occasionally and have someone cut a small good luck piece off his red underwear. He used to pour ice water on his arm before a game, claiming that if he didn't he'd throw so hard he'd burn up the catcher's mitt. He was serious about that. You never knew what Rube was going to do next, and neither did Rube. Loftus didn't mind—with the way Rube was pitching, how could he? The opposition would join in the zaniness, too. Some thought they were swept up in the fun and force of personality. Sam Crawford had a different slant on it. 'He was always laughing out there on the mound.... The other side tried to keep him in good humor, even if he was striking them all out. They figured he was tough enough to hit against when he was happy; get him mad and there was no telling.... If ... he'd really bear down ... you wouldn't have a chance. Not a chance.'"[9]

From Grandville, Kentwood, Walker, Cutlerville, Jamestown, Holland, and Wyoming (Michigan), from all over Western Michigan folks turned out by the thousands to see the Prodigals. The team was so-so though Sam Crawford began to hit like a fiend (he batted over .400 that summer). On August 1, the Prodigals were in third place, 45–38, a half-game ahead of Detroit. Rube's record was 25–6.[10]

Crawford finished with 87 hits. On August 1, 1899, he slammed a double while batting third and playing left field against, of all teams, Detroit, in an 8–5 loss. His second day was even better as he scattered three singles. "On September 9, Sam Crawford was gone. His spectacular line-drive hitting won him a contract with the Cincinnati Reds. There he began a 19-year career in the big leagues. Rube would see him again.... Rube was slated to pitch on the 10th, but didn't show. He hadn't gone on another toot. He had simply gone; he didn't even say good-bye to Loftus. He had actually left with Sam Crawford. While Crawford stayed in Cincinnati, Rube met the Louisville Colonels there en route to a game in Baltimore. Someone had persuaded [Pittsburgh manager] Fred Clarke to give the 30-game-winning 'big slob' another look."[11] Two of the most dominant players of the first decade of the new century were on their way.

2. BOTH BIG LEAGUES

As the 1899 National League season began to wind down, Sam Crawford's career was winding up. On Sunday, September 10, 1899, Crawford made his major league debut for Cincinnati. Crawford batted fourth and played left field against Cleveland. He went 2-for-4 with a run scored in a 10–2 rout of Cleveland pitcher Harry Colliflower. It was the first game of a doubleheader, but not the traditional kind. Both Cleveland and Louisville played consecutive games in Cincinnati. The Reds beat Louisville, 8–7. Future Hall of Fame catcher Buck Ewing was the manager of the Reds, and the team boasted two more future Hall of Famers—second baseman Bid McPhee and first baseman Jake Beckley—at the time of Crawford's arrival.

Crawford quickly learned that the public viewed baseball players much differently than people inside the game did, despite living a clean lifestyle. Crawford said, "Baseball players were considered pretty crude. We couldn't get into the best hotels. And when we did get into a good hotel, they wouldn't boast about having us. They would shove us way back in the corner of the dining room so we wouldn't be so conspicuous."[1]

Baseball was continuing to gain more and more attention, making players more conspicuous, especially as the rise of an upstart American League came into play. Players began to jump to the new league formed by Ban Johnson. Crawford followed suit, but not right away.

He left Cincinnati reluctantly. It will be remembered that in 1900 the American League began, in a small way, to launch out on its career of expansion. But 1901 found the war in full sway and most of the players in the National League who were of major reputation, firmly ensconced in the pay roll of the younger circuit. Crawford, however, was not one of these. With all the glamour of larger salaries he remained true to his club. And he consented to join the Detroit team only when in his own mind the American League was an assured success and the need of a settlement between the leagues a crying necessity of baseball. "It appeared to me," says Crawford, "that the cause of the National League in its effort to dominate the situation was a lost cause. I stuck to them longer than almost any other ball player, but at the end I could see no reason why I should compromise my own future and at the same time be powerless to further the interests of my employers. The ball player is not as greedy as some people think. But the ball player is not a fool. And he will not knowingly relinquish several thousand dollars when nothing good to anyone will result from this act. The policy of sticking to the ship is the only policy. But that doesn't mean that you have got to stay aboard and go down with a scuttled craft when the outlook is hopeless. That was my position on the American League situation. I remained with my employers as long as there was any prospect of their succeeding even at a considerable financial sacrifice to myself. When it seemed to me to be a certainty that further resistance was useless I saw no reason why I should jeopardize my own interests any further."[2]

Crawford had offers in 1901 and 1902 once the American League became a major league, but continued to play for the Reds. In four seasons in Cincinnati, Crawford batted .312 with 60 triples. In 1903, Crawford finally made the move to the American League and the Detroit Tigers. It would be a fitting bond that would last for 15 years. Meanwhile, Crawford entered another long-lasting bond in 1901, marrying Ada Lattin in Omaha, Nebraska. She had lived in Wahoo since 1894. They had two children, Virginia and Sam Jr.

After a strong start to his major league career, Sam Crawford was looking to make his mark in the American League, especially after signing a lucrative $3,500 offer from the Detroit Tigers. It wasn't going to be an easy transition. In addition to getting to know a new set of teammates, Crawford would have to learn about the pitchers of the new league, as well as the hitters when he was in the outfield.

Crawford got a rude awakening in his American League debut on April 22, 1903, though the Detroit crowd cheered him well. The Tigers faced Cleveland, and Crawford had to face future Hall of Fame pitcher Addie Joss, perhaps the greatest pitcher in the American League's first decade. The American League was full of future Hall of Fame hurlers during the first decade of the century, and Crawford fared about as well as any hitter facing Joss for the first time. He went 0-for-3, but the Tigers rallied behind pitcher George Mullin to beat Joss and the Indians, 4–2. While Crawford didn't manage a hit, his sacrifice fly knocked in what turned out to be the winning run. The Tigers won the next game, 11–1, without much help from Wahoo Sam, who was 0-for-4. It was frustrating for Crawford, who was expected to be the big bat in the Detroit lineup. He wouldn't go a third game without getting his first hit as a Tiger.

"Samuel came with a reputation as a batsman, and had been sorrowing for three days over his failure to meet the ball safely," the *Detroit Free Press* said.

There is really no cause for this on the part of the left fielder, for no one doubts that he will be there when his time comes. Moreover, his work in bringing in the winning run of opening day is gratefully remembered by several thousand fans. Winning runs are his long suit to date, for it was he who made the tally that told yesterday. It was in the fourth inning, with one man out. One of Moore's benders just suited the Nebraska slugger, and he flogged it far over the head of [Harry] Bay and the roped-off crowd that stood between the fielder and the club house. It was a three-base hit at least. The rules held it to a double.... Kid Elberfield came to the rescue,

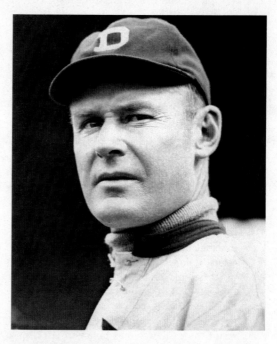

Sam Crawford joined the Detroit Tigers in 1903 after beginning his major league career with the Cincinnati Reds in the National League. Crawford was one of the most prominent stars to jump from the National League to the American League (National Baseball Hall of Fame Library, Cooperstown, New York).

however, pushing Crawford over the plate by a wicked drive that tagged the first sack as it went whizzing down to right field. That run won the game.[3]

Slamming a double for his first American League hit was all Crawford needed to get his bat going. Wahoo Sam had his first multi-hit game the following day, in the series opener against Chicago on April 27. He singled and scored in the eighth inning to cap a three-hit game in an 8–1 victory over the White Sox. Things were looking up for Crawford and the Tigers, who started the season 4–0. Crawford had two more hits the following day, but the Tigers dropped their first game of the season, a 6–4 loss to Roy Patterson of the White Sox.

The Tigers got back on track the next day as Wild Bill Donovan threw a gem and the Tigers pounded Davey Dunkle in a 10–1 victory. Crawford had a single and tripled home a run in the third inning. It was his first three-bagger as a Tiger. There would be many more to come. The White Sox closed out the four-game series with a 5–1 victory over the Tigers. Wahoo Sam had his fourth consecutive multi-hit game, but the rest of the Tigers couldn't get their bats going against Patsy Flaherty.

Crawford's first road trip as a member of the Tigers began in St. Louis, where he and his Detroit teammates would play a quick, two-game series. Crawford's multi-hit streak ended when he managed just one hit in a 5–1 victory against Browns ace Ed Siever, who had started his career with the Tigers and would return to Detroit after two years in St. Louis. Crawford's hitting streak continued with a 1-for-3 performance in the second game, but the Tigers lost, 3–1. Detroit would face the White Sox again, after only two days of playing another team. Crawford would make his first appearance in Detroit as an American Leaguer. After tagging Flaherty for two hits on May 1, Crawford slapped three against him three days later in Chicago. But the White Sox roughed up Donovan and won, 6–5. The loss dropped the Tigers to 6–4 and out of first place for the first time in the young season. The White Sox took over the top spot in the standings at 7–3. The White Sox won the next two games, 8–1 and 10–9, to build their lead after sweeping the Tigers. In the final game of the series, Crawford went hitless, snapping his hitting streak at nine games.

Detroit headed to Cleveland, where things didn't get much better. The Indians took three of four from the Tigers, who returned home after losing six of seven. The New York Highlanders, who later became the Yankees, came to Detroit on May 11 and took the first two games of the series. Crawford was hitless in the first game before managing one hit off future Hall of Famer Jack Chesbro.

The Tigers had lost eight of nine and were in a tailspin. They took their frustrations out on New York pitcher Lewis "Snake" Wiltse on May 13. Crawford led the charge with his first four-hit game while wearing the Old English D. He peppered Wiltse with four singles and scored twice to lead the Tigers to a 7–1 victory, as Donovan held the Highlanders in check. Crawford and the Tigers didn't let up in the fourth game of the series either. Three more singles and two runs by Crawford helped the Tigers win, 9–6.

Crawford didn't have another multi-hit game the following day against Boston, but he made his one hit count. He slammed his first Tigers home run against Tom Hughes in the first inning to lead the Tigers to victory, 8–6. After the losing streak, the Tigers had finally climbed their way over .500 at 11–10. They were quickly put back to .500 by Cy Young, who beat George Mullin 9–6 on May 16. Crawford managed two hits in his first appearance against Young, who would go on to become baseball's all-time wins leader with 511.

Crawford would get his first opportunity against another future Hall of Famer next as Philadelphia came to town, following Detroit's series split with the Red Sox. Left-hander Eddie Plank started the first game for the Athletics and stymied Crawford but not the rest of the Tigers in a 3–1 win for Detroit. Crawford went hitless against "Gettysburg Eddie," who would become Wahoo Sam's nemesis for the rest of his career. It was a friendly rivalry, with no ill feelings, but a rivalry nonetheless. Sometimes Crawford got the best of Plank and sometimes Plank was the victor. But the rivalry would take off to a higher level when both the Tigers and Athletics became perennial contenders for the American League pennant, beginning in 1907.

For the first time in his career, Crawford would face future Hall of Famer pitchers back-to-back. Albert "Chief" Bender was Philadelphia's No. 2 starter, and Crawford's bat woke up with two hits in a 5–3 victory. It wouldn't be the last time Crawford would face Hall of Famers two games in a row. It would happen many times when the Tigers faced Philadelphia over the next decade.

The Tigers took two of three from Washington before St. Louis came to town on May 26. Crawford drove a "Wahoo special" (a triple) off three-time 20-game winner Jack Powell in a 3–0 Tigers victory. Crawford powered two more triples in the next five games, but unfortunately for the Tigers, after winning the first game of the series with the Browns, St. Louis took the next six games, which dropped the Tigers to 17–19.

The Tigers were having their problems off the field, too. Kid Elberfield had been in several shouting matches with manager Ed Barrow. Barrow, known as "The Bulldog," would go on to become the general manager of the Yankees and build a dynasty that would later see New York win five straight World Series championships. Barrow never backed down from a fight, verbal or physical, and Elberfield apparently didn't either. Elberfield was sick of Barrow and played a game in the outlaw California League, something strictly against club and major league rules. "Elberfield went on record yesterday as positively refusing to wear a Detroit uniform during the incumbency of Barrow, and also said he would not consent to figure in any trade with any other club unless his fine is remitted," the *Detroit Free Press* reported on June 1. Then the trade rumors started to fly, and Sam Crawford's name came into the mix. "With the suspension of the player less than a day old, the Cincinnati National club came looking for him. This team yesterday made an offer to the Detroit club that involved the transfer of Elberfield and Sam Crawford to the Reds."[4]

Now, Crawford had just left Cincinnati and was enjoying the American League. However, if a trade was ever in the works, going back to a familiar team and city would have been a comfortable choice. The Tigers made the best choice and kept Crawford, who would be the cornerstone of three straight pennants, 1907–1909, and go on to be one of the greatest players in baseball history.

Despite not giving up their best players, it was a horrible way to end a homestand, and the Tigers went on the road to Philadelphia on a low note. Crawford helped the Tigers to a 6–4 win in the first game against the Athletics on June 4, but the Tigers faced back-to-back future Hall of Famers in the next two games, this time Crawford's old teammate Rube Waddell, then Eddie Plank. Wahoo Sam managed a pair of hits off his old teammate and one off Plank but the Tigers lost two close ones, 5–4 and 3–2.

Crawford was known as a slugger, but he had great speed, too. He stole 366 bases in his career and started to show it now for the Tigers. He stole two bases after getting two singles against Boston on June 9, part of a three-game sweep by the Tigers. But just as Detroit thought it was putting it all together, the season unraveled quickly, leaving the Tigers scratching their heads.

After sweeping the Red Sox, the Tigers lost four in a row and dropped to seventh place at 20–26. If that wasn't enough, they faced four legends in a span of six games. On June 23, Cy Young shut out the Tigers in a great pitchers' duel to beat Wild Bill Donovan, 1–0. Two days later, Eddie Plank hung on to beat the Tigers, 3–2, in ten innings. "Gettysburg Eddie" went the distance despite allowing two singles and a triple to Crawford. Two days later, Donovan found himself in another duel, this time with Rube Waddell. Donovan emerged the victor, topping the Athletics, 3–1. But Chief Bender beat the Tigers, 7–3, the next day and the Tigers remained close to the cellar in seventh place.

Detroit showed some signs of strength. After managing a split with Philadelphia at Bennett Park despite facing three future Hall of Famers, the Tigers beat Washington three out of four before hitting the road again. But again, it was to Philadelphia. On the Fourth of July, the Tigers and Athletics played a doubleheader, as was tradition for the holiday. Eddie Plank allowed two hits to Crawford but edged George Kitson, 4–2, in the opener. Crawford continued to hit in the second game, tagging Waddell for two hits. With Donovan pitching, he again topped Waddell, who had left Louisville, 5–3. Philadelphia manager Connie Mack sent Waddell to the mound again the next game, after an off-day, and Waddell edged George Mullin, 6–5. The Tigers won the final game of the series, beating Andy Coakley, 8–7. The Tigers were happy to pull out the victory and even happier to be getting out of Philadelphia, which never seemed like the City of Brotherly Love to Tigers fans.

The Tigers reached the nation's capital on July 8 and closed their road trip by taking three of four from the Senators. The Tigers then went to New York on such a high that they beat future Hall of Famer Jack Chesbro, 4–3, on July 13 with Donovan again earning the victory and Crawford again hitting the legends well. He had two singles as the Tigers returned to .500 (33–33) for the first time since May 30, when they were 17–17. The Tigers took two of the next three against New York to reach fourth place. At 35–34, it was the first winning record for Detroit since they were 17–16.

Detroit lost again, 5–3, to Boston on July 18, despite Crawford slapping three hits, including a triple, against Cy Young. It was one of Crawford's best games of his early career, but without another hitter to put the pressure on the opposing pitchers, Crawford could hit all he wanted, but would be left on base much of the time. That would all change when a youngster from Georgia joined the team a couple of years later. But in 1903, Crawford was basically alone. He went 5-for-5 with a double and triple against New York's Jesse Tannehill on August 16, the most hits any Tiger got in a game all season.

The Tigers hovered around .500 the rest of the season before falling to 65–71 to end the season in fifth place. Boston won the pennant at 91–47 and won the first-ever World Series by beating Pittsburgh. The Tigers needed to take a few steps before they could contend for this new invention known then as the World's Series. It wouldn't come the following year, but it seemed the Tigers were on the right track. They just needed a little help.

Unfortunately for the Tigers, that help was a year away. Tyrus Raymond Cobb was a rookie at Detroit's spring training in 1904, though he wouldn't make the big league club for another year. He would become one of the most intense competitors the game has ever known, but was still a kid in 1904, just 18 years old. He was eager to learn and make himself better.

Cobb stayed anchored on the bench. That didn't stop him from closely watching Detroit's rangy center fielder, a left-hander like himself—Wahoo Sam Crawford.... Cobb saw Crawford, a .322 batting star in the previous season, leisurely trot to first base after drawing a base on balls, then suddenly switch into high gear and race for second. The Tourists [Augusta] were caught napping. While they scrambled to nail Crawford at second, where he threw up a broad cloud of dust, a Tiger runner who had seconds earlier wandered down the line from third base sped home to score by inches. Cobb stored away that delayed, closely timed play for future use.

He noted, too, that while at bat Crawford seemed to be sneaking peeks at the mitt of the Augusta catcher. Was he stealing the catcher's finger signs to the pitcher? It looked that way to Cobb, although he had never seen this trick. In the outfield, on a wallop heading for the fence, Crawford drifted under the ball, leaped at the exact right moment, and picked the chance off the boards, making the play look easy.

After the Tourists were beaten, Cobb hesitantly walked up to the future Hall of Famer Crawford to say, "That was a great catch, Mr. Crawford. What's the best way to judge long fly balls?" Crawford didn't mind talking about his specialty. While giving the rawboned boy his first big-league coaching, he also offered the first friendly words that Cobb had heard recently. Wahoo was a town barber in the offseason and had a wheat-belt twang, and Cobb's speech was filled with "cain't" for "can't," "ah" for "I," and "yuh" for "you." Still, they understood each other. Crawford said, "You go [on flies] by the sound of the bat. A sound like a gun going off means the ball's hit hard.... You start back in a big hurry. Use the crossover step, left or right, on the getaway. Run on the balls of your feet.... Look over your shoulder to tell where the ball's headed, so's you run under it.... Don't do any backpedaling, that gets you nowhere." He went on, "Use both hands whenever you can.... If you get a real good jump on a ball hit to your front, be moving forward on the catch so as to make a stronger throw." Liking Cobb's concentrated interest, the loquacious Wahoo passed on other tips: "Make up your mind in advance to what base you'll throw.... Throw on one hop to the bag, not on the fly.... Before a road game bounce a ball off the fence in different places, testing for force and direction of the rebound."

Cobb wanted to hear more. "Hell, I can't gab all day," said Wahoo. "Break in a backup glove or two in case your number-one leather is ripped." Cobb didn't admit that he could barely afford one old glove.

Cobb was encouraged to show Wahoo his own particular glove. As an experiment, he had cut the leather out of the palm to expose raw flesh, so that any catch essentially was a bare-hander. Crawford grinned, saying, "I did that as a kid—to keep balls from sliding off the leather. No more, though."

"It works for me," said Cobb.

"Then keep it until you can't stand the blood it'll draw," said Wahoo. Then he admonished, "Don't drink on game days."

Trying not to stammer—one of the holdover curses of his boyhood—Cobb thanked Crawford before going off to contemplate what he had learned. Some of it was basic. But at least half of what he had heard was new to him. He would always remember Crawford's kindness.[5]

Crawford didn't start off on the right track in 1904. After five games, he sustained a boil on his throwing arm, forcing him out of the lineup on April 20. Without a strong-hitting outfielder on the bench, Tigers manager Hughie Jennings started pitcher Wild Bill Donovan in right field. Crawford would miss the next seven games and the Tigers opened the season 6–6.

Crawford returned to the lineup on May 2 and hit a double and a triple to lead the Tigers to a 6–2 victory over Cleveland. But the Tigers would soon lose eight straight games, including a 15-inning, 1–0 loss to Cy Young despite masterful pitching from Ed Killian. It didn't matter how good Killian was, or anyone else in the American League in 1904. Young dominated the entire season, but for five consecutive starts, he was untouchable. On May 5, he threw the first perfect game in the history of the American League.

There was an even more impressive accomplishment during these five great games.

For if the 45 straight scoreless innings that link the games constitute a feat that has occasionally been exceeded, and if his perfect game represents an achievement that has sometimes been equaled, there was a third record that emerged from these games that Cy Young—over 90 years later—still holds all by himself. Before he hurled his perfect game he had already pitched nine straight hitless innings; in his first post-perfection start he reeled off another six hitless innings before Sam Crawford stroked a single to end the string. So Cy Young pitched 24 consecutive innings without yielding a base hit. No one has ever equaled that mark.[6]

Crawford ended Young's streak but was batting .227 in mid–May and struggling to get on track. The Tigers finally won, beating New York 11–6 on May 16. But Jack Chesbro beat Donovan 5–1 the following day, despite two hits by Crawford. Killian bounced back in his next start to beat Chief Bender 6–4 on May 24. The Tigers lost the next game to the Athletics and faced Rube Waddell in the series finale on May 26. Waddell—Crawford's former teammate—pitched a four-hitter and shut out the Tigers, 5–0. Wahoo Sam went 0-for-3 against the lefty.

Killian and George Mullin each won their next starts before the Tigers went on another losing streak, with two losses coming to Chesbro. Detroit was 13–26 and in a dismal seventh place. It wasn't the direction the Tigers thought they would be heading. Crawford's average had risen, but just to .233. He managed just 32 hits and 16 runs by June 12.

Crawford's struggles continued. He tallied just three hits and one run the following week and his averaged dropped back to .227. The Tigers finished the week with a series against Philadelphia and faced Plank, Waddell and Bender—three future Hall of Famers—in a row. Surprisingly, the Tigers beat Plank, 6–5, behind Mullin and Bender, 7–3, behind Donovan. Waddell won, 7–1, in between.

The Tigers' struggles continued against Chicago. Nick Altrock shut out Donovan and the Tigers, 4–0, on June 24. The Tigers won the next day but were swept in a doubleheader, then routed, 18–6, before losing the series finale, 4–3, on June 28—dropping five of six to the White Sox. In Cleveland, Joss beat Mullin, 4–2 on July 7 and the Tigers fell to 27–36 to remain in seventh place.

Crawford's best game of the season came on July 18 in New York, his only four-hit game of the season. He smashed a two-run homer in the seventh inning after slapping two singles earlier in the game and capped the performance by doubling home Matty McIntyre in the ninth inning to seal Detroit's 8–4 victory over Tom Hughes. Unfortunately for Crawford and the Tigers, it was one of few highlights during the season. The Tigers once again had to face Happy Jack Chesbro the following day and he edged Donovan, 2–1. Chesbro beat the Tigers all eight times he faced them in 1904, including a 13-strikeout performance on August 3.

In late July, the Tigers tried to shake things up by making a trade. In a three-way deal, Detroit sent Charley O'Leary, Clyde "Rabbit" Robinson and Ed Greninger to Louisville of the National League and received Bill Coughlin from Washington. On July 26, the new-look Tigers beat Eddie Plank, 5–1, behind the pitching of Killian. But again, the Tigers couldn't build any momentum as Waddell shut the Tigers out, 5–0, the following day. It got worse for Detroit as Weldon Henley shut them out, 4–0, the next day and Plank got his revenge with a 2–0 shutout. Waddell was again on the mound in the finale and the Tigers actually managed to score a run against him, but still lost, 4–1. It was the worst stretch of the season for the Tigers, who were shut out 22 times in 1904 and played four scoreless ties. Crawford got a hit off Waddell to up his average to a still dismal .246 with 32 runs scored and 75 hits.

The Tigers never recovered from the shutout streak. They moved up to as high as sixth place in August, but finished in seventh place, where they spent most of the season. Crawford had his worst full season in the majors. He batted .254 with 49 runs, 143 hits, 22 doubles, 16 triples, two home runs and 20 stolen bases. The Tigers needed something to change. Little did they know that change would come from a small, fiery ballplayer who would become the greatest hitter of all time.

3. Ain't He a Peach

To call the 1904 season disappointing would have indeed been an understatement in Detroit. With a strong pitching staff and potent lineup, led by Sam Crawford, the Tigers were dead set on contending for the American League pennant, if not winning it. But they didn't win it. They didn't even put up a fight. They weren't the dominant team they expected to be. In fact, they weren't even a good team. Detroit finished in sixth place, not even making it into the first division (top four teams), as it was called when leagues consisted of just eight teams.

If a roster full of talent like Detroit's couldn't even approach the first division, management had no choice but to implement some changes to shake things up. Manager Bill Armour tried to shuffle things around in an attempt to put together a better ball club than was seen in 1904. The biggest change involved Sam Crawford—the Tigers' best player. Armour moved him from right field to first base. Crawford made it no secret that he preferred the outfield, but he conceded to do what was best for the team after their lousy finish the season before. It was still an interesting move for the Tigers. It is always a gamble to shake things up, especially when it involves a team's best player.

Detroit started out the 1905 season just as it had left 1904—with a disappointment. George Mullin was tagged for six runs and Crawford went hitless in a 6–1 loss to Cleveland on April 15. It turned out to be a one-game series thanks to some April snow showers in Detroit. Four days later, Chicago came to town. Wild Bill Donovan had been itching to get on the mound and responded by shutting out the White Sox, 3–0, with Crawford notching his first hit of the season.

Two more days off because of the weather followed, forcing the Tigers to play 16 games in a row without an off-day. On April 22, Crawford doubled and scored against Chicago's Nick Altrock and the Tigers beat the White Sox, 6–3, behind the pitching of Ed Killian. Cleveland was back in Detroit next and the four-game series featured dominant pitching from both teams in four consecutive shutouts. On April 24, George Kitson shut out the Naps, 2–0. Crawford doubled and scored one of Detroit's runs. Donovan lost a 1–0 shutout to Bob Rhoads the following day. But the most surprising shutout came in the third game of the series on April 26. Killian squared off with Addie Joss, who was perhaps the greatest American League pitcher in the first decade of the century and would end up in the Hall of Fame. Killian did his part but Joss could not get Crawford out. Wahoo Sam pounded Joss for two singles and two doubles to lead the Tigers past Joss, 5–0.

Detroit hit the road for the first time on April 28 and got destroyed by the White Sox in a three-game sweep. The Tigers lost, 10–5, 15–5 and 6–0, leaving town with their tails between their legs. St. Louis shut out Detroit, 6–0, to start a home-and-home series. The Tigers lost four of the seven games and were still a disappointing 8–10. The Tigers got back to .500 by beating Boston two games in a row. Crawford figured in both games with two singles, a stolen base and two runs scored in a 5–1 win on May 12, and a double and run scored against Cy Young in a 3–2 win the following day. Crawford was hitting .294 after one month of the season with 20 hits in 20 games.

Crawford went on a tear at the end of May. On May 18, he laced three hits in a 5–0 win over Washington. Two days later he pounded a single, double and his first home run of the season off New York pitcher Al Orth. The clout in the first inning was unlike most home runs the Detroit fans had seen, in fact it was the first one hit over the fence that season. Most homers were of the inside-the-park variety in those days. The *Detroit Free Press* described the scene: "In round one of yesterday's conflict with New York, the man from Wahoo … placed on exhibition the first four baser seen in these parts since 1905 broke out on the calendar. It was a shot for the score-board whose bounding finish eluded Mr. Dougherty…. The drive with its consequent two runs, ultimately proved to be enough for all purposes."[1] Donovan shut out New York and the Tigers won, 6–0.

Crawford clouted 19 hits in his next ten games, including six multi-hit games, to up his average to .361 on May 27. He had collected ten doubles and scored 17 runs in the first 31 games of the season. Despite his offensive heroics, the Tigers were still fluttering around .500 and on May 29 found themselves in fourth place at 16–16. Detroit hung near .500 for the next two months. Crawford put them two games above on June 3 when he singled in the ninth inning and scored the tying run in St. Louis. Bobby Lowe followed with a single to score Bill Coughlin and the Tigers beat the Browns, 5–4, to improve to 20–18. But the Tigers dropped the next two. By June 11, Crawford's averaged had dipped to .329, still a solid mark, but he wasn't getting much help from his teammates.

Armour wanted to shake things up again, so he moved Crawford back to his usual position in right field and moved Charlie "Piano Legs" Hickman back to first base on June 14. The Tigers lost, 4–1, to Eddie Plank and the Athletics but beat Cy Young the following day, 5–1, thanks to an underappreciated aspect of Crawford's game. Wahoo Sam stole two bases, putting himself in scoring position to tally two runs for the Tigers. The Tigers dropped the first game of a doubleheader on June 17 before rallying to win the second, improving to 25–22, the first time they had been three games above .500 all season. The *Detroit Free Press* praised the position switch as leading to the success: "The Tigers are going very strong. The switch of Crawford to right and Hickman to first has worked out admirably. The strain upon Hickman's eyes, due to the bad sun in some of the lots back this way, has been relieved so that he is getting back to his batting form. He is doing well upon the sack. Crawford is perfectly at home in his old patch, and if he keeps up his present batting gait all of the pitchers will be walking him."[2]

The press jinxed Crawford with their praise of the situation and he went hitless the next three games. In the second game, New York's Jack Chesbro pitched a 7–0 shutout, which began a five-game skid for the Tigers. Armour, wishing to get things back on track, switched Crawford and Hickman again, moving Wahoo Sam back to first base. It worked— at least initially. Crawford singled and scored while Hickman walloped a home run to beat the Indians, 4–1. But Detroit faced Addie Joss in the next game, lost 8–3, and lost four of their next six games to fall below .500 at 30–33. It was back to right field for Crawford after that, and he played there the rest of the season except for July 22, when he played right field the first game of a doubleheader, then first base the second game.

Crawford was happy to be back at his normal position. He didn't show it right away, however. He managed just one hit in the next eight games. The Tigers were lucky to break even and even beat Chesbro, 6–4, on July 13 after being shut out again by the future Hall of Famer three days earlier. The Tigers built off the momentum of beating Happy Jack by knocking off another future Hall of Famer—Eddie Plank—the next game, 5–2. Crawford managed a single and run scored off "Gettysburg Eddie" but Detroit dropped the second game of the twin bill to stay below .500 (36–37). Detroit reached .500 the next day by beating another future Hall of Famer in Rube Waddell. Crawford singled and doubled off his former Grand Rapids teammate and scored a run to spark the Tigers offense. Plank got his revenge the following day with a 6–3 win. Washington came to town next and started a five-game series on July 19. The Senators, who were still two years away from having legend Walter Johnson on the mound, struggled with their pitching. The Tigers took advantage and scored 33 runs in five games to sweep the Senators, to improve to 42–38 and reach four games over .500 for just the second time all season.

The success was short-lived, however. Cy Young shut the Tigers down in a 6–1 win to start a four-game series with Boston that was played in Columbus, Ohio. Young won again two days later and the Tigers dropped three of four. It got worse for the Tigers as they traveled to the nation's capital. The Senators, seething from the five-game sweep, busted out their own brooms and beat the Tigers four straight. Crawford managed just two hits in the series. It was on to Philadelphia and Connie Mack's always dominant pitching staff. The Tigers dropped the first game, 3–2, as Andy Coakley outpitched George Mullin in a close game. Detroit faced the daunting task of facing three future Hall of Famers in a row. Eddie Plank shut the Tigers out, 8–0, and Waddell got the best of Kitson, 4–3, but the Tigers jumped on Chief Bender to win, 9–3.

The road trip wasn't over. Detroit traveled to Boston and beat Cy Young, but lost the other three games in the series, despite Crawford coming out of his hitting funk. He had four hits in the series and started off in New York with four hits in a twin bill with Chesbro winning the opener and Mullin taking the nightcap. Crawford finished the road trip strong with a single, double, triple and three runs scored to power the Tigers to a 6–4 win in support of Killian.

It was the worst road trip of the year, and in recent history, for the Tigers, who started the trip four games over .500 and finished five games under.

The Tigers finally returned to Detroit on August 17 and were rudely welcomed by Eddie Plank, who beat them 6–2 in a makeup game with the Athletics for his third win in a month over the Tigers. Cy Young was next as defending American League champion Boston came to Bennett Park. The Tigers knew they wouldn't score often against the all-time wins leader, but took advantage of the hitting by Sam Crawford. Wahoo Sam doubled and tripled off Young in the second and seventh innings, and both times came around to score on suicide squeeze plays as Wild Bill Donovan hung on to beat Young, 2–1. "Turning loose the 'squeeze' play whenever W. Sam Crawford peopled the third sack—it happened twice during the afternoon—our boys yesterday possessed a pair of tallies that proved to be just enough to nose out the Boston Champs in the first game,"[3] the *Detroit Free Press* reported. Detroit couldn't build off the successful use of small ball, however, and lost six of their next seven games to drop to their lowest point of the season at 51–60, capped by a 5–4 loss to Plank and the Athletics.

The Tigers needed a boost and needed someone to play aggressively and fiercely. Someone who could hit well to support Crawford in the lineup and give Detroit an edge. On August 26, the Tigers called up Tyrus Raymond Cobb from the Augusta Tourists of the Sally League. The youngster was still nearly four months shy of turning 19. Little did the Tigers know just what they were getting—a ferocious player who was equally ferocious off the field.

Cobb immediately made an impact when he debuted in center field on August 30 against the New York Highlanders and future Hall of Famer Jack Chesbro. "Ty Cobb, late of Georgia, selected the afternoon for his big league debuting, and acquitted himself nobly," the *Detroit Free Press* said.

> For a young man anxious to get along in the world it was not an especially auspicious occasion, as Mr. Chesbro is not the softest twirler in the country, and Tyrus, in an addition, had the luck to face (Jack) on two occasions when there were two men out and a man waiting to score, a base hit being the only thing that would be of any value. First time the Georgian whaled the ball over "Noodles" Hahn's head for a two-baser, scoring his man. Second time he drew a pass and died in an attempt to double steal. On the fielding end he grabbed off both flies that came his way. He had no chance to show us whether his speed is what the papers said about it, excepting on the occasion of his attempted steal, which was a failure. Tyrus was well received and may consider a two base pry-up a much better big league opener than usually comes a young man's way.[4]

Ty Cobb joined the Detroit Tigers in 1905 and changed the fortunes of the team. His brash, aggressive play took baseball by storm as he led the Tigers to three consecutive pennants. Cobb and Sam Crawford immediately became one of the best one-two punches in baseball history (National Baseball Hall of Fame Library, Cooperstown, New York).

It was a relief for Cobb, who had many problems before he made the majors. His father was killed by his mother, who thought he was a prowler, with a shotgun.

His father's death, the pressures of big-league play, and hazing by his teammates threatened to end his career before it began. The other players locked him out of the bathroom, tore the crown out of his straw hat, and sawed in half the bats that had been especially fashioned for him by his hometown coffin-maker. Sam Crawford recalled his reaction: "Every rookie gets a little hazing, but most of them just take it and laugh. Cobb took it the wrong way. He came up with an antagonistic attitude which in his mind turned any little razzing into a life-and-death struggle. He always figured everybody was ganging up on him. He came from the South ... and he was still fighting the Civil War. As far as he was concerned, we were all damn Yankees before he even met us."[5]

Cobb never fully suppressed those feelings, which added to the fire he brought to the ballpark every day. The "Georgia Peach" sparked the Tigers, who won six of their next seven games, the only loss being a 3–2 defeat in ten innings against the Browns in Eddie Cicotte's debut. Cicotte would be a valuable pitcher for the Tigers before joining the Red Sox, and finally the White Sox. He is most remembered not for his dominant pitching, but because he was one of the Black Sox who threw the 1919 World Series.

Cobb played the rest of the season in center field, next to Crawford, who quickly realized what a player they had gained. The two became the best one-two punch in baseball but did not always get along. "We had our spats on the field, sure, and some off the field," Crawford confided in later years to Fred Lieb. "Ty was a hot-tempered Southerner who let his emotions show. And we were mostly Northerners on those old Tigers. But Ty mellowed with the years, and I always respected him and his great ability."[6]

Most importantly, the Tigers started winning. On September 12, Cobb and Crawford hit and ran past Addie Joss and Cleveland. Crawford had two singles, a double and a stolen base, while Cobb had two singles and a steal, and both scored runs in a 4–3 win. Crawford still provided most of the extra-base hits. On September 18, he clobbered Bob Rhoads and the Naps. "Three times Wahoo Sam Crawford came to bat with a runner on second in today's game, which Detroit won 3 to 0, and each time he lined to the outfielders," the *Detroit Free Press* reported. "The first went to Harry Bay in deep center. Otto Hess took care of his second attempt. Elmer Flick leaped into the right field bleachers to take in the third line drive. It was luck, to say the least, but when Crawford came up in the ninth inning, he was the first man up, so broke the monotony, and incidentally, 'Dusty' Rhoads's heart, by sending one where the fielders could not get it. The ball started for the right field pocket, which is always good for at least two bases, and probably three. But fortune smiled on Sam, for the ball struck on the top rail of the extension of the bleachers, and bounded into Lexington Avenue and the Tigers scored the first run of the game."[7] It was all Killian needed, though the Tigers added two more in the 3–0 shutout.

In a very even American League, the Tigers improved to 68–65 with the win but dropped to sixth place after being swept in the following doubleheader by Cleveland. Detroit beat Washington, 5–1, the next day and jumped all the way to fourth place. Cobb smashed three hits off John "Happy" Townsend and Detroit beat the Senators, 6–4, the following day and jumped to third place. It is where they would remain the rest of the season thanks to Cobb and Crawford, who both batted over .300 in September. The Tigers beat Cy Young again, 4–3, on September 28, and topped Chesbro one more time, 7–2.

The Tigers were looking for something to put them over the top—or someone—and that someone was Cobb. In the final five weeks of the season following his debut, the Tigers went 27–14 to move from sixth place to third. The Tigers still thought they could have challenged Connie Mack's Philadelphia Athletics for the pennant, but were happy with the finish. A new-found confidence radiated in the Tigers' clubhouse after the finish. With Cobb around for a full season, next year was their year to contend.

1906: *Juggling Lineup*

Tigers manager Bill Armour had a problem managers like to have in 1906. He had four outfielders that were good enough to be starters. Sam Crawford, Davy Jones and Matty McIntyre had been the mainstays, but youngster Ty Cobb proved at the end of the 1905 season to be a valuable commodity, so valuable in fact that he signed a contract for $1,500. The trouble was, Armour had to figure out what combination would give the Tigers their best shot at contending. It wasn't easy and Armour tried just about every combination. Crawford, who was making $2,500, played right field, center field and first base at times, while the other three played all three outfield positions at some point.

Armour was a tinkerer. In 1905, he forced Crawford to play first base because he thought it would give him a better lineup. It did on paper, but Crawford was so unhappy at first base, he wasn't the player he had been. In addition to tinkering with the outfielders, Armour changed the batting order around often in 1906. Crawford usually batted third or fourth but Cobb shifted from fifth to first and everywhere in between. The problem was there was no consistency. Nobody knew when or where they were playing and where they were hitting in the lineup.

On Opening Day, however, Crawford was in his usual spot in right field and his usual cleanup spot in the lineup. Playing before a crowd of 13,875 at Bennett Park in Detroit on April 17, Crawford started his season 1-for-4 in a 5–3 loss to the Chicago White Sox. Crawford had his first multi-hit game the next day with a 2-for-4 performance against future Hall of Famer Ed Walsh, leading the Tigers to a 3–2 victory. Crawford followed with a home run in the sixth inning off Frank Smith the next day as the Tigers beat Chicago, 3–1. Cobb was not in the lineup and would be the odd man out the first week of the season.

The second week of the season, Cobb was in the leadoff spot, playing right field, and it was Crawford who was on the bench because of a strained leg muscle. Sent to right field, Cobb showed nothing special, went hitless at St. Louis, and made a costly error on a fly ball against Cleveland.[8] Cobb went 6-for-21 before moving to center field to get Crawford back in the lineup. Crawford did not like being on the bench. He also didn't like that the Tigers started the season 7–7. After being back in right field for four games, Crawford finally got into his groove. On May 3, he clubbed four hits, including his first triple of the season. The Tigers pounded Nick Altrock in a 9–2 win over the White Sox.

Crawford soon found his power stroke. He doubled in each of the next two games and upped his average to .312 for the season. More importantly, the Tigers were 10–8 and things were looking up, especially with Cobb and Crawford in the lineup. Cobb brought something to the ballpark that was truly rare—a player whose baseball IQ equaled his talent.

Cobb had a "persecution complex," Sam Crawford told Lawrence Ritter in *The Glory of Their Times.* "He came up (to the big leagues) with an antagonistic attitude, which in his mind turned any little razzing into a life-or-death struggle. He always figured everybody was ganging up against him…. Well, who knows, maybe if he hadn't had that persecution complex, he never would have been the great ballplayer he was. He was always trying to prove he was the best, on the field and off." Everything about Cobb—the Colt pistol he packed was only part of it—left his teammates feeling uneasy. Sam Crawford, the club's best run producer until Cobb's arrival, once told how Cobb suspected him of not bearing down at bat when the Peach was on base and positioned to score. Cobb already had a beef with Crawford, believing he had been one of those who earlier smashed his bats. "He walked up to me red in the face and wanted to fight," Crawford said. "I didn't know what he might pull on me—a knife, brass knucks, or a gun. I waited until some other players came along and said, 'Let's go.' He changed his mind pretty fast then."[9]

Crawford, however, didn't have trouble getting along with anyone else on the team, especially fellow outfielders Davy Jones, Matty McIntyre and Sam Thompson.

"(Joining the Tigers) was a real break for me, of course, because, as you well know, we won the pennant in 1907, '08, and '09, and for seven years I got to play in the same outfield with two of the greatest ballplayers who ever lived, Ty Cobb and Sam Crawford," Davy Jones told Lawrence Ritter in *The Glory of Their Times.*

> Of course, playing by the side of two fellows like that was a good deal like being a member of the chorus in a grand opera where there are two prima donnas. I always got along with Sam just wonderfully. In a lot of ways we were very much alike. He's still one of my very best friends. Cobb, though—he was a very complex person—never did have many friends. Trouble was he had such a rotten disposition that it was damn hard to be his friend. I was probably the best friend he had on the club. I used to stick up for him, sit and talk with him on the long train trips, try to understand the man. He antagonized so many people that hardly anyone would speak to him, even among his own teammates.[10]

But despite the personality conflicts, the Tigers outfielders got the job done on the field, for the most part. By mid–May of 1906, Crawford was hitting .327 while Cobb was well below at .266. That would change quickly. Cobb surged to .318 by the end of May while Crawford went hitless in five of six games and plummeted to .250. Part of it was the pitching he faced. On May 16, the Tigers opened a four-game series with the Philadelphia Athletics, who had the best pitching staff in baseball. Crawford went hitless against Chief Bender in a 9–2 loss. Crawford's old teammate Rube Waddell was next, and he shut out the Tigers, 5–0, and held Wahoo Sam hitless. Crawford finally managed a single against Eddie Plank in the next game, but Gettysburg Eddie hung on for a 4–3 win. It was difficult for any hitter to face three future Hall of Famers in a row, but it was especially tough on someone already in a slump. Andy Coakley completed the sweep for the Athletics with a 3–1 win on May 19, dropping the Tigers to fourth place at 13–13.

After the sweep, Armour tinkered with the lineup again. Crawford sat out a game and Davy Jones moved to right field. Cobb moved from leadoff to third in the batting order and pitcher George Mullin hung on to beat Boston, 2–1. Crawford returned to right field after a day off and smoked a triple to help the Tigers win, 6–3. Despite two wins in a row, Armour continued to shuffle the lineup. Crawford moved from fourth to third in the batting order and Cobb moved from third to second. It worked for Cobb, who batted 7-for-14 (.500) during his four games in that spot. Crawford also shined in the three-spot, going 6-for-15 with a double and a home run off future Hall of Famer Jack Chesbro. But the Tigers, after sweeping Boston, got swept by New York with that lineup and remained even at 16–16.

Crawford and Cobb were tearing the cover off the ball, but it wasn't enough for Armour. Cobb was moved back to lead off, which put him into a 3-for-13 tailspin (all three hits came in one game as he went hitless in the others). If Crawford thought he was moved around too much already, he hadn't seen anything yet. On May 30, he batted cleanup and had a double off Chicago's Doc White. The next three games, he batted third and went 3-for-13. Two days later he was playing first base. Armour thought his best lineup would have all four outfielders in it, so he moved Crawford back to first base for the next 12 games. Crawford moved his average from .250 to .283 while at first base. Meanwhile, Cobb moved into Crawford's post in right field, dropped to fifth in the lineup, and recovered from his slump by going on a tear which raised his average to .324.

Detroit crept above .500 but was still in fifth place on June 6. On June 9, the Tigers beat Cy Young, 7–6, in 11 innings with Crawford lacing three hits and Cobb singling and doubling. Three days later, the Tigers got to Bender for eight runs in an 8–7 win. Crawford smashed three hits off Plank the following day, but the Tigers could not beat all three future Hall of Famers in a four-day period and lost to Philadelphia, 4–3. The Tigers topped Coakley the next day to improve to 26–21, their best win percentage of the season.

On June 18, Crawford was back in right field. Cobb, who was struggling with an injury, would not start the next seven games, though he pinch-hit twice. When Cobb returned on June 24, he was in left field and Armour moved him to cleanup, batting behind Crawford. Cobb played six games in left field, then moved back to center, and the Georgia Peach went into a 1-for-22 slump. It was obvious Cobb was playing hurt, so Armour rested him for most of July and August and only used him as a pinch-hitter if the game was on the line. Crawford was forced to pick up the slack without Cobb in the lineup. He responded with four multi-hit games in a six-game span and raised his average to .301. The Tigers were still hovering just above the .500 mark at 36–33 when Cobb was forced to the bench.

It was tough to gain any ground on Philadelphia and Chicago without one of their stars. Plus, the Athletics and White Sox had strong pitching which kept them in every game. The Tigers were used to facing three future Hall of Famers in a row every month or so when playing Philadelphia, but from July 25–30, they faced four straight future Hall of Famers from three different teams. In the second game of a doubleheader in New York, the Tigers lost, 9–0, to Jack Chesbro. They beat Cy Young 7–4 the next day in a makeup game with Boston, and two days later lost 8–2 to Chief Bender. Eddie Plank was next up for the Athletics and beat the Tigers, 6–3, dropping their record to 45–44. Three days later Chesbro was on the hill again and beat the Tigers, 11–1, at Bennett Park. Detroit lost nine of 11 games and dropped to 50–54. In the middle of that run was a doubleheader sweep at the hands of the Senators that put the Tigers at 48–50. It was the first time the Tigers had a losing record since June 2 at 18–19.

Crawford, who had dropped to .271, snapped out of his slump in late August, going 17-for-34 with two triples from August 16–27, helping him to a .286 mark by the end of the month. With Cobb out, Crawford got to play briefly alongside another future Hall of Famer and legendary RBI man, Sam Thompson. Thompson had starred with the Detroit Wolverines from 1885–1888, helping them win the championship in 1887, before the team left Detroit after the 1888 season. He knocked in 100 runs eight times and led the National

League with 166 in 1887 and 165 in 1895. He also led the NL in RBI in 1894 with 147. The Tigers brought him back to Detroit in 1906 to play eight games while Cobb was on the shelf. He batted just .226, but his presence was welcomed in Detroit by the fans and Crawford. On September 1, Crawford tripled in a run and scored on a single by Thompson to give the Tigers a 3–0 win over Jack Powell and the St. Louis Browns.

"Looked like pictures from the past at Bennett Park yesterday when fans who were wont to cheer the Champs of twenty years ago turned out to show that they had not forgotten those heroes," the *Detroit Free Press* said of the September 1 game.

> Detroit beat St. Louis 5 to 1. The winning or losing of the game, however, seemed to be a minor consideration with most of the fans, who were there primarily to see how Sam Thompson would look and act back in fast company. After the fifth inning, in which Sam tore off a base hit that of itself proved sufficient to win the game, the old boys ... who sat quietly when Sam struck out in his first at bat, perked up and told the folks that it was just what they expected of the product of a day when there were giants in the land. Sam (Thompson) came to bat in that fifth with the sacks full and hit one past Tom Jones so fast (scoring two) that the big first sacker's diving stab for the ball looked like a yokel's grab for the shell that he thinks the pea is under.[11]

Cobb returned to the lineup on September 2. He played center field with Crawford in left, and Wild Bill Donovan lost a 1–0 game in a rain-shortened six innings. The following day, Crawford, Cobb and Thompson all played together for the first time, but it wasn't in the outfield. Crawford was on first with Cobb in center, Thompson in right and McIntyre in left. On September 4, Crawford tagged St. Louis pitcher Jack Powell for three hits, Cobb laced a pair and Thompson launched a triple, but the Tigers couldn't hang on and lost, 4–3. Even with three future Hall of Famers in the lineup, the Tigers lost the first eight games after Cobb's return and dropped to a dismal sixth place at 56–67. Detroit's Red Donahue out-pitched Chicago's future Hall of Famer, Ed Walsh, 2–1. The Tigers won the next two. Joss shut them out 8–0 on September 13, then in the second game of a doubleheader the next day, Hess pitched a three-hit shutout to beat the Tigers 6–0. The latter started the Tigers on another skid, this time of five games.

Armour tried everything to stop the bleeding. He moved Crawford back to right field and into the cleanup spot, with Cobb batting leadoff. On September 17, Crawford moved back into the third spot and Cobb moved to fourth. The Tigers finally got to Chesbro on September 24. Crawford had four hits, including a triple, to lead Detroit past New York, 7–4. New York dropped to 85–55, which put them into a first-place tie with both Chicago and Philadelphia right on their heels.

Fitting with the kind of season the Tigers were having, their home finale was washed out on September 29. The Tigers traveled to Cleveland and won the first game, 3–2, behind the pitching of George Mullin, a homer by Cobb and a single and run scored from Crawford. The Tigers lost the next two in Cleveland and got swept in a doubleheader by the Browns on October 6 before finishing their season with a 6–1 win over the pennant-winning White Sox on October 7. The White Sox (93–58) edged the New York Highlanders by three games and Cleveland by four. The Tigers finished 71–78 in a dismal sixth place.

Detroit had high hopes in 1906, and after the finish, some of those hopes diminished. The Tigers would have a new manager in 1907 and a new outlook. They almost had a new superstar. Detroit's new manager, Hughie Jennings, knew Cobb was a handful and tried to make a deal to get a more gentlemanly star. He offered a deal to Napoleon "Larry" Lajoie, the brilliant second baseman who just missed winning the batting championship in 1906 in his first year as Cleveland manager. Jennings wanted to make a straight trade, Cobb for outfielder Elmer Flick. Flick had led the league himself in batting average in 1905, had hit even better last year, but now was at odds with Lajoie and had not yet signed his contract. Meanwhile Cobb told the reporters, "I'm in the right and so long as I know that fact I don't care what is done or said."[12] The next day Jennings announced that Lajoie, convinced Cobb was a troublemaker, wouldn't make the trade. Under no circumstances, added Jennings, would Cobb be sold; if he couldn't be traded for a first-rate ballplayer, than Cobb would stay with Detroit. Three days later Flick signed with Cleveland. It turns out some of the best trades are the ones that don't get made.

4. Birth of an American League Dynasty

Coming into the 1907 season, the Tigers knew they were capable of better than the sixth-place finish they showed in 1906. Offensively, Detroit had Ty Cobb and Sam Crawford, and with "Wild Bill" Donovan, Ed Siever and George Mullin leading the pitching rotation, the Tigers were one of the best well-rounded teams of the Dead Ball Era. The team also added one of the best managers in baseball history in Hughie Jennings (sometimes spelled Hughey in Detroit newspapers), taking over for the constantly tinkering Bill Armour. Detroit just needed to find a way to play up to its potential, something the Tigers would finally figure out under Jennings.

As well-rounded as Detroit was, the Tigers depended on Cobb and Crawford, who between them would lead the American League in hitting, runs scored, hits, stolen bases and runs batted in. The Tigers would also depend on Jennings, who in his first season as manager, would uniquely capture the attention of his team, opposing players and fans everywhere. It started in the first game of the season.

Herman "Germany" Schaefer lined a double into left field and Ty Cobb streaked home with the Detroit Tigers' first run of the 1907 season. "In the third-base coaching box the team's new manager pulled up two handfuls of infield grass. With clenched fists raised over his head, he leaned his torso back, raised his right leg with bent knee, let loose with a piercing cry of 'ee-yah' and threw the grass in the air like confetti. The fans howled with laughter and yelled back, trying to imitate the mysterious cry. Thus began a love affair between a baseball manager and baseball fans which was unequalled before and remains unequalled since."[1]

During the early years of Hughie's 14-season tenure as Tiger manager, sports writers, fans, managers and players around the country speculated wildly about the origin of Hughie's dance and signature yell. He gave contradictory hints about what it meant, but never revealed the true origin of the yell.

A logical conclusion is that "ee-yah" was an outgrowth of Hughie's days as a mule driver in the mines. Mule drivers used voice commands to steer their mules, "giddap" for go, "whoa" for stop, "gee" for right turn, and "wah-haw" for left turn. Hughie never confirmed nor denied that his "ee-yah" was based on mule driving commands.... A magazine story claimed the cry, and the dance-like gyrations that accompanied it, originated from a trip to the circus. "In his early youth Hughie attended a one-ring circus and was much impressed with a Cherokee Indian rain dance. In a side show, on the same occasion he witnessed a snake dance from the Far East. Hughie has combined these two dances with some original steps." … It is a mixture of Arabian slang and Swedish court tongue," wrote one. "Eyah, eyah, eyah a shrill series of suppressed warhoops, a few of the dancing steps particular to the flying dervishes of Persia or a Cherokee rain dance will give a fair description of Jennings on the coaching lines," wrote another. So what was the purpose of these crazy yells? Eddie Collins, the Athletics' Hall of Fame second baseman, also believed Hughie was up to something. "Judging from his results it's not illogical to suppose that 'ee-yah' contained some signs and secrets of team play such as steal, hit and run or sacrifice." Hughie never denied that he was conveying secret signals but Ty Cobb did. "Many fans think Hughey gives his players orders through his famous 'ee-yah' yell. That's not the case though. He gives signals the same as other coaches. I heard two players trying to 'dope' out what 'ee-yah' meant. 'When he follows it up with a whistle that means hit-and-run,' they said, and 'he puts emphasis on the 'yah' for a sacrifice. Even if I told them that Jennings was not giving signals through 'ee-yah' they would not have believed me. Some baseball players are convinced there is something behind the cry and Jennings is perfectly willing for them to continue to think it, too. I don't know what 'ee-yah' means. Jennings has also studied Spanish and used that with his pitchers so umpires and other players wouldn't know what it meant. The coaching of Jennings has a certain affect on his players. It kind of buoys them up and makes them dig in and work hard. We have made seven, eight and nine runs in an inning many times. On successful days, we had 10-run innings. Innings like that were due to Jennings' aggressive coaching."[2]

The 1907 season didn't start well for the Tigers, however. On April 4, outfielder Davy Jones was arrested and charged with assault of a paper boy who shoved a newspaper at him and demanded a nickel for it. According to the *Detroit Free Press*, Jones was acquitted that very evening because the bulk of the charge came from Jones calling the boy a profane name, and Jones was known as a player who never swore.[3] In addition, Donovan missed the first two months of the season.

There also was a position up in the air. The Tigers had to decide who would be their regular first baseman. Crawford had worked a lot to learn the position, playing from time to time in the past and fielding the position well. He was an outfielder by trade, but with Cobb, Matty McIntyre and Jones in the outfield, perhaps it would be best for the team to have all four bats in the lineup. Jennings eventually decided against this and started Claude Rossman at first base. Crawford started the season in center field, Cobb in right field and McIntyre in left. Jones would be a platoon outfielder.

> There has been much talk about Sam Crawford's first base play, and occasional contrast with that of Rossman. It is only fair to say that Sam, who has been practicing around the bag for three years, and playing occasionally, is more finished in his infield work than Rossman. But the latter has been on the bag but one season—more truthfully, part of a season—in a major league and did not have much coaching at that time. He does not claim to be a polished first sacker yet, but he plays the bag well, is studying and improving all the time, and has a reach that makes him the sort of mark as which infielders like to throw. And this with his stickwork means he will be the regular first baseman of the Detroit team, and Sam will be back in the outfield.[4]

There was another reason. Cobb and McIntyre hated each other. Favoring Matty McIntyre (who finally signed his contract two days into the season) over Davy Jones, Jennings decided to put Cobb in right field and shift Sam Crawford to center. Crawford was no gazelle, and he had his own unhappiness with Cobb. In his autobiography, Cobb remembered still another bat-sawing incident in the 1907 season and blamed Crawford for instigating that particular petty vandalism. Yet if prideful and sometimes arrogant, Crawford was also generally a professional, a man ultimately willing to subordinate personal feelings to team considerations. Thus the blond, broad-shouldered native of Wahoo, Nebraska, moved to center field, separating Cobb from McIntyre in left. It was a solution elegant in its simplicity.[5]

It was the best move for the Tigers, who would use Crawford at first base at times during his career when someone was injured or slumping. However, Crawford himself seemed to struggle at bat when he played first base. Crawford would turn in another stellar season in 1907, but it brought a rollercoaster-like feel. He started the season slowly, then went on an offensive tear the last two weeks of May. He was streaky in June and July, but had another dominating couple of weeks in September to lead the Tigers to their first pennant.

After all of the anticipation of a contending season, Detroit opened the season at home against Cleveland on April 11. Cleveland had the American League's other top player, second baseman Napoleon Lajoie. Cobb and Lajoie would battle for many batting titles the next decade and the Indians were known as the Naps while Lajoie was playing. The Indians also had another future Hall of Famer, Elmer Flick.

Mullin started the opening game for Detroit and dominated the Naps. Lajoie went hitless and Flick managed one of Cleveland's three hits. Mullin pitched a complete-game shutout with six strikeouts and two walks. It was just the beginning of a great season for Mullin and the Tigers. Crawford managed one hit while Cobb had two hits and scored both Detroit runs.

Cleveland got even the next game, winning 9–3 behind George Stovall's five hits. Crawford and Cobb each scratched out a single. After two days off, Crawford got his first multi-hit game of the season, slapping two singles in a 2–1 win over the defending World Series champion Chicago White Sox. Both teams were tied atop the American League standings at 2–1. It wouldn't be the last close game these two pennant contenders battled out against each other. The White Sox won the second game of the series, 4–1, on April 17 at Bennett Park. Crawford laced another hit while Cobb went hitless but scored a run.

Detroit traveled to Cleveland to face the Naps again. Mullin was back on the mound for the Tigers and again shut out the Naps as the Tigers won, 2–0. He struck out five and walked three to improve to 2–0 with a 0.00 ERA. Cobb and Crawford each singled and scored in the eighth inning on an error by Harry Bay to seal the victory.

Cleveland won the next game, 4–1. Detroit had a day off and Crawford made the most of his rest. Playing a Sunday exhibition game against Sandusky, Crawford slapped three singles and scored each time, leading the Tigers to an 18–1 victory. It wasn't major league competition, but Crawford needed something to get him going at the plate.

Detroit returned to its season April 22 with a 9–4 win over Cleveland. Crawford had another multi-hit game with two singles. He scored one of Detroit's runs in the next day's victory. Cobb managed one hit again. It wasn't the start Cobb and Crawford were hoping for, and it would be a while before each found his groove in the batter's box.

Cobb led the Tigers to a 7–4 win over the St. Louis Browns the next day, slapping two hits and scoring a run. Crawford was 1-for-4 with a run and Mullin earned another victory. On April 24, Detroit pitcher Ed Siever allowed just two hits—both to St. Louis pitcher Beany Jacobson—in a complete-game shutout, leading the Tigers past the Browns, 3–0. Cobb singled twice, scoring both times, and Crawford singled and came around to score on a Cobb base hit. Although Cobb and Crawford were leading the Tigers to wins, they were still not batting as high as they had hoped, and Detroit's 6–4 record put them in fourth place. Cobb and Crawford each went hitless the next day against the Browns in a 3–1 victory, though Crawford did score a run after walking.

The Tigers rolled past the Browns, 13–5, in the series finale and, with Philadelphia and New York losing, the Tigers found themselves tied for first place with the White Sox and Athletics at 8–4. Crawford had a hit and scored while Cobb scored after one of his two hits. First place would be a familiar one for Detroit, not only the rest of the season, but the rest of the decade. What's more important is that the Tigers knew that they were capable of playing much better than their 8–4 record showed.

While first place was somewhere the Tigers would be most of the season, they dropped right back into fourth place with a 3–1 loss to the White Sox the very next day. Future Hall of Fame spitballer Ed Walsh gave up just four hits—one to Cobb—and Detroit dropped to 8–5. The White Sox took over sole possession of first place at 9–4 and with better percentage points, and the Philadelphia Athletics (8–4) and the New York Highlanders (7–4) also moved ahead of Detroit.

The Tigers split a doubleheader with the White Sox on May 3. It was more notable who didn't play than who did. The Tigers played the twin bill without Crawford, while the Sox were without pitcher "Big Ed" Walsh, who would miss more than a month after injuries sustained in a collision at the plate. Several of the White Sox accused the Detroit manager of calling Walsh a coward and a quitter. Jennings was incensed by the accusation. Here is what he told the *Detroit Free Press* after the game on May 6 was postponed by rain: "Whatever might have been said in the heat of battle, all of the Detroit players, including myself, regret exceedingly that Walsh is badly hurt. Often times a player who is seriously injured appears to be all right at the time. We might have kidded the big fellow a little but we are extremely sorry that he is seriously hurt."[6]

The Tigers-White Sox rivalry didn't need any more fuel added to the fire, but this incident stuck with both teams the rest of the season. It was put on hold, however, since it happened at the end of the series. Detroit had more things to worry about, like rising out of fourth place. Crawford's struggles continued as he went 0-for-4 in a 4–3 makeup win over St. Louis on May 7. Cobb had two hits and scored twice to spark the Tigers.

The Boston Americans came to town next and Cy Young topped Mullin, 3–2. If Crawford thought his tough time was bad before, he was completely frustrated after going hitless against Oberlin College in an exhibition game on May 10. His performance, or lack thereof, against the small college turned out to be the best thing that could have happened to "Wahoo" Sam. Crawford reeled off eight multi-hit games in the next two weeks, beginning with a 2-for-4 performance on May 11 against the Americans. He hit a "Wahoo" special three-bagger in the game and scored a run, leading the Tigers to a 4–1 victory. Four days later, Crawford repeated his 2-for-4 with a run scored performance against New York but the Tigers lost, 5–3.

The Tigers' offense came together to beat the Philadelphia Athletics, 15–8, on May 18. Crawford contributed another multi-hit game with a single, double and two runs scored. "Wahoo" Sam was swinging the bat very well, but was overshadowed by Cobb's four hits and the failure by Philadelphia aces "Chief" Bender and Jack Coombs to get any of the Tigers out. Bender, a future Hall of Famer, went just 2⅓ innings while Coombs lasted just 1⅔. The win pushed Detroit into third place.

The Tigers had to face another Athletics future Hall of Fame pitcher in Rube Waddell in the series, and Waddell held Crawford to one hit as Philadelphia won, 3–0. One-hit games were prevalent in Crawford's first month, but not the past two weeks. He still managed a hit off Waddell, who threw a complete-game shutout and struck out seven Tigers.

Third baseman Bill Coughlin tripled in Davy Jones in the 11th inning to give Detroit a 6–5 win over Philadelphia on May 22. Crawford helped Detroit get to extra innings with a single, double and run scored. Crawford had two hits and a run scored against Bender the next day to lead Detroit to a 3–2 win. The tear continued for Crawford with two more hits and two runs scored, however even another multi-hit game could not stop Detroit from losing to Cleveland, 9–5 on May 29. Cleveland took the second game of the series, 1–0, the first game of a doubleheader, but Detroit stormed back behind Crawford and Cobb to beat future Hall of Fame pitcher Addie Joss and the Naps, 6–0. Crawford had two singles, a double and two runs scored. One of those runs came on a Cobb home run off Joss, which again stole the show.

Crawford ended his May tear on the 31st when he hit a game-tying home run in the ninth inning off Jake Thielman. Coughlin again was the extra-inning hero, singling in Jimmy Archer in the tenth inning to give Donovan the victory 2–1 over Cleveland. Donovan allowed just three hits—two to Flick—to earn the complete-game victory with five strikeouts.

Unfortunately for Crawford, June didn't start out like May ended. Crawford's streak came to a halt. He went 10 for his next 43, and although he was hitting less than .250, he made the most of his hits and scored 11 runs in his next ten games.

On June 1 in Chicago, the bad luck wasn't just with Crawford's hitting. He collided with fellow outfielder Red Downs in the ninth inning, allowing the only run of the game to score. Though it was Downs's fault, the Tigers still fell to 20–15 (.571), still well behind the White Sox, who improved to 27–11 (.711). Jiggs Donahue lifted a fly ball to short left center field which looked as though it would be an easy play for Crawford. Downs caught the ball after colliding with Crawford, but couldn't throw the ball to the plate in time to get the runner tagging from third. Here's how the *Detroit Free Press* described the game-changing play: "There were twenty reasons why Crawford should have been allowed to handle Donahue's hit. It was in his territory, and he called for it, which was Downs's cue to keep away. Sam would have thrown Ed Hahn out by forty feet. In fact, the ball, held back by a strong wind, could have been taken by the shortstop almost, it was in so close."[7] The next day, Crawford was 1-for-5 and the Tigers beat the White Sox, 4–3, to end the series.

The Tigers traveled to Boston and Crawford went 1-for-4 with a double in a 7–5 loss to the Americans. George Mullin allowed four Boston runs in the eighth inning, after pitching seven strong innings. The Tigers were still in third place, and things didn't look good on the horizon, facing Cy Young the day after a loss. But the Tigers rallied to beat the all-time wins leader, 6–2. Crawford had a single and a run scored against his fellow future Hall of Famer. Cobb, on the other hand, had a single, double and two runs scored against Young. Ed Killian earned the victory for Detroit after allowing two runs and seven hits in a complete game. He also singled and scored off Young. Detroit took the final game of the series, 5–3, behind Crawford's double and run scored. Cobb just outpaced him with two hits and a run scored against the Americans.

It was on to the Big Apple for the Tigers, who were hoping to continue the win streak against the Highlanders when the series began June 8. George Mullin made sure the Tigers would keep rolling with a complete-game shutout. Crawford slapped two hits—his first multi-hit game since May. His performance lifted his batting average to .311 for the season, which was first on the team and fifth in the American League. Cobb was seventh at .306, but he, like Crawford, would catch fire again during the second half of the season.

Crawford made it back-to-back multi-hit games with a single, double and two runs scored against Joe Doyle and the Highlanders, but Detroit lost, 9–3. The Tigers' offense bounced back to beat New York, 10–2, the following day. Crawford was 1-for-4 with a run scored, but the hero of the day was Cobb, who had two singles, a double and two runs scored. The offense continued to roll in the series finale as Detroit pounded New York, 16–4. Crawford had two singles and scored twice while Cobb had one hit and two runs scored. "Wahoo" Sam was keeping pace with Cobb at the plate, which spelled trouble for opposing pitchers. By June 16, Crawford was up to .316 while Cobb was at .305.

It was Washington's offense which proved mightier in the opener of Detroit's first series of the season in the nation's capitol. The Senators scored ten runs while Cy Falkenberg worked on a shutout of the Tigers. The following day, Downs and Cobb hit doubles in the top of the tenth inning to beat the Senators, 5–4. It was the only hit of the game for Cobb, who helped the Tigers climb to 27–18 (.600). It still meant third place behind Chicago (32–17, .653) and Cleveland (32–19, .627).

Crawford did not play in the game. It was the first of six games he would miss with an undisclosed minor injury. The Tigers missed his .321 average greatly in several games, but Detroit didn't need Crawford in its first game in Philadelphia. The Tigers beat Waddell and the Athletics, 6–2, behind Cobb's two hits and two runs scored. The next day, however, the Tigers lost, 4–1. It was then another future Hall of Famer who stymied the Crawford-less Tigers. Lefty Eddie Plank threw a shutout to beat Detroit, 4–0. The southpaw had his way with the Tigers for most of his career. In fact, he had his way with every team, finishing his career with 326 wins, still a record for left-handed pitchers in the American League. Here's how the *Detroit Free Press* described Detroit's bane with a biblical reference: "Detroit's ancient Jonah, Eddie Plank, was invincible after the fourth inning today, and Detroit was beaten 4–0."

Again the Tigers faced Waddell and again, "Wild Bill" Donovan got the best of him, Waddell allowed five runs and the Tigers beat Philadelphia 5–2, despite a rare 0-for-5 game for Cobb, dropping his average to .303.

Crawford returned to center field June 23 as the Tigers opened a series in St. Louis. He had a hit and scored a run in a 2–1 win over the Browns. St. Louis returned the favor with a 4–2 win the next day in the first game of a doubleheader, despite Crawford's first multi-hit game since his return. He had a single, double and run scored. In the second game of the twin bill, Crawford had two more hits, but the Tigers lost to the Browns, 4–2 again. The Tigers were upset at losing both games to a second-division team and equally upset that with the two losses, Detroit fell into fourth place.

The only solace the Tigers had was that they would finally return home after a long road trip. "Wahoo" Sam continued to show his old form with two more hits in the opening game of a series against Cleveland, but despite his recapturing his stroke at the plate, the Tigers were not winning. The Naps won the first game, 4–1.

It didn't get any better in the next game as Addie Joss outpitched Killian and Cleveland won, 5–4. Joss held Crawford hitless and allowed two singles to Cobb. To add insult to injury, Joss himself doubled and scored a run off Killian. The Tigers finally knocked off Cleveland, 2–0, in the third game with John Eubank pitching a shutout.

Detroit evened the series with the Naps with a 12–2 victory, but tempers flared and caused some fists to fly. It is no surprise that Cobb was in the middle of it. Here's how Joe Jackson of the *Detroit Free Press* described the incident:

> There was a hint of slugging that wasn't done with swatting sticks that really was the main feature of the afternoon. It came in the second inning of the game and was an unprovoked attack by Catcher Bemis on Ty Cobb, which nearly precipitated a general fight between the teams.... Bemis had no excuse for his actions and lost his temper simply because he was "shown up" by a player who outguessed him.... Cobb tripled to the scoreboard. Crawford scored easily. Cobb rounded third ... figuring that [Bradley] would expect him to stop at third, and would turn to that bag, Cobb kept going for home. Bradley made a perfect throw. The ball was in Bemis's hands when Cobb was three steps from home. Bemis blocked off the plate, presumably expecting Cobb to walk in and be put out. Instead Cobb made a head-first slide ... struck Bemis with his shoulder ... and the catcher dropped the ball. As Cobb lay across the plate, face downward, Bemis hit him in the head with his fist two or three times. There was a near-riot in a minute.[8]

Cobb finished the day 4-for-5 with a double, triple and four runs scored. Crawford also had a superb game, going 3-for-5 with a double and two runs scored. The strong game upped his batting average to .325 for the season, fourth in the league and well ahead of Cobb's .304.

After battling with Cleveland in a series with a bench-clearing brawl, the Tigers were tired. Unfortunately, Detroit had no days off and had to travel to Chicago to face the first-place White Sox. The exhausted Tigers hitters were shut out by Doc White, despite a strong performance on the mound by Ed Siever, who allowed just two runs and six hits. Crawford was 1-for-4 against White while Cobb had two hits, but the next six batters combined for just two hits and the Detroit sluggers were stranded on base. The next day, the Tigers lost, 4–2, to Frank Smith and the Sox. Crawford and Cobb scored the two Tigers runs, but again, without anyone else contributing, Detroit's offense wasn't helping get the team out of fourth place or gain any ground on the White Sox.

After losing the two-game series in Chicago, the Tigers desperately needed to return home. Luckily, the sixth-place St. Louis Browns were in town and Detroit bounced back to win, 8–5. Crawford was 3-for-4 in the game, contributing to the scoring in the third inning. He doubled in Coughlin and scored when Cobb singled to the same spot in right-center to give the Tigers a 5–1 lead. Bigger than the victory itself was the fact that other hitters stepped up for the Tigers, not just the sluggers. Davy Jones and Charley "Boss" Schmidt each scored twice and pitcher "Wild Bill" Donovan even got into the act, going 3-for-3 with a run scored on top of striking out five in a complete-game victory.

The Tigers couldn't start a win streak, however, losing to the Browns, 8–4, the following day. Crawford went 0-for-5, Cobb 1-for-4, and Mullin was knocked around by the St. Louis hitters, who totaled 15 hits.

Third-place Philadelphia traveled to Bennett Park for a makeup game and the Tigers, sensing the urgency, won 9–5 to puddle-jump the Athletics and move into third place at 36–28 (.563). Philadelphia was 37–30 (.552). Donovan was on the mound again and out-pitched Waddell, who despite his Hall of Fame arm, was struggling against the Tigers. It was his third loss of the season to Detroit. Cobb smacked three hits and scored twice, also knocking in Crawford, who had a single, triple and a run scored off Waddell.

Cy Young and the Boston Americans were next to come calling. Knowing they would have to win to keep ahead of the Athletics for third place, Detroit beat Young, 6–3. Crawford continued to hit well against Young, pounding three hits and scoring a run to lead the Tigers' attack. He knocked in Killian and Jones with a single in the fourth inning. Cobb added two hits but never got past second base. Once again, the luck didn't last as Crawford went hitless in a 7–3 loss to Boston. Detroit dropped to 38–29 (.567), just ahead of Philadelphia for third place. The Athletics were 38–32 (.543).

New York was the next to arrive, and Donovan was ready. He only struck out one Highlander, but scattered six hits as the Tigers won, 9–4. Crawford and Cobb each laced three hits while Coughlin paced Detroit with four. The Tigers split a doubleheader with New York on July 12, and in the first game, Cobb became the first player to reach 100 hits that season. Crawford scored the game's only run in the opener, reaching on an error, then coming all the way around to score on a bad throw. Both Crawford and Cobb each managed one hit in the second game while the Highlanders knocked George Mullin around and won, 8–3. Detroit was only one game ahead of Philadelphia after the split. The Tigers came back to win the final game of the series, 7–3, to take three of four from New York. Crawford again had a pair of hits, including a triple, leading Donovan to another victory. "Wahoo" Sam singled in Cobb in the sixth and tripled in Coughlin in the third inning. Crawford promptly scored on Cobb's infield single.

Cobb had been on a tear during the first two weeks of July, upping his average from .304 on July 1, to .344 on July 16 to lead the league. Crawford was right behind at .343, and his 84 hits were behind only Cobb and Cleveland's Elmer Flick's 93. With Cobb and Crawford on a roll, the Tigers thought they were finally ready to make a serious run at the pennant. But the bats cooled off and the pitching weakened as the Tigers fell back into fourth place.

Ed Siever shut out Washington, 3–0, in the first game of a July 16 doubleheader with Crawford providing most of the offense with two hits, an RBI and run scored. Crawford scored the lone Tigers run in the second game as Detroit fell, 6–1. Washington chased John Eubank and crushed the Tigers, 13–2, the following day. Both Crawford and Cobb went hitless, a rarity. Detroit played another doubleheader against the Senators on July 18 and won both, pulling them one game behind Philadelphia, which had jumped back into third place.

Then the Tigers got just what they needed—a head-to-head matchup with Philadelphia and future Hall of Fame manager Connie Mack, the "grand old man" of baseball, who would pilot the Athletics to back-to-back World Series championships in 1910–1911. Detroit beat the Athletics, 6–1, and retook third place at 45–32 (.584) while Philadelphia moved to 45–33 (.577). Crawford again was the hero, lacing three hits and scoring twice. Most teams wouldn't be excited to see a future Hall of Famer pitch against them with third place on the line, but the Tigers were happy to see Rube Waddell. His struggles against Detroit continued as the Tigers beat him and the Athletics, 4–3—Waddell's fourth loss in a row to the Tigers. Detroit managed only six hits, but made the most of them. Siever got another victory for the Tigers, who moved three games ahead of Connie Mack's A's.

Batting averages for Cobb and Crawford dropped to .334 and .336, respectively, for the Tigers sluggers, both moving behind Flick in the batting race (.341). But averages weren't as important as winning, and despite the sluggers dropping ten points off their averages, the Tigers had safely climbed into third place and were looking for more. The Tigers beat Philadelphia again on July 22, 6–3, finally getting the better of Plank, who had single-handedly stopped several Detroit winning streaks during the past two seasons. Crawford singled, tripled, knocked in a run and scored twice off Plank. At 47–32, the Tigers were just one-half game back of Cleveland for second place in the American League. After an off-day, Detroit would quickly drop one game behind Cleveland with a 4–3 loss in Boston on July 24. Crawford had three hits and a run scored, but he was one of the few bright spots, as Donovan took a rare loss for Detroit.

Things didn't stay down for very long. The Tigers roared back to sweep both games of a doubleheader with the Americans, surging into second place for the first time since the early weeks of the season. This time, it was not Crawford who was the hero, as he managed just one hit in the twin bill. In fact, it was the pitchers who were the heroes of the day, holding Boston just enough for the Tigers to scratch out a win both games by one run. Killian was the star in the first game, allowing one run in a 2–1 victory, while Siever allowed two runs to beat Cy Young, 3–2, in 11 innings. Detroit's record improved to 49–33 (.598). Cleveland, which lost to New York, 9–4, dropped to 50–35 (.588) and into third place. Detroit was still 1½ games behind the first-place White Sox, but beginning to peak at the right time.

Detroit would move back before it moved forward, however. The Tigers lost, 3–1, to Boston on July 26 and moved back into third place by a game thanks to a doubleheader sweep by Cleveland over New York. Here is how close the standings were:

Team	W	L	Percentage
Chicago	53	35	.602
Cleveland	52	35	.598
Detroit	49	34	.590
Philadelphia	49	35	.583

Only two games separated first place from fourth place, and with Chicago's slight decline and Detroit and Cleveland playing well, the race was far from over. Detroit won its 50th game of the season by beating Boston, 5–4, despite getting just one hit from Crawford and none from Cobb. Donovan earned some revenge by beating the Americans after losing his previous start to them.

Rain halted the Tigers' march, but that seemed to be all that could stop them. On the last day of July, the Tigers beat the Highlanders in New York 6–1 to move back into second place. Cobb took matters into his own hands with four hits and three runs scored, playing with the fire that Detroit needed to overtake Chicago. Here's how the standings looked after Detroit's victory:

Team	W	L	Percentage
Chicago	55	36	.604
Detroit	51	34	.600
Cleveland	53	37	.589
Philadelphia	50	36	.581

Detroit lost 21–2 to New York's Doc Newton on July 31, but with a two-game lead on the Naps coming into the game, the Tigers remained in second place. Newton held both Crawford and Cobb hitless in the game and gave up just three hits in his complete-game victory. Crawford again went hitless against the Highlanders the following day, August 1, but Cobb smacked a pair and Detroit beat New York, 4–3. Cleveland got smoked by Boston, 14–1, and actually dropped to fourth place behind Philadelphia, which shut out St. Louis, 2–0. The Tigers were getting help from other teams which beat the White Sox and Naps while the Tigers continued to win on a regular basis. First place was not far away.

In fact, the Tigers roared into first place the very next day, but it wasn't easy. Detroit swept Washington in a doubleheader on August 2 while New York beat the White Sox, pushing the Tigers into the top spot for the first time since the third week of the season. Here are the August 2 standings:

Team	W	L	Percentage
Detroit	54	35	.60674
Chicago	57	37	.60637
Philadelphia	53	36	.596
Cleveland	54	39	.581

It was by mere percentage points that Detroit took its first real lead in the pennant race, but they earned it. Crawford belted a home run off future Hall of Fame pitcher Walter Johnson in the eighth inning of the first game. It was Johnson's major league debut. He would go on to win 417 games in his career and become arguably the greatest pitcher in baseball history. But he was just a rookie August 2, and had to deal with two of the greatest hitters in the game. Here is how the *Detroit Free Press* described Crawford's clout: "In the eighth, 'Wahoo Sam' Crawford broke into the limelight with great brilliancy in knocking a home run to the score board his speed in going around the bases matching … with the mighty hit."[9]

> On August 2, Detroit beat Washington (in) a doubleheader at American League Park in the capital and took the league lead for the first time that year. The major significance of the date, however, turned out to be that it marked the major-league debut of a gangly nineteen-year-old pitcher with remarkably long arms, brought up directly from Idaho semipro ball, named Walter Johnson. In facing Johnson that day, Cobb later said, "I encountered the most threatening sight I ever saw on a ball field." As the rookie right-hander took his windup and came around with an easy sidearm motion, Cobb barely saw the ball. "The thing just hissed with danger," he thought. Not only was Johnson the fastest pitcher Cobb had ever met; he soon demonstrated that he had nearly pin-point control, most extraordinary in a raw rookie. His first time at bat, Cobb was able to lay down a bunt that the awkward newcomer could not field. Then he went from first to third on Rossman's bunt single and scored on a fly ball. After Washington tied the game in the sixth inning, Crawford hit to the scoreboard in distant left field for a homerun. Meanwhile Cobb threw out a runner at home and another at first. Johnson left for a pinch hitter in the ninth after giving up seven hits and striking out three, with the score 3–1, Detroit. That inning Cobb misplayed a single into a two-base error and let in a run, but Washington's rally fell a run short. Although Walter Johnson took the loss in his first major-league appearance, Cobb and the rest of the Tigers "knew we'd met the most powerful arm ever turned loose in a ball park."[10]

It was Crawford's only hit of the game, but it counted the most. Johnson allowed ten Tigers hits while Siever allowed just five to earn the 3–2 victory for Detroit. Killian relieved Eubank, who was pulled after giving up three runs in the first inning, to earn the victory in the second game, 9–6. Crawford only had one hit—a double—but again made it count as he came around to score.

"Of course, the greatest of them all was Walter Johnson," Crawford told Lawrence Ritter, during an interview for *The Glory of Their Times*. Boy, what a pitcher Walter was! He was the best I ever faced, without a doubt. Did you know I was playing with Detroit the day Walter Johnson pitched his first major-league game? His very first. In fact, I beat him. I'm not being egotistical, you know, but it's a fact. I hit a home run off him and we beat him–I believe the score was 3–2. I think it was late in 1907. We were after the pennant that year, our first pennant, and we needed that game badly.... That's all he pitched, just fast balls. He didn't need any curve. We had a terrible time beating him. Late in the game I hit one—I can remember it as though it were yesterday—it went zooming out over the shortstop's head, and before they could get the ball back in I'd legged it all the way around.... That Walter was fast! I batted against him hundreds of times after that, of course, and he never lost that speed. He was the fastest I ever saw, by far.... He had such an easy motion it looked like he was just playing catch. That's what threw you off. He threw so nice and easy—and then *swoosh*, it was by you![11]

Manager Hughie Jennings was as ecstatic as his players about their recent play, but cautioned them that there was still a long way to go in the season and the standings were so close that anything could happen if they didn't fight every inning of every game. But he still had the confidence in his team that they would win the pennant if they continued to hustle and play like they had been. "At last we are there but we are on pretty thin ice and everybody realizes there is lots of work yet to be done. There is not a band of players in the league that has anything on my boys in the way of fighting spirit, and I really feel that we are there to stay.... The club is in great shape and we will continue to make them all hustle."[12]

Jennings wasn't the only one excited about the Tigers finally reaching first place. The Detroit fans had been waiting for this all season. Meanwhile, that same day, Philadelphia was on the verge of being put out of the race without even being on the field. Rube Waddell, perhaps the greatest raw-talented pitcher of all time, was up to his antics again. He was known for leaving games to chase fire trucks, and on this occasion disappeared entirely for a time, much to the frustration and anxiety of manager Connie Mack, who was still hoping his Athletics had a run left in them. Waddell eventually was found and his antics caused Mack to trade him to St. Louis in 1908. But the Athletics fell out of the race after the latest disappearing act.

Detroit didn't want to let Chicago retake first place and took it out on Washington again, winning 12–4. Crawford had a single and scored while Cobb had a hit and two runs scored, but it was Mullin who was the all-around star for the Tigers. He slapped two hits of his own, scoring twice, and struck out four. He pitched out of jams all day, scattering 13 hits and allowing just four runs to earn the victory. However, the Tigers did fall out of first place, through no fault of their own. The White Sox swept a doubleheader from New York and just as the Tigers had crept into first place in that fashion, Chicago returned the favor the very next day. Here are the August 3 standings:

Team	W	L	Percentage
Chicago	59	37	.615
Detroit	55	35	.611
Philadelphia	53	37	.589
Cleveland	55	39	.585

The Tigers weren't happy about losing first place because of a doubleheader, so knowing they themselves had one on August 5, Detroit went out and swept Washington, 8–2 and 5–2, to retake the lead.

Team	W	L	Percentage
Detroit	57	35	.620
Chicago	59	38	.608
Philadelphia	55	37	.598
Cleveland	55	41	.573

Crawford went hitless in the first game but hit a sacrifice fly, then slapped a pair of hits in the second. It was Cobb who led the way for the Tigers, smacking six hits and scoring two runs in the twin bill. Siever and Donovan each allowed just two runs to pick up the victories.

The Tigers traveled to Philadelphia to face a team that was not out of the race by any means, despite having to deal with the off-the-field antics of Waddell. The Athletics won the series opener, 4–2, despite a strong game from Crawford, who had a single, smacked a triple and scored a run off Chief Bender. The Tigers were still in first place, however, and remained there after facing another future Hall of Famer and known Tiger-killer, Eddie Plank. The Tigers were not fazed, topping Gettysburg Eddie, 5–3. It was Cobb who smacked a double on a pitch that was supposed to be ball three of an intentional walk from Plank. It scored Coughlin and Crawford, who had doubled.

More future Hall of Famers awaited Detroit on the mound in this series. Waddell was slated to start the next game, but it was actually Bender, who shut out the Tigers and jumped the Athletics over Chicago for second place.

Team	W	L	Percentage
Detroit	58	37	.611
Philadelphia	58	38	.604
Chicago	61	42	.592
Cleveland	57	43	.570

The Tigers had a chance in the ninth inning. Davy Jones walked and Crawford smacked a line drive that had double written all over it. However, another future Hall of Famer, Eddie Collins, snagged the line drive at second base to end the game with a 1–0 victory for Philadelphia. Bender allowed just three hits and struck out five in his complete-game shutout. "Wild Bill" Donovan was on the short end of the stick, allowing just three hits and striking out four, but giving up a run in the first inning to take the loss.

The Hall of Fame assault on the Tigers continued as Waddell returned for his first start since his disappearance and beat the Tigers to push the surprising Athletics in first place—ahead of the Tigers.

Team	W	L	Percentage
Philadelphia	59	38	.608
Detroit	58	38	.604
Chicago	61	43	.587
Cleveland	58	43	.574

Waddell didn't look as sharp as he had at times during the season but broke his four-game skid against the Tigers in a 7–3 victory. He struck out seven and walked three in his complete-game victory. This was the performance Connie Mack and the Athletics were hoping for all season, and instead of being the scapegoat for a failed season, Waddell literally pitched Philadelphia into first place. He held Crawford hitless and showed his true Hall of Fame form.

It came as no surprise to anyone in baseball that Philadelphia was fighting the Tigers tooth and nail for the pennant. The Athletics already had two pennants under their belt in the first decade of the century and were on their way to winning three straight after the Detroit mini-dynasty. The reason for their sustained success was pitching. Baseball at the time had a three- or four-man rotation. The Athletics had Eddie Plank, Chief Bender and Rube Waddell—all future Hall of Famers—atop their rotation with Jack Coombs usually taking the fourth spot. Coombs won 158 games in his career and led the AL in victories in 1910 and 1911.

It was Plank's turn and he earned some revenge against the Tigers, pitching a three-hit shutout as the Athletics won, 3–0, and moved another game ahead of the Tigers. Crawford, who had Plank's number most of the season, had two of the three hits by the Tigers but "Gettysburg Eddie" struck out Cobb three times. The Plank-Crawford matchup is still one of the most intriguing historical matchups between two players, especially as a lefty-lefty matchup. Such matchups don't happen in the specialized game of today. Maybe someone like Ken Griffey, Jr., or Barry Bonds could have had one with a lefty like Tom Glavine or Randy Johnson, but they are few and far between. Starting pitchers, especially lefties, don't face the dangerous left-handed hitters as much in today's game, and face them even less with the game on the line. If he is a superstar, he stays in and hits, but more often the left-handed hitter would be lifted from the game for a right-handed pinch-hitter.

The Tigers knew that the Athletics and their pitchers were for real. That was enough of a spark to light a fire in the Tigers dugout for the series finale. Detroit jumped on Waddell for three runs in the first inning, chasing the lefty after he recorded only one out. Crawford had two hits and scored two runs in the 9–2 victory. Cobb recorded another four-hit game and scored once.

The spark was short-lived as New York came to Detroit next and won the first three games. Doc Newton beat the Tigers, 2–1, in the first game. It was the kind of loss that hurt being so close, but stung even more after the tough series with Philadelphia which knocked the Tigers out of first place. Crawford went hitless while Cobb was 1-for-5. The Highlanders won the second game, 4–2, and the Tigers incredibly found themselves in third place.

Team	W	L	Percentage
Philadelphia	62	40	.608
Chicago	64	44	.593
Detroit	59	41	.590
Cleveland	60	46	.566

Crawford had a hit and a run scored, but it wasn't nearly enough to keep the Tigers in second place, though all four of the top teams were still within a few games of each other.

This was one of the best four-team pennant races baseball had seen, and it was helping boost baseball's already growing popularity.

The race in the National League wasn't anywhere near as close. The Chicago Cubs were in first place on August 16 with a 78–29 record (.729), well ahead of the second-place New York Giants and Pittsburgh Pirates, who were each 61–41 (.598).

Detroit still had two more games against New York, but faced future Hall of Fame pitcher Jack Chesbro, who still holds the modern record for most wins in a season with 41. Chesbro beat the Tigers, 5–3, with Killian taking the loss. The fireballer held Crawford to one hit in five at-bats, while Cobb managed two hits.

The Tigers were able to salvage the fourth game, 13–6, and avoid the sweep and climb back into second place. Crawford broke out of his mini-slump with two hits and two runs scored. The American League standings as they looked after August 18:

Team	W	L	Percentage
Philadelphia	62	41	.602
Detroit	60	42	.588
Chicago	64	46	.582
Cleveland	61	46	.570

The Tigers were happy to see another team come into Bennett Park after Philadelphia took four out of six and the Highlanders took three of four from them. Boston was next, and George Mullin decided to take matters into his own hands. Mullin shut out the Americans, 3–0, giving up just six hits. Crawford did his part to help Mullin with two hits and an RBI. With a win the following day, the Tigers could have jumped into first place, but they lost to Boston, 5–4, and dropped into third place in the wild American League race. Crawford went 0-for-5 while Cobb was 1-for-6. The August 21 standings:

Team	W	L	Percentage
Philadelphia	63	43	.594
Chicago	67	46	.593
Detroit	62	43	.590
Cleveland	64	47	.577

So the Tigers were somehow in third place while just a half-game out of first place. Each team was having its ups and downs, moving between first and fourth place. Cleveland had not been in first place for the bulk of the season but the Naps were hanging around within striking distance.

Crawford hadn't been hitting at the level he had shown most of the season, and the Tigers knew he and Cobb would both have to be swinging the bat well for Detroit to swing the close-knit standings in its own direction. Crawford led the Tigers to an 8–7 win over Boston on August 22 with three hits, including a triple, and two runs scored. Cobb had two hits, scored once and knocked in Crawford after his triple. The victory, coupled with a Chicago loss to Philadelphia, moved the Tigers back into second place behind the Athletics.

The Tigers flip-flopped with Chicago again when the White Sox beat New York and Detroit lost, 3–1, to Washington. One game after their offensive output led Detroit to victory, Washington's Cy Falkenberg held both Crawford and Cobb hitless. The Tigers beat the Senators, 8–5, the next game but remained in third place since the White Sox won. Crawford managed a hit and Cobb had a pair. Boston was back in town for a makeup game, and Ed Killian dominated on the mound for Detroit in a 7–1 victory. Crawford and Cobb each powered the Tigers with two hits. Cobb scored a run and Crawford knocked one in.

Despite their rollercoaster August, all the Tigers needed was a win to jump back into first place, which came with a 7–4 win over Washington at home. In the fifth inning, Crawford tripled and scored on a Cobb single, one of two hits for each, while Siever took the victory on the mound. The August 26 standings:

Team	W	L	Percentage
Detroit	66	44	.600
Philadelphia	67	45	.598
Chicago	70	47	.598
Cleveland	66	49	.574

Crawford's slump returned as he went 0-for-8 in a pair of Detroit victories which moved the Tigers to 69–44, ahead of Philadelphia's 67–46. Detroit won its 70th game on August 31 thanks to an Ed Siever shutout over St. Louis. Crawford had a hit and a run scored in the 5–0 victory.

The next day, Detroit visited Chicago and lost to Doc White and the White Sox. Crawford went 0-for-4. A doubleheader with the third-place Sox was next, on September 2, and the Tigers split, winning 6–5 and losing 4–2. Crawford continued to struggle with a 1-for-8 performance. A 1-for-5 game for Sam Crawford helped the Tigers to a 9–6 win over Chicago.

Crawford finally swung his way out of his slump with a single, double, triple, two RBI and run scored. It was something the Tigers needed desperately, however it wasn't enough to beat Cleveland, which edged Donovan and Detroit, 6–5. To make matters worse, the loss dropped the Tigers out of first place again. Philadelphia was 73–47 while Detroit was 72–47, just a half-game back of the Athletics.

It had been a while since the Tigers faced Cleveland, and they renewed their rivalry with future Hall of Fame pitcher Addie Joss, who promptly shut them out, 3–0. The game was monumental for two reasons. First, it kept the Tigers out of first place even after a Philadelphia defeat. Second, and more importantly for Joss, it moved Cleveland into third place ahead of the White Sox. Here is how the race shaped up September 5:

Team	W	L	Percentage
Philadelphia	73	48	.603
Detroit	72	48	.600
Cleveland	72	51	.585
Chicago	73	52	.584

With one shutout victory by Joss, Cleveland had thrown a big monkey wrench into the pennant race. They could now be a major player in the final month of the season.

After the shutout, the Tigers needed offense immediately. Crawford stepped up to the plate and provided it in a 7–4 win over the Naps. He dominated the game as no Detroit batter had all season. "Wahoo" Sam had a hand in all seven Tigers runs. He had two singles, a double, two runs scored and five RBI. Joe Jackson of the *Detroit Free Press* called it an "exhibition of game busting that has the local fans talking."[13] The Tigers needed this, but moreover, Crawford needed to prove to himself and his teammates that he could win some games for them down the stretch.

George Mullin silenced the Cleveland fans for the last time in 1907 by beating the Naps, 4–3, and sending them back to fourth place behind Chicago. It was again Crawford who provided the sparks in the victory. He had a single and a triple, scored once and knocked in two runs. "He really won the contest," Jackson wrote in the *Detroit Free Press*.

Crawford continued to swing a hot bat as the Tigers traveled to Chicago on September 7 to face the White Sox, who had just returned to third place. He belted a home run in the sixth inning off Ed Walsh, another future Hall of Famer, as Detroit won, 6–3, in 11 innings. Crawford knocked in another run with a single in the top of the 11th and eventually came around to score. Siever had started the game and lasted seven innings. In such an important game, Jennings called on Mullin out of the bullpen. He pitched three innings before giving way to "Wild Bill" Donovan, who earned the victory in relief—his 20th win of the season. It wasn't how Donovan expected to reach that plateau, but it was an important victory for Detroit, which at 75–48 was still a half-game back of Philadelphia (76–48).

That Sunday game on the South Side of Chicago drew more than 20,000 fans, a big accomplishment since the Cubs, who were in first place in the National League, were playing a doubleheader and fans got two games there for the price of one. The *Detroit Free Press* noted that the Tigers had played to more than 100,000 fans in a week. That might seem unimpressive by today's standards where that may be accomplished by most teams in a four-day period, but it was a big deal in 1907.

Crawford and the Tigers met their match again in Doc White of the White Sox, who beat Detroit, 5–3, in the series finale. The Tigers managed just seven hits and Crawford went hitless as Detroit dropped to a full game behind idle Philadelphia.

Cleveland returned to Detroit next and Joss greeted the Tigers with another 3–0 shutout, the same score he had blanked them by six days prior in Cleveland. He struck out only two, but allowed five hits, including none by Crawford and one by Cobb. The Naps played a doubleheader on September 12 in Detroit. The Tigers won the opener, 3–2, and played to a 2–2 tie before the second game was called because of darkness. Crawford bounced back from two consecutive hitless games to slap three hits and score a run, leading Detroit to the opening victory. Another doubleheader concluded the series with the Naps, and the Tigers swept both games 4–1 and 10–0. Crawford moved from his usual third spot in the batting order to second and responded with two hits, a run scored, and he also threw a Cleveland runner out at the plate from center field. Crawford also had a hit and a run scored in the second game, which had a controversial finish. With darkness looming, and needing five innings to make it a complete game, the Naps took every measure possible in trying to delay the game so it couldn't be completed and would have to be made up at a later date. Their efforts were in vain as Detroit pummeled the Naps, 10–0.

Another doubleheader was in store the following day, but this one was not so fortunate for the Tigers. Traveling to St. Louis on September 14, the Tigers were swept by the Browns. Even more depressing was that with Chicago's win over Cleveland, the White Sox had jumped into second place, pushing the Tigers back to third. The standings after the September 14 games:

Team	W	L	Percentage
Philadelphia	80	50	.615
Chicago	79	54	.594
Detroit	77	53	.592
Cleveland	75	57	.568

Crawford tallied two hits in the first game but went hitless in the second game, pushing his average to .312 with three weeks to go in the season. Cobb's average was at .337, still trailing Cleveland's Elmer Flick, who was hitting at a .346 clip.

The Tigers were getting sick of doubleheaders wreaking havoc on the standings, but had to play another twin bill against the Browns the following day. Crawford singled and scored in the first game then smashed a home run as part of his two-hit game in the afternoon. The Tigers split, winning 6–3 and losing 3–2, but moved back into second place by percentage points. The September 15 standings:

Team	W	L	Percentage
Philadelphia	80	50	.615
Detroit	78	54	.591
Chicago	79	55	.590
Cleveland	76	57	.571

The Tigers returned home for their final series of the season at Bennett Park, facing an important test in the Chicago White Sox. Detroit needed a fast start to set the pace for the series. Crawford contributed when he doubled and scored in the first inning, helping Detroit chase Doc White from the game before he could get out of the inning. That was all Donovan needed as he completed a shutout and the Tigers won, 7–0. Philadelphia also lost, helping Detroit inch a little closer to first place.

After playing so many doubleheaders, the Tigers got a quick victory when the September 17 game was called because of darkness in the sixth inning. Detroit won, 9–1, behind its two sluggers—Crawford and Cobb—who each went 3-for-4 with one and two runs scored, respectively. It was the 80th win of the season for the Tigers, matching Philadelphia's total. Here are the September 17 standings:

Team	W	L	Percentage
Philadelphia	80	52	.606
Detroit	80	54	.597
Chicago	79	57	.581
Cleveland	77	59	.566

The Tigers had one more doubleheader to finish their home season. Detroit split with the White Sox, losing 3–2, then winning, 3–2. Crawford had three hits on the day and the Tigers moved ahead of idle Philadelphia in the win column with 81, but the Athletics were still in first place with Detroit closing in.

The Tigers began their final road trip of the season in New York, where Bill Donovan threw his third shutout in a week, this

The left-handed Sam Crawford was a mainstay in the Detroit Tigers outfield for 15 years and was the first player to lead both the National League and American League in home runs (National Baseball Hall of Fame Library, Cooperstown, New York).

time allowing just two hits, and giving the Tigers a 1–0 victory. Crawford did his part with two hits and the Tigers crept closer to the Athletics. Here are the September 20 standings:

Team	W	L	Percentage
Philadelphia	80	53	.602
Detroit	82	55	.599
Chicago	82	58	.586
Cleveland	79	60	.568

As close as the Tigers were getting to the Athletics, the White Sox were gaining that much on Detroit, creeping just a half-game behind the Tigers. Detroit and New York split another doubleheader the following day with Mullin losing, 8–2, and Killian winning, 7–2. Crawford scored three runs in the twin bill. The Tigers moved to Boston but were stalled by rain, postponing the series opener to September 24. The wait was worth it. The Tigers thumped Boston, 8–3, and passed Philadelphia to move into first place:

Team	W	L	Percentage
Detroit	84	56	.600
Philadelphia	81	54	.600
Chicago	84	58	.592
Cleveland	80	61	.567

"It was Detroit's game from the time that the Tigers' one best bet in the scoring way, Crawford and Cobb, put two runs over with two out in the fourth, on a base on balls and a triple, which, with an error, proved to be just as good as a home run,"[14] the *Detroit Free Press* reported. Crawford and Cobb did their damage against Cy Young, each scoring twice.

Both the Tigers and Athletics won the next day, keeping atop the American League standings. Crawford again led the charge for the Tigers with two hits and a run scored. Detroit won again in Boston on September 26, keeping pace with the Athletics, who won again. Crawford was still on fire, slamming four hits, scoring twice and knocking in two runs. He walked his fifth time up, which didn't sit well with him. "As a matter of fact, the way Wahoo Sam Crawford was landing the ball there wasn't much chance for any twirler to stop the team. The big fellow got four clean clouts in as many times up, and lost a chance for his coveted record of five in one game because Elmer Steele wouldn't put it over to him in the ninth,"[15] the *Detroit Free Press* stated.

The Tigers were finally putting it all together at the right time because the season would be decided in the next series as Detroit moved to Philadelphia. On September 27, the Tigers opened their series by beating the Athletics, 5–4. Crawford had two hits and two RBI off nemesis Eddie Plank, but it was his fielding that saved the game for Detroit. The *Free Press* described his fielding prowess: "In the Athletics' half (of the fourth inning) the side went out in order, on three great catches by Sam Crawford. The last one was on Danny Murphy. Sam came tearing in for the ball, reached it with his gloved hand just as it was touching the ground, batted it into the air ten feet and caught it as it came down." The victory built Detroit's lead on Philadelphia:

Team	W	L	Percentage
Detroit	87	56	.608
Philadelphia	83	55	.601
Chicago	85	60	.586
Cleveland	83	62	.572

Cobb had one hit in the game, but it was enough to keep him ahead of Crawford in the batting race. Both players had surged ahead of Cleveland's Elmer Flick, who was hitting .323 September 27. Cobb bolstered his average to .337 while Crawford was second in the league at .324.

The Saturday, September 28 game was rained out and rescheduled for Sunday, but rain postponed both games. If that wasn't enough, the Tigers and Athletics played to a 17-inning tie Monday with darkness calling the game knotted, 9–9. The Tigers wasted superb hitting from their two stars. Crawford and Cobb each had three hits and two runs scored, Crawford belting an RBI double and Cobb smashing a home run. So the Tigers left Philadelphia with two rainouts and a 17-inning tie, a game that the great Rube Waddell pitched (it turned out to be his last game at Columbia Park as a member of the Athletics). It would be the game that symbolized the season for the Athletics and their missed opportunities. The game all but decided the pennant race. Here is how the *Philadelphia Inquirer* described the game:

> Jimmy Dygert started for [manager Connie] Mack in game one. Detroit countered with Bill Donovan, who had beaten Plank on Friday. Dygert shut down the Tigers in the first. The A's countered with four hits and three runs, batting eight men in their half of the inning. The fans were delirious. In the second inning, the pressure got to Dygert. The first batter singled. The next man grounded to Dygert. He threw to second, but his toss landed wide and in the dirt, pulling Murphy off the bag, leaving all safe. A sacrifice advanced runners to second and third. The next batter chopped back to Dygert. The runner on third had advanced too far and Dygert had him in a rundown. Again, however, Dygert threw wildly. The run scored and the runners advanced. Dygert then yielded a walk, filling the bases full with only one out. Mack decided to make a move.
>
> With the bases loaded and one out, Mack sent for the Rube. He wanted Plank for game two. Bender was ill and Jack Coombs was hurt. Fans were more than a little nervous as Rube took the mound. His phenomenal play of earlier years was a distant memory. As was normal in those days, Rube took no warm-ups; Bang! Rube immediately struck out Detroit's next two hitters, their leadoff and second batters, no less. Detroit left the inning with three runners standing. The crowd roared. Rube seemed to have his stuff and he had a lead, to boot. Confidence grew even more as Rube struck out four in the next two innings, thus fanning six of the first eight he faced. The A's, meanwhile, hit Donovan for two runs in the third and two more in the fifth. Going into the seventh inning the A's lead remained 7–1.
>
> Then came the weird seventh. Donovan led off the inning for Detroit with a pop to center. Rube Oldring was camped under it but, inexplicably, he flat dropped it. Perhaps a little rattled, Rube walked the next batter, the only man he would walk all day. Then Simon Nicholls muffed a grounder at shortstop that would have been a double play. Were it not for the dropped fly and the muff at short, Rube and the A's would have been out of the inning. As it was, the bases were loaded with nobody out. Up stepped Sam Crawford. Crawford was as dangerous a line-drive hitter as ever played the game. He could hit 'em low, high, inside, or out, it didn't matter. A reporter once asked Chicago's Ed Walsh, "Is there any place where you can throw the ball where Crawford won't hit it?" "Yeah," Walsh cracked, "second base." Walsh was not far off: Crawford knocked Rube's first pitch for a double, scoring two. Ty Cobb stepped in. Cobb was leading the league in hitting for the first time that season (he would do it a few more times) but Rube worked him for an infield grounder. Murphy elected to toss it to first, however, and a run scored. Murphy could have gone to Ossee Schreck, but he apparently preferred to keep Cobb off the base paths. He didn't want to risk being spiked again. It was one of countless ways that Cobb's terror tactics worked in Detroit's favor. With Crawford now on third and no one on first, the next

batter grounded to second. He was thrown out but Crawford scored.... Rube struck out the next batter to end a long inning. Crawford's double had been the only hit of the inning, yet Detroit had scored four.

The A's got one back in the bottom of the seventh, and Detroit hustled one in the top of the eighth on a double, a steal and a grounder. Going into the ninth, the score was 8–6. Rube again faced Sam Crawford, who singled to start the inning and set things up for Ty Cobb. Rube worked Cobb carefully, throwing him three straight curves. Each offering just missed. At 3 and 0 Rube would not yield. He threw two more curves, and each cut the corner. Cobb usually leaned his shoulders toward the plate to hit more for contact than power. This time he pulled slightly away, guessing, with the count full, that Rube's next delivery would be a fastball. He guessed right. Cobb pulled back and connected, knocking the pitch over the crowd and over the fence. In his 24 years in baseball, Cobb never hit more than nine home runs in a season. He hit only one off Rube Waddell, and this was it, one of two home runs Rube yielded all season. The score was now tied. Connie Mack fell off his seat on the bench and landed in the bat rack.

The mess of the seventh was not Rube's fault. And there was no disgrace in the ninth, given who had touched Rube for the two runs. Crawford and Cobb were the best one-two punch in the game, as good as any at any time, including Ruth/Gehrig and Maris/Mantle. Sam Crawford was a future Hall of Famer. He is (and likely always will be) baseball's all-time leader in triples. And Ty Cobb was—Ty Cobb. Some wondered how Cobb could hit a pitch so far, particularly since he hit a ball that had been in use since the fifth inning. The answer was in his body motion. With Cobb pulling his shoulders away from the plate, he was connecting with more than just the weight and strength of his arms. Such a swing is not the way to hit for a high average, and Cobb seldom hit that way. But it is one way to jerk the ball a long way. Whatever the reason for Cobb's homer, the fact was that Rube had failed to hold a substantial lead, and people were angry. Whether Rube could have held Detroit from there, we'll never know, for Mack sent in Eddie Plank. No one realized it then, but they had just witnessed Rube Waddell's last appearance for the A's at Columbia Park.

The 8–8 tie held up through the tenth inning. In the 11th each side scored one. In the 12th, Detroit loaded the bases but didn't score. Some real controversy came in the 14th. The outfield was still ringed with people with no barriers but squads of police. The police were supposed to move the crowds back in case a play came their way so there would be no interference. In the top of the 14th, the A's big first baseman Harry Davis led off with a high drive to center field. Sam Crawford was out there. He raced for the ball; it grazed his glove and glanced into the crowd. Normally, a ball hit into the crowd under such circumstances is ruled a ground rule double. Davis anticipated this and jogged into second. Plate umpire "Silk" O'Loughlin ruled, however, that a policeman had interfered with Crawford and ruled Davis out. The second umpire of the day had ruled it a ground rule double, but O'Loughlin overruled him. The A's put up a fearsome argument. Even Connie Mack grew red-faced. He would not speak to O'Loughlin for over a decade because of the call.

The Detroit players streamed out and threw their two cents into the discussion. With both teams out, shouting and pushing started.... Rossman and Monte Cross were tossed out of the game.

The police were able to restore order.... Plank pitched the rest of the way for Philadelphia. Donovan went the distance for Detroit, throwing over 200 pitches. After the 17th inning, O'Loughlin said it was too dark to see the ball. There would be no second game, and in those days teams did not make up ties. An A's victory would have put them on top. Now they were still percentage points behind.

The A's-Tigers game of September 30 was one American League fans talked about for years. It was a critical game, it was well played, it had stars like Crawford, Plank, Cobb, and Waddell, and it was full of excitement and controversy.

The A's were not out of the race, but now their chance was merely mathematical....

Their chance for a pennant entailed their winning both games against the Senators and St. Louis sweeping all three games they still had to play with Detroit.[16]

Crawford later remembered the incident in a letter to a friend. It read in part: "It was strictly a one man interference and the crowd had nothing to do with it. This policeman was sitting on the grass in front of the ropes. When he saw the ball coming he jumps up and runs in front of me just as I have my arms out to catch the ball. He brushes my arms aside and of course, I miss it. This happened 10 to 15 feet in front of the ropes so you see the crowd couldn't have had anything to do with it. The umpire saw the interference."[17]

A trip to the nation's capitol was next for Detroit. The Tigers beat Washington, 5–3, behind three hits from Cobb, pushing him past 200 hits for the season, and quality pitching from Ed Siever. Detroit posted its 90th victory of the season on October 2, by sweeping a doubleheader from the Senators, 9–5 and 10–2. The pennant looked like it was coming to Detroit:

Team	W	L	Percentage
Detroit	90	56	.616
Philadelphia	84	56	.600
Chicago	86	62	.581
Cleveland	84	65	.564

The Tigers finished off the sweep of the Senators with a 9–3 victory on October 3. A trio of hits by Cobb and a run scored by Crawford did a bulk of the damage as Bill Donovan again pitched well.

The Tigers had an off-day October 4, but still lengthened their lead in the American League when Walter Johnson and the Senators beat the Athletics in ten innings in the first game of a doubleheader. Philadelphia needed to sweep to get back into the race.

Detroit clinched the pennant the next day with a win over St. Louis, 10–2. Crawford doubled in a run while Davy Jones scored three runs and pitcher Ed Siever scored two, as many as he allowed in his complete-game victory. The Tigers were 92–56 (.622) and couldn't be caught by Philadelphia, which was 88–57 (.607).

The entire city of Detroit, and state of Michigan, was excited for the Tigers to be in their first World Series. It was exactly 20 years earlier when the Detroit Wolverines had won their first championship behind future Hall of Famers Big Dan Brouthers, Foxy Ned Hanlon and another Sam: Sam Thompson, who is still one of the best RBI men to ever play the game with 1,305 in just 1,410 games, leading the league three times including 166 in 1887. There was no World Series back then, so Tigers fans were in for a treat when Detroit faced the Chicago Cubs, who had won 107 games—16 more than the second-place Pirates and 15 more than the Tigers won in the AL—to take the National League flag.

The Tigers came in a hot team, hitting when it counted and winning when it counted. They had Ty Cobb, who won the batting title at .350, becoming the youngest batting champ in history at age 20 (since broken by Tiger Al Kaline in 1955). Sam Crawford finished second at .323. More impressive was Crawford leading the league in runs scored with 102. He also knocked in 81 runs. Meanwhile, Cobb led the league with 212 hits, scored 97 runs and led the American League with 119 runs batted in.

But the Cubs had the most famous double play combination in baseball history: Tinker to Evers to Chance, which became the subject of a famous poem "Baseball's Sad Lexicon" by Franklin Pierce Adams. More than that, Joe Tinker, Johnny Evers and Frank Chance were great ballplayers and future Hall of Famers. The Cubs also had a great catcher in Johnny Kling, and one of the best pitchers in the National League: Mordecai "Three Finger" Brown. Brown went 20–6 in 1907 on his way to a 239–130 (.648) career record and a spot in the Hall of Fame. The Detroit pitchers also had a terrific season as a group, led by "Wild Bill" Donovan's 25 victories. Ed Killian matched Donovan with 25 while George Mullin posted 20 victories and Ed Siever added 18.

Game 1 of the World Series was October 8 in Chicago. "In the Series opener, 24,337 packed and slightly overflowed the Cubs' West Side Grounds at Polk and Lincoln (later Wolcott) Streets. It was the biggest crowd in Series history up to that time. As Cobb approached the plate for his first at-bat, umpire Hank O'Day stopped play so a representative of a St. Louis jewelry company could present an ornate diamond-studded medal, the prize the company had put up for the batting champion in each league. Cobb then grounded meekly to Frank Chance. After that Bill Donovan battled the Cubs' Orval Overall and Ed Reulbach to a 12-inning, 3–3 tie, made possible when Charley Schmidt's passed ball on a called third strike let in the tying run in the ninth. Cobb went hitless in five times up."[18]

Cubs fans and Tigers fans alike went home disappointed as the game ended in a 3–3 tie after 12 innings. Playing well before lights were implemented, any game after the sun set was called so nobody got hurt, and so fans could actually see what was happening. It was very disappointing for Crawford, who slapped three hits and drove in two runs for Detroit. He wouldn't hit that well again in the Series.

The Cubs beat the Tigers, 3–1, the following day. George Mullin allowed three runs despite pitching well, but not as well as Chicago's Jack Pfiester—14–9 during the season— who allowed one run and held Crawford hitless.

Game 3 was more of the same as the Cubs won, 5–1, behind Ed Reulbach, who had gone 17–4 during the season to lead the National League with an .810 win percentage. Crawford and Cobb each managed a hit, but that was all. Meanwhile Evers slapped three hits to lead the Cubs, who again didn't need to score much the way their pitchers were performing. Siever pitched the first four innings for the Tigers, then gave way to Killian, who allowed one run. But the damage was done.

Orval Overall was the next Cub to take the mound, after going 23–7 during the regular season. He followed the example set by his teammates and shut down the Tigers for a 6–1 victory. Crawford again went hitless while Cobb had one hit and scored Detroit's lone run. Overall struck out six Tigers while Tinker scored twice to give the Cubs the edge, and a commanding 3–0 lead in the series. Donovan allowed three earned runs to take the loss.

The Tigers had feared "Three Finger" Brown, who had injured his pitching hand in a farm accident as a youngster, but had used his one-knuckled index finger to develop a devastating curve ball. Despite this fear, the Tigers were not expecting to get shut down by Pfiester, Reulbach and Overall. The last thing the Tigers wanted to see was Brown when they were already down 3–0. But that's what happened, and Brown shut out the Tigers, 2–0, with four strikeouts to clinch the first World Series championship for the Cubs.

It was a depressing showing by the powerful Tigers offense. The four Chicago starters held Detroit to just six runs in four games. Cobb batted .200 with four hits. Only Claude Rossman (.450) and Davy Jones (.353) batted higher than .250 for the Tigers. Meanwhile, light-hitting Johnny Evers batted .350 and third baseman Harry Steinfeldt batted .471 to lead the Cubs to the championship.

Hughie Jennings kept up his spirit to the final out, prancing in the coaching box and hollering his "atta boys" and "ee-yahs," and when it was over he was positive. "Another year is coming," he told the players. "And we'll be up there again. Next time we will be world champions. As it is there are honors enough."[19]

It was a poor Series for Crawford, not unlike the rest of his Detroit teammates. He was disappointed with his hitting—batting just .238 for the Series with five hits—but he would have more chances to make good for the Tigers in the coming years and would remain one of the elite players in the game for another decade.

The Tigers and their fans were left to ponder about Detroit's chance of repeating as American League champions. It turned out, the chance was pretty good.

5. Another Pennant, Another Disappointment

Sam Crawford and the Detroit Tigers entered the 1908 season with mixed emotions. Detroit had won its first pennant in 1907 and made its first trip to the World Series. But Crawford and Ty Cobb, two of the best hitters in baseball history, did not perform up to their abilities in the series and the Tigers were swept by the Chicago Cubs. But like every spring in baseball, there is hope, and the Tigers had much more hope than most teams in the American League. They were still on the rise with more pennants in the future.

Another trip to the World Series would happen for Detroit in 1908—another matchup with the Cubs. But first, the Tigers would have to fight through another close pennant race to prove they were once again the best in the American League. Crawford knew, as all baseball players know, that there would be a close pennant race almost every year. The Tigers were just hoping they would be in it—with fewer than four teams with a chance at a pennant in September as in 1907.

To defend their pennant, the Tigers would need the same one-two punch that Cobb and Crawford provided in 1907. Cobb won the batting title and led the league in hits, stolen bases and runs batted in, while Crawford led in runs scored and finished second to Cobb in the batting race. Cobb would go on to win an astounding 12 batting titles in his career, including 1908. The only question was: could Wahoo Sam keep pace again?

It didn't start well for the Tigers in spring training. The club had abominable weather in Arkansas, and not only Cobb, but Crawford, missed most of the training. Crawford was called home by the serious illness of his wife.[1]

The season began on April 14 against another Chicago team, the White Sox. Doc White and Nick Altrock pitched for the White Sox and escaped with a 15–8 victory, despite a pounding from the Tigers offense. Crawford had a single and a double and scored two runs while Cobb had a single, double and home run, also scoring two. It was a good start for the Detroit duo but not for the Tigers.

The second game was rained out but the Tigers earned their first victory of the season on April 16 with a 4–2 win over the White Sox. Crawford and Cobb weren't the heroes, each tallying one hit on the day. It was the start of a slow season for Crawford, who would manage only three multi-hit games in the next month. Cleveland was next for Detroit, Crawford went 0-for-6 and the Tigers lost, 12–8. While Crawford was slumping, so were the Tigers. They would lose eight of their next 11 games and be buried in last place. Even when Crawford looked to break out of his slump, it didn't seem to do much good. On April

24, he posted a single and a triple off future Hall of Fame pitcher Addie Joss, but Joss beat the Tigers, 2–1. It was the first time the Tigers faced a Hall of Fame pitcher that season. It wouldn't be the last. Detroit faced future Hall of Fame starters a stunning 42 times—close to one-third of their games in 1908. It didn't look promising, but things were starting to look better for Crawford. The next day, he won a 3–2 game over the Naps with a home run in the top of the tenth inning. The *Detroit Free Press* described the action in the tenth: "Big Sam Crawford, terror of Cleveland pitchers on their home lot, put another one over for Detroit today. In the tenth inning he won the game for his side by smashing the first ball pitched by [Glenn] Liebhardt into right field bleachers for a home run."[2] Ed Summers held Cleveland scoreless for eight innings and allowed two runs in the bottom of the ninth inning to tie the game. Detroit (3–6) climbed out of the cellar, a half-game ahead of the last-place Washington Senators (3–7).

The Tigers lost the next three—two to Cleveland and one to the White Sox. Crawford managed just two hits in the three games and his batting average plummeted to .222. Cobb also wasn't hitting his best and took out his frustrations on his opponents on the base paths and on umpires. On May 1, Cobb was thrown out of a game after being called out at the plate, trying for a home run. He knocked in two runs with the hit, and had doubled in two more runs earlier in the game to beat the White Sox, 4–2. Here's what Joe Jackson of the *Detroit Free Press* saw:

> Tyrus Cobb, darling of Detroit's diamond devotees, featured some reversible ructions at Bennett Park yesterday, thereby winning one game for the Tigers 4 to 2, and on the other hand putting himself in danger of being banished from a few yet to be played. His pardonable ambition to be the first Tiger to smite a four sack smash on the revised ball park was the cause of his undoing, and, incidentally, also of that of the Chicago club....
> Umpire O'Loughlin called Cobb out. Tyrus jumped to his feet, rushed at the umpire, and made the fatal error of putting his hands on the arbitrator.[3]

Crawford's old friend Rube Waddell, now pitching for the St. Louis Browns, was up next for Detroit. Crawford smacked two hits to help the Tigers beat Waddell, 1–0. The success was short-lived as Crawford went 0-for-4 in a 2–1 loss to the Browns the following day before rain postponed the third game.

Next the Tigers traveled to Cleveland, where more rain postponed the first game with the Naps, resulting in two consecutive doubleheaders on May 9 and 10. Joss started the first game for Cleveland and beat the Tigers, 4–3. Crawford, beginning to heat up, went 3-for-4 against the future Hall of Famer, who held Cobb hitless. The next day, it was back to St. Louis for a makeup doubleheader. Crawford had one hit off Waddell in the first game and the Tigers won, 6–2. "Wahoo" Sam pounded Bill Dineen in the second game with a single, double and three runs scored in an 11–4 win over the Browns. Things were slowly turning around for the Tigers.

On May 11, it was off to Boston to face Eddie Cicotte, who was at the start of his career in Boston, and the Tigers beat him, 4–2, thanks to Crawford. "Wahoo" Sam tripled in two runs in the eighth inning to tie the game, then scored the go-ahead run on a single by Cobb. "It was Sam Crawford's rallying triple in the eighth that sent two men over the rubber with the score a tie and gave the visitors a lead that the locals could not overtake," the *Detroit Free Press* reported.

The next day, Crawford went 2-for-4 with three runs scored as Detroit thumped

Boston, 10–3. Cy Young was the next pitcher to face the surging Tigers and he went down, 6–4. Young held Crawford hitless but Cobb had two hits and a run scored to spark the offense.

Moving to New York, the Tigers lost the opener to the Highlanders, 7–6, but scored an 11–6 victory May 18, jumping on future Hall of Fame pitcher Jack Chesbro. Crawford came up in the eighth inning with the bases loaded and promptly cleared them with a double to put the game away for the Tigers. The Highlanders won the series finale 6–1 to end a Tigers streak where they won six of eight games.

The nation's capitol was next for Detroit, and they weren't welcomed well by the Senators as Bill Burns threw a two-hit shutout to beat the Tigers, 1–0. Crawford got one of those hits and added one in each of the next two games as Detroit beat Washington, 4–1 and 3–2. In the finale, Crawford went 0-for-4 but Ed Siever pitched a complete-game shutout to return the favor to Burns and the Senators, 1–0.

It was on to Philadelphia, where Eddie Plank and the Philadelphia Athletics awaited the Tigers. Plank always pitched well against the Tigers and did just that on May 26, but lost 1–0 as "Wild Bill" Donovan posted the second consecutive shutout for the Tigers. Crawford managed two hits in the next game, but the Athletics rallied to win when first baseman Harry Davis knocked in the winning run with a groundout. Another two hits by Crawford helped the Tigers beat Philadelphia, 10–2, to close out the series and move into second place (17–15).

But Detroit wasn't interested in second place after winning the pennant a year ago. The Tigers instantly made a move to the top by sweeping the White Sox, 6–3 and 9–5, in a doubleheader to tie New York for first place at 19–15. In the first game, Doc White intentionally walked Sam Crawford with runners on second and third to get to Ty Cobb in the first inning. The strategy backfired as Cobb singled in two runners, Crawford moved to third and scored on a hit by Coughlin, propelling Detroit into first place.

The Tigers wouldn't be in first place for long, however. Incredibly, Detroit lost four of its next five games and plummeted to fifth place at 20–19. After Ed Walsh beat the Tigers, 1–0, with a four-hit shutout, the Tigers beat the White Sox, 2–1, in the second game of the twin bill. It was Cleveland they were more concerned with, however. The Naps had made a move up the standings and beat the Tigers in the first three games of their four-game series to take first place at 22–18. Crawford went 2-for-11 in the games, scoring just one run. As if it wasn't enough that the Tigers were getting manhandled by Cleveland, they had to face Addie Joss in the series finale. He had stifled Detroit earlier in the season, 2–1, and was one of the best pitchers in the American League—maybe the best. Crawford managed two hits off Joss and the Tigers beat him and the Naps, 3–1. As big as the win was for Detroit, they moved up only to fourth place.

Joss wasn't the only problem the Tigers had to deal with in Cleveland. That June, Cobb's prejudice against blacks had surfaced, this time landing him in a court of law as the defendant.

> He was leaving the Pontchartrain Hotel in June when a streetworker who was spreading fresh asphalt shouted at him for walking too close to the gooey stuff. A bit spilled on Cobb's trouser cuff. A discussion over this led to Cobb knocking the black worker, one Fred Collins, on his back. Collins's head was injured. Forty-eight hours later Cobb faced a judge on assault and battery charges. Although handed only a suspended sentence, he was

ordered to pay Collins seventy-five dollars to cover court costs or face a damage suit. Cobb's testimony that Collins had been out of line and had spoken insultingly to him was good enough reason for Judge Edward Jeffries—a Tiger fan—to hand down no more than a suspension without fine.

At the same Pontchartrain, as reported by the *Chicago Defender*, an early news organ for blacks, Cobb had kicked a chambermaid in the stomach and knocked her down some stairs because she flared back when he called her "nigger." The hotel's manager protested and ordered Cobb to leave the place. The story was suppressed by the newspapers, but years later Harold Seymour was moved to track down the details for his book, *Baseball: The Golden Age*. Seymour's research showed that the press had finessed the incident, and that because of Cobb's prominence the woman was quietly paid off in exchange for dropping a ten-thousand-dollar lawsuit.[4]

The Tigers had to keep their focus on the field if they were going to stay in the pennant race. The pitching in the American League was too good to overlook in any game. Another legend awaited the Tigers as Boston came to town. Cy Young promptly sent the Tigers back to fifth place with a 2–1 victory. He held Crawford hitless and Cobb managed just one hit off the career wins leader. The Tigers jumped into third place by scoring two runs in the ninth and beating Ed Cicotte, 8–7. However, it was Young again the next day as Boston won, 10–5, then finished the series with a 9–5 victory to send the reeling Tigers into sixth place with a 22–22 record.

The Tigers dugout was not a happy place during this stretch. How could this team with all that talent on the mound and in the field be sitting in sixth place? It was inconsistency. The Tigers started the season by winning some, then losing some. When they pitched well, they couldn't hit, and vice versa. Hughie Jennings and his ball club knew they had the makings of another pennant-winning team, but they would have to climb out of the hole they dug themselves into.

A loss to the Highlanders put the Tigers below .500 at 22–23. It was the breaking point for Crawford, Cobb and the Tigers. Though it took a losing record to wake up the Tigers, they finally woke up and slowly crept back into the race. The Tigers won the next three games against New York, including a 3–1 victory over Jack Chesbro. Before the final game of the series on June 12, the Tigers raised their 1907 pennant at Bennett Park. It inspired them to continue their winning ways, beating the Highlanders, 5–2. Crawford was 2-for-4 with a run scored and had six hits in the series. "Wahoo" Sam was at first base because of an injury to Claude Rossman and would hold down the bag for the next ten games while Cobb was joined in the outfield by Matty McIntyre and Davy Jones.

Philadelphia was next and the Tigers took three of four from the Athletics to move into fourth place at 28–24. The biggest evidence of a turnaround came on June 16, when the Tigers faced their old nemesis Eddie Plank. The Tigers chased Plank from the game after just 2⅓ innings and beat the Athletics, 7–3. Crawford powered Detroit with two hits, a run scored and an RBI, while Cobb went 1-for-5 with a run scored.

Washington's Bill Burns shut out the Tigers, 5–0, two days later, before the Tigers won the next two from the Senators and swept a two-game series with the White Sox, including a 6–1 win over Ed Walsh. Once again, the Tigers would have to face two future Hall of Fame pitchers in a row when Crawford's old teammate Rube Waddell and the St. Louis Browns came to town. Waddell held Crawford and Cobb hitless and beat the Tigers, 7–1. Waddell's performance sparked the Browns, who won the next two games, 4–1 and 4–2, to take first place in the American League. The next game (June 27) Crawford was back in center field and had two hits as the Tigers beat the Browns, 1–0, to avoid the sweep. The Tigers were 33–28 and still in fourth place.

Finally back in the outfield where he belonged, Crawford began to tear up the American League pitchers as the Tigers faced a daunting 26-game road trip. He knocked around Ed Walsh the next day for a single, a triple and two runs, while Nick Altrock gave up three hits to Crawford two days later as the Tigers took two of three from the White Sox. Next it was on to Cleveland, where Crawford slammed a double and a home run and scored three times to spark an 11–1 win. He tripled and scored the next day as the Tigers won, 6–0. Joss was on the mound again for the Naps in the first game of the July 4 doubleheader. Again he pitched masterfully, holding Cobb and Crawford hitless, but lost 1–0 because the Cleveland offense got nothing going against Summers. The Tigers were back in business in third place and weren't showing any signs of slowing down, cruising to a 20–6 record on the road trip.

After winning a makeup game with Chicago, 5–3, the Tigers moved their record to 39–30—tied with Cleveland for second place. Detroit moved to the Big Apple, where they won both games of a doubleheader to move alone into second place (41–30). Crawford pounded a double and a triple and scored three times in the 11–4 drubbing in the second game. The Tigers beat Chesbro, 5–3, the following day and again two days later, 8–2, completing the five-game sweep of the Highlanders and climbing all the way back to first place. The Tigers moved their record to 44–30 after going 12–2 in the previous 14 games and found themselves tied with St. Louis atop the American League standings on the morning of July 8.

Detroit was still tied with the Browns on July 11, but split a doubleheader July 13 to drop into second place (45–32). St. Louis won to improve to 46–31. A 5–3 win in ten innings the following day tied Detroit with St. Louis, who lost. In the finale with Boston, Crawford had a hit and a run scored, upping his average to .282 for the season. The Tigers beat the Red Sox, 5–1, and since the Browns lost, Detroit was alone in first place at 47–32.

As close as the race was with St. Louis the first half of the season, and would be until September, the Tigers would remain in first place most of the way. It was a relief to be on top for so long in 1908 after battling until the final week of the 1907 season, with not just one team, but four, which all had a shot at the pennant.

Detroit traveled to Philadelphia to face the Athletics, the same team that fought until the end the season before. Plank started the opener and struck out four on the way to a 4–3 victory. Crawford didn't manage a hit and Cobb tallied just one. But the Tigers got their revenge the next day, slamming the Athletics, 21–2, chasing Harry "Rube" Vickers after he was able to get only one out in the first inning. Crawford had his biggest game of the season. He slapped three singles and a triple and came around to score three runs. Again he was outdone by Cobb, who posted five hits and scored three times.

The offensive explosion was short-lived for the Tigers as they were routed, 11–5, by the Athletics. Philadelphia manager Connie Mack sent Plank out to the mound the following day and, once again, "Gettysburg Eddie" held Crawford hitless, but the rest of the Tigers picked up the slack and knocked off Plank, 4–1. After two more victories at Washington, the Tigers were 51–34. St. Louis lost a doubleheader on July 21 and was 49–37, struggling to keep pace with the surging Tigers.

If there was any chance for the Browns to make up some ground, it was the next three games. The Tigers had to face three future Hall of Fame pitchers in a row. In the last game of the series in Washington, Detroit faced Walter Johnson. Then it was a makeup game against Addie Joss and the Naps, followed by the first game in New York against Jack Chesbro. The Browns won their two games during those three days, but the Tigers didn't flinch. They beat Johnson, 4–2, on July 23 with Crawford tallying a single. He had another three-hit performance against Joss, knocking a single, a triple and belting a home run into the right field bleachers to lead the Tigers to a 4–0 victory. It was their 19th victory in the last 25 games. The *Detroit Free Press* described the atmosphere: "The long trip of the Detroit Tigers was wound up here today in style…. It was enlivened by the presence of a small, but loud lunged, bunch of Detroit rooters, who went crazy every time Sam Crawford hit the ball safely, and who rooted steadily for the good young pitcher who was making the home team look bad."[5] That young pitcher was Eddie Summers, who shut out the Naps while allowing just four hits. But it was Crawford who was the real hero, hitting the home run to win the game. Here's what the *Detroit Free Press* said about Crawford's clout: "Crawford of course had to get his customary four base hit here…. The two runs were superfluous but 'Wahoo Sam' could not be expected to break himself of his home run habit, to which he has fallen a victim persistently on his trips to Cleveland. The other two runs scored in the third and fifth, would have been enough. Neither was earned, and maybe Crawford decided the Tigers should earn enough to win."[6]

Next up was Jack Chesbro and the Highlanders, but it was Cobb's turn to be the hero against a future Hall of Fame pitcher. "The Georgia Peach" slapped two singles and a triple, scored a run and knocked in four runs in a 5–3 victory. Crawford scored on Cobb's triple after singling. With his performance, Cobb upped his average to .342, while Crawford, despite his strong hitting of late, was batting .283. Detroit finished out the series in New York with 6–2 and 4–2 victories over the Highlanders.

Boston came to Detroit next with another legend: Cy Young. Young held Crawford without a hit while Cobb had another three-hit game and the Tigers won, 3–2. Stunningly, the Tigers had won 24 of their last 30 games—including nine in a row. More impressively, Detroit beat eight future Hall of Famers in the process, moving their record to 57–34, three games ahead of the Browns (55–38).

The streak finally ended on July 31 with a 9–5 loss to the Red Sox. Detroit split the next two games with Boston before facing Philadelphia. Eddie Summers pitched the Tigers to a 4–3 victory with a little help from Crawford, who was back in right field. Joe Jackson of the *Detroit Free Press* gave his opinion of Crawford's move from center:

> There must be something in the atmosphere of that northeast section of the local ball-yard. In the absence of Cobb, to be bound with silken fetters, W. Sam Crawford was shifted over into the conversational corner, where a man gets a chance to fan and field at the same time. On the home lot of late things have not been breaking as well for Sammy as his efforts deserve. But the change of scene acted as an immediate tonic. First time up Crawford cracked out a double. And on his second appearance he practically decided the result of the contest, pulling off a play that not only had all of the daring of the most desperate that Cobb has shown, but that also was excellent head work on the part of its maker. It turned a single into a play that paved the way to two runs.[7]

Those two runs scored on a throwing error by left fielder Topsy Hartsel. Crawford took third on the play and scored on a single by Coughlin.

Cobb didn't make the trip home with his teammates. He instead married Charlotte Marion Lombard at the country home of the bride's father, nine miles from Augusta. "The marriage was characterized by extreme simplicity, and only the close relatives of the bride were present, a few very intimate friends and a representative of the press. 'Tyrus Cobb is to desert his teammates to get married. He will return to Detroit accompanied by his wife.... The couple will spend the greater part of the winter abroad." Mention was made that the absentee had obtained Hughie Jennings's permission to take off. No such permission had been given, said Sam Crawford when Al Stump visited the 77-year-old Hall of Famer at his Pearblossom, California, home in 1957.

> "He just walked out and left us flat in midseason," said Crawford bleakly. With his team fighting for the pennant, Cobb proceeded to absent himself for six days, without even bothering to notify the management of his intentions until shortly after he had left. To Frank Navin and Detroit co-owner Bill Yawkey, the departure of Cobb was inexcusable. In a subsequent dispute with Cobb, Navin spoke of his 1908 defection as the most arrogant act he had ever heard of in baseball. Cobb's leaving the team was one of the earliest of a series of acts by Cobb establishing him as a special case, exempt from the usual organization rules, and presaging his eventual status as law unto himself.[8]

Playing without Cobb, the Tigers relied on Crawford to supply the punch in the lineup. The day after Cobb's wedding, Crawford clubbed two hits, scored twice and led the Tigers to a 5–3 win over the Athletics. The next day, it was Eddie Plank again on the mound and he got his revenge for the 4–1 loss he took on July 20. He shut out the Tigers, 3–0, and held Crawford hitless. Plank gave up four hits and struck out three. Facing Plank was the only setback in Crawford's leading role while Cobb was away. Washington came to town the next day and Crawford lined three singles, slammed a triple and scored three runs as the Tigers rocked the Senators, 18–1. "Wahoo Sam" had his average back up to .291 with his four-hit performance. Joe Jackson of the *Detroit Free Press* praised Crawford's hitting prowess: "There was no gent whose bludgeon work stood out over that of his fellows unless it was W. Sam Crawford, who hit safely four times in a row, winding up with a triple. If Sam could have poled this a little farther, for a home run, we would have seen almost everything that a game of ball can bring forth. Sam figured in every scoring session excepting the opener."[9]

Cobb returned to the lineup August 9 in the second game of the Washington series. He and Crawford provided that one-two punch the Tigers had been missing. Crawford had a single, a double and scored a run while Cobb picked up right were he left off, building his batting average to .348 with a triple and two runs scored in a 5–2 Detroit victory.

Next up for the Tigers was Walter Johnson, who, like Plank, got some revenge for a loss he took against the Tigers during their impressive streak. "The Big Train" allowed five hits and struck out two as the Senators won, 3–2. Crawford and Cobb each scored a run for the Tigers. The Senators won the series finale, also by a 3–2 score, and Detroit headed to Boston with a 62–39 record. St. Louis closed some ground and was right on the Tigers' tails at 61–42.

During an off-day, several of the Tigers played in a Cy Young tribute game in Boston. Every team had at least one representative in the game, honoring Young's great career. This was 25 years before the All-Star Game was put into practice, and fans flocked to the park to see the great stars of baseball on one field. More than 20,000 fans packed the Boston stadium to pay their respects to the greatest pitcher of all-time. (At this point, Young had no equal in longevity and dominance, but Walter Johnson was in his first full season and later earned the "best pitcher of all time" nods from the majority of baseball historians.) Crawford and Cobb did not play in the game but watched Davy Jones, George Mullin, Red Killifer and George Winter perform.

Two days later, they faced Young in a real matchup and lost, 4–3, in ten innings. Crawford had a single and a double against the legend but it wasn't enough against the Red Sox. The Tigers won the finale, 1–0, before heading to New York, where they won the first game of the series, 7–3. Jack Chesbro was waiting on the mound in the second game of the series on August 19, and shut out the Tigers, 8–0. Like Plank and Young, Chesbro got a little payback for losing to the Tigers during their nine-game win streak. He scattered 11 hits and two walks but didn't let anyone come around to score. The Highlanders won the next day, 4–3, sending the Tigers to Washington on a two-game skid.

Walter Johnson beat the Tigers, 3–1, in Washington on August 21, giving the Tigers their third consecutive loss and dropping their record to 65–43. The St. Louis Browns were still in second place at 63–46, well within striking distance.

The Tigers were getting complacent and needed to snap out of it and play like a first-place team, or they would lose that spot. Once again, it was Crawford who took matters into his own hands, going 4-for-5 off Tom Hughes as the Tigers beat the Senators, 6–4. Matty McIntyre scored two runs after slapping three hits and walking once. "Wahoo Sam Crawford and Matty McIntyre had a grand battle for the honors in the matter of number and timeliness of hits, and the center fielder (Crawford) just nosed out his friendly rival, though the latter got on just as often," wrote Joe Jackson of the *Detroit Free Press*. Cobb also chipped in with three hits and a run scored. It was just the kind of offensive output the Tigers needed going into the stretch run of the season.

Johnson pitched again on two days' rest and lost, 1–0, to the Tigers. He struck out six and scattered ten hits, including two apiece from Crawford and Cobb. Cobb tripled in Crawford with the game's only run. Meanwhile, "Wild Bill" Donovan dominated the Washington hitters, allowing just two hits in a shutout performance.

Two future Hall of Famers awaited the Tigers on the mound in Philadelphia as the Tigers had to face Plank and Chief Bender in a doubleheader on August 28. Plank was again at his best against the Tigers, holding Cobb hitless. Detroit managed only eight hits as the game went into extra innings. Plank and Eddie Summers locked horns for ten scoreless innings. In the 11th inning, Crawford led off and quickly provided the winning score when he launched a line-drive home run over the center field fence. Though the Tigers had eight hits in 11 innings, Crawford had three hits himself and was clearly the hero of the day. But the day was not over. Detroit still had to face Chief Bender in the second game. Crawford managed just one hit but knocked in a run against Bender, and the Athletics rolled past the Tigers, 11–2. Detroit seemed tired in the second game and would be so again the following day as another doubleheader was scheduled in Philadelphia. Jack Coombs shut out the Tigers in the first game and Rube Vickers beat them in the second game, 4–3, despite three hits and a run scored by Crawford, who pushed his average over the .300 mark for the first time all season at .302.

Detroit hosted Cleveland next and lost their fourth straight game, 9–1, and lost again on August 31, 7–3, to the Naps thanks to six Detroit errors. The Tigers were once again reeling. Not only was their offense sputtering, they were starting to field poorly, something that had not been a problem all season. Just about the last person they wanted to see on the lineup card was Addie Joss, but of course, when the Tigers were struggling, Joss always seemed to be waiting in the wings to take advantage. Detroit didn't commit an error but Joss threw a one-hitter to shut out the Tigers, 1–0, and spoil great pitching by Winter. Cobb's biggest rival at bat during the decade was Napoleon Lajoie, who was so popular the Indians became known as the Naps for a time. Lajoie scored the lone run of the game after singling.

Crawford got his third straight day off on September 2 because of a leg injury and the Tigers beat Cleveland, 5–3. "Wahoo Sam" took full advantage of the rest, smacking three hits, including the game winner, in a 2–1 victory in the series finale. Joe Jackson set the scene:

> One soulful swat by Wahoo Sam Crawford started and ended the ninth inning of the final game with the Naps. When the Wahoo person went to bat it was a tie game 1 to 1. Before another hitter could get to the plate it was all over, a three-base smash that probably would have been a home run had Sam not been lame, being converted into a run while you wait for a bad relay to the plate. It was a field day for the big fellow from the Nebraska wilderness, who, after three afternoons of enforced rest, came through with three hits, two of which threatened to become runs, and the last of which, as shown, decided the outcome.[10]

The Tigers were glad to have Crawford back in the lineup because the pennant was on the line in the following series as Detroit traveled to St. Louis to face the Browns in a four-game set beginning September 4. The *Detroit Free Press* called it "The series that counts."[11] Crawford was obviously less than 100 percent as he went hitless in the first two games. The Tigers lost the opener, 4–2, then dropped the second game, 2–1, in ten innings. The Browns were close, just a half-game out.

Team	W	L	Percentage
Detroit	70	51	.579
St. Louis	70	52	.574

The next game was the most important game of the season. If the Tigers lost control of first place, they might never regain it. Facing them on the mound in the must-win game was Rube Waddell. The future Hall of Famer didn't have his best stuff and Crawford, his former teammate, knew it. He laced three hits and scored twice as the Tigers won, 6–4. Joe Jackson's take on the game:

> Waddell got what he was handed so frequently last year, when the Tigers drove him to the bench on five different occasions. He lasted six innings today. He was hit hard all the way, especially by McIntyre and Crawford. His downfall really resulted from the classiest exhibition of base running the team has shown in a month, Schaefer, Crawford and Cobb figuring in the dizzy dash around the paths that netter the two tallies that represent victory.... Waddell retired after the sixth inning had yielded Detroit three hits and two tallies.... McIntyre tore off his second double. Schaefer walked. Crawford singled, and Matty died at the plate.... Cobb hit to Jones and beat Waddell to the bag, and Schaefer went all the way from second home. The throw by Rube was wild and Crawford followed Schaefer over on the error.[12]

There was more bad news for the Browns. The American League race had tightened up with the Chicago White Sox and Cleveland Naps surging into contention. While the

Tigers kept their stronghold on first place, the Browns, just 1½ games behind the Tigers, fell into third place. The standings after September 6:

Team	W	L	Percentage
Detroit	71	51	.582
Chicago	71	53	.573
St. Louis	70	53	.569
Cleveland	67	58	.536

The Browns were in trouble, and if the Tigers strayed one bit, they would be too. But the Tigers smelled blood and knew they could put the hurt on a tumbling Browns team. Detroit won both games of a doubleheader the next day, 4–3 and 9–3, over St. Louis. Crawford tallied a single and double and walked once, scoring all three times he reached base in the second game.

After such an important series, the Tigers were grateful but had no time to celebrate the victory or their homecoming. The Chicago White Sox, now in second place just three games out and looking for more, were at Bennett Park the next day to begin a more important series. Each team would be able to throw its ace twice in this series of five games. Both teams wanted to show their best, which was evident since four of the five games would require extra innings.

The first game didn't go into extra innings, but the Tigers wished it had. Doc White shut the Tigers down and the White Sox won, 5–2. The next four games needed more than nine innings. The Tigers won the first in comeback fashion, tying the game in the seventh and winning 7–6 in the 12th. Crawford contributed two hits and a run scored. Chicago ace Ed Walsh took the mound in relief of Doc White and lost 6–5 in the tenth inning. Crawford knocked in the tying run in the ninth inning. As expected, the White Sox started Walsh again the following day and again he pitched a complete game, this time beating the Tigers, 4–2, in 11 innings. Walsh and Crawford had many battles. Walsh said,

> I used to think that when my spitter was breaking right no one … could drive it out of the infield. Even if they hit it, its tendency to whirl and swerve would drive it down to the ground. But I had one experience that cured me of this. It was in a game against Detroit and I was called upon in the ninth inning to relieve a pitcher. There were three men on bases and Crawford was at bat. This is not an enviable position in which to place a pitcher, but I had been warming up and felt that my spitball was breaking at its very best. So I faced Sam with some assurance. I wound up slowly. I had everything. I put everything on the ball and threw it with all my strength. And Sam met it square on the nose with all of his. And it sailed and sailed like a sky rocket out over the outfielders heads and over the fence while four runs romped across the pan. All I have to say about the spitball is made with the mental reservation that Sam Crawford doesn't meet it fair with his bat.[13]

The White Sox won the final game of the series, 2–1, in ten innings. Crawford went 6-for-29 in the series and his average dropped to .315 for the season. Here are the standings after the series:

Team	W	L	Percentage
Detroit	75	54	.581
Chicago	74	57	.565
Cleveland	73	59	.553
St. Louis	71	59	.546

The Tigers lost the series, 3–2, to the White Sox but were still in control, unlike the Browns, whose slide continued, dropping them into fourth place. They still were in contention, especially since they hosted the Tigers again starting September 13. After playing four straight extra-inning games, the last thing Detroit needed was a long game, but as fate would have it, the first game in St. Louis went into extras. Waddell was on the mound for the Browns and hung on to win, 3–1, in 11 innings. The Tigers lost again, 5–2, the next day, sending the American League standings into a logjam—at least in the win column—on September 14:

Team	W	L	Percentage
Detroit	75	56	.573
Chicago	75	59	.560
Cleveland	75	60	.556
St. Louis	73	59	.553

The Tigers beat the Browns again the next day, 8–7. With the way Chicago and Cleveland were playing, the Tigers faced another must-win game in the series finale, which was no easy task with Waddell back on the mound. But the Tigers had shown their resilience all season and did so once more, beating Waddell, 4–1.

It was back to Detroit for the Tigers and a showdown with the Highlanders. Crawford busted out of a slump with three hits in the opener to lead Detroit to a 7–4 victory. Jack Chesbro was next on the hill and he held Crawford hitless to beat the Tigers, 5–1. Crawford had slumped to a .308 average, but the Tigers together were facing a bigger slump, especially with three teams on their heels. The September 19 standings after the Tigers lost, 6–5, to the Highlanders:

Team	W	L	Percentage
Detroit	78	58	.574
Cleveland	80	60	.571
Chicago	78	61	.561
St. Louis	75	62	.547

Not only had Cleveland surged into second place, they were behind the slumping Tigers by mere percentage points. Fortunately for the Tigers, there were no more matchups that Addie Joss or Napoleon Lajoie could ruin since there were no more games between the two teams for the rest of the season. Detroit salvaged the final game against the Highlanders, 2–1, hanging on to first place by a thread.

That thread finally broke September 21, when the Tigers lost, 4–3, to the Red Sox thanks to a late home run by Charlie Wagner. It was the seventh game in the last 11 that Detroit had lost, and it cost them first place. Here are the standings:

Team	W	L	Percentage
Cleveland	81	60	.574
Detroit	79	59	.572
Chicago	80	61	.567
St. Louis	77	62	.554

Crawford was the only Tiger with a multi-hit game. That would have to change if Detroit wanted to climb back into first place. Unfortunately for the Tigers, Eddie Cicotte and Cy Young shut them down the next two games and the Tigers dropped into third place on September 23:

Team	W	L	Percentage
Cleveland	83	60	.580
Chicago	81	61	.570
Detroit	79	61	.564
St. Louis	78	63	.557

With no scheduled days off remaining in the season, the Tigers needed something to break up the losing. It didn't look like that would happen with Philadelphia coming to town and Jack Coombs on the mound. The Tigers jumped on him for three runs in the third inning, but the game ended a 4–4 tie, called because of darkness. It would have to be made up the following day as part of a doubleheader. It was a strange circumstance, but for the Tigers, any change was good at this point.

Detroit went on to sweep both games of the doubleheader, winning 7–2 behind two hits and a run from Crawford in the first game, and getting a 1–0 shutout by Eddie Summers in the second game. Athletics manager Connie Mack threw Jack Coombs the next two games and the Tigers beat him both times with Crawford slamming three hits off him in the first game to win, 3–2, moving Detroit back into second place. The Tigers won the next game over Coombs, 5–2, and regained the lead in the American League:

Team	W	L	Percentage
Detroit	83	61	.576
Cleveland	84	62	.575
Chicago	83	62	.572
St. Louis	79	64	.553

Their lead was mere percentage points, but first place was first place. The Tigers got the train rolling and would have to keep it rolling against "The Big Train," Walter Johnson, and the Washington Senators, who were in town next. Detroit swept the four-game series, including a 7–3 victory over Johnson. Crawford was 6-for-11 in the series and scored five runs to spark the Detroit offense. But Cleveland kept winning, too. The Naps were still on Detroit's heels with just five games to go. Detroit was 87–61 (.588) while Cleveland was 87–62 (.584). Anything could happen in the last five games.

Detroit faced the Browns on October 2 and were able to handle the great Rube Waddell. The Tigers actually chased Waddell and won the first, 7–6, thanks to Crawford, who doubled in the tying run in the ninth inning.

"With little more than a mathematical possibility remaining, the Browns opened that series in Detroit. Anticipating a pennant, Detroit fans packed the stands of old Bennett Park and ringed much of the outfield. St. Louis was leading 7–5 going into the bottom of the ninth with darkness quickly approaching. Detroit led off its half of the inning with a single. Sam Crawford doubled and Ty Cobb followed with a single. The next batter, Claude Rossman, hit one down the left field line. The umpire ruled it fair, as it rolled into the crowd lining the field. 'Into the crowd' usually meant a ground rule double, just as it was supposed to in the previous year's contest between the Tigers and A's. Rossman's hit, however, had rolled into an exit tunnel. Normally, few people would be there, and the fielder was to do the best he could with it. On this crowded day, the exit tunnel was packed with people. As the ball got lost in the crowd, Cobb scampered home behind Crawford with the winning run. The umpire had ruled that Rossman's hit was a double, hence Cobb had to go back to third. Cobb began screaming at the umpire to such a degree that manager Hugh Jennings had to restrain him. (Jennings actually grabbed Cobb and threw him on the plate.) The field umpire weighed in on the discussion. He and the plate umpire conferred, and the decision was reversed. Cobb's run counted, the ball game was the Tigers,' and just like that, the Browns were out of the pennant race."[14]

The victory kept Detroit up a half-game over Cleveland and 2½ over Chicago. Meanwhile, at Cleveland's League Park, 10,598 fans witnessed one of the greatest baseball games ever played as Cleveland defeated Chicago, 1–0. Big Ed Walsh of the White Sox struck out 15 and threw a four-hitter. In any other game Walsh's effort would have been an easy victory. But Naps hurler Addie Joss was better. He pitched a perfect game and kept his team within a half-game of the Tigers. During his masterpiece, Joss delivered only 74 pitches to the plate.[15]

Detroit then rode a shutout by "Wild Bill" Donovan to a 6–0 win to sweep the short two-game series. The season all came down to the final three games in Chicago. While Detroit had won both games against St. Louis, Cleveland split its two games, giving Detroit a three-game lead with three to play. The Tigers just had to win one of their final three games with the White Sox to win their second straight pennant.

It was a good thing the Tigers had swept the Browns because the White Sox won the first two games of the final series behind the pitching of Ed Walsh, one of the most effective spitball pitchers to play the game. He would often fake the spitter for effect. Hall of Famer Sam Crawford described the Walsh delivery aptly: "I think the ball disintegrated on the way to the plate and the catcher put it back together again; I swear, when it wasn't past the plate it was just the spit that went by."[16] Walsh shut them down, 6–1, on October 5 with nine strikeouts to force the Tigers into a must-win situation in the season finale. After losing out to the Tigers in 1907, the White Sox would have liked nothing more than to recapture the flag they earned in 1906 by beating the Cubs in the only Chicago-Chicago World Series in baseball history.

Doc White took the mound for the White Sox, facing "Wild Bill" Donovan on October 6. Usually, when those two locked horns, a low-scoring pitchers' duel was in store and one run could decide the game. Luckily for the Tigers, that wasn't the case—Crawford made sure of that. The Tigers scored four runs in the top of the first inning to set the tone. They chased White out of the game after Crawford doubled in a run, then scored on a triple by Cobb. Crawford singled in the second inning off Ed Walsh, who had relieved White, and came around to score when Walsh tried to pick off Cobb at first base and threw wildly. Crawford knocked in McIntyre in the ninth inning to cap the scoring. Meanwhile, Donovan completely dominated the White Sox, allowing just two hits and pitching a complete-game shutout and a 7–0 victory.

"It only took us one inning for us to realize that White didn't have his usual stuff," Crawford wrote in a first-person story for the *Chicago Daily News*.

He wasn't a very big fellow and couldn't come back with one day's rest. It was all over in the first inning. I was hitting third and hit one over Eddie Hahn's head and it rolled into the crowd along right field for a double. Now few pitchers ever gave Cobb more trouble than White, but Ty was ready for him this time and he shot a line drive into left center that went for a triple. McIntyre and I scored and that would have been the game…. The four runs we made that inning were three more than we really needed. Donovan was fast as ever. He fanned nine of the Sox and allowed only two singles. We went on and got three more runs and I got three more hits…. I guess that was as big a day as I ever had for I made those hits when the chips were down and it was the last hand.[17]

During that period of baseball, games not played could make a big difference in the pennant race. Games that were postponed and not made up during the season were not made up, sometimes leaving a team, like Chicago, without a chance to catch another, like Detroit. The White Sox used Walsh in relief in the final game. It was his 14th appearance in the final 17 games.

"Horns and squawkers, drums and blazing torches waved aloft, with Hugh Jennings's familiar cry of 'wee-ah' on every tongue," was how one scribe described the scene in Detroit after the Tigers clinched. The mayor called the pennant race the most gallant fight in the history of baseball and issued a proclamation: "Resolved that we on behalf of the people of Detroit extend to manager Hugh Jennings and the team hearty congratulations." The resolution asked that city merchants and citizens decorate their businesses and homes for the World Series. A city clerk delivered a certified copy of the resolution to Jennings the next day. The team arrived in the morning and was greeted at Michigan Central station by several thousand fans. Donovan was carried on the shoulders of the fans. A brass band played and automobiles waited to take the players to the Hotel Pontchartrain for a party. The fans and band marched behind. Downtown Detroit was decorated in Michigan blue and yellow for the World Series opener on October 10. There were tigers in every window display, many sitting alongside teddy bears with black patches over their eyes and black mourning bands in their arms. Men wore yellow neckties and ladies' yellow chrysanthemums. One fan from Chicago said, "the only civil answer you could get from a policeman was 'wee-ah.'" Cleveland, by beating St. Louis, finished in second place, half a game behind Detroit and one game ahead of Chicago. It was the closest three-team race in major-league history. The Tigers won because they ended up playing only 153 of their games, while Cleveland played its full 154. Rules later adopted in both leagues would have required the Tigers to make up their missing game and, if they lost and thereby finished tied with Cleveland, forced a playoff. …

It was Matty McIntyre, having his best year in the majors thus far, who led the Tigers in runs scored, with Crawford and Schaefer behind him. Crawford topped the league with only seven home runs. The Tigers' pitching load was a little more evenly distributed than in 1907. Donovan, hampered by chronic rheumatism, won 18 games; Mullin, considerably less effective than he had been in recent years, went 17–13; and Edgar Willett and Ed Killian won 15 and 12, respectively. Ed Summers, a tall left-hander up from Indianapolis, where he had developed an effective knuckleball, led the staff with a 24–12 record and a brilliant 1.64 E.R.A.[18]

While the Tigers barely hung on to win the pennant, they won the final game in spectacular fashion. Every aspect of their game came through with the season on the line. The Tigers saw their ace pitch a spectacular game—his best of the season. Crawford dominated at the plate with four hits and two runs scored. Cobb was almost as impressive with three hits and a run, upping his average to .324 and giving him another batting title. After slumping in September, Crawford's final week upped his average to .311 for the season. The power hitter led the league with seven home runs and scored 102 runs while smacking 184 hits, including 33 doubles and 16 triples. "Wahoo Sam" was also retroactively credited with 80 runs batted in, though it wasn't an official statistic at that time. Thanks to Crawford's power, Matty McIntyre lead the American League in runs scored with 105. Cobb led the AL with 108 RBI.

The Tigers would again face the Chicago Cubs in the World Series and were looking for payback. The Cubs had breezed to the pennant in 1907, but 1908 was different. The New York Giants fought back-and-forth with the Cubs and their pennant also came down to the wire, highlighted by a the play that would live forever in baseball infamy—the "Merkle boner"—tops on the list until the ball went through Bill Buckner's legs in the 1986 World Series.

The Merkle boner didn't happen on the last day of the season, but its outcome forced the two teams to play a playoff game with the Cubs winning, 4–2. It actually happened September 23: Christy Mathewson and Jack Pfiester locked themselves into a classic pitchers' duel. The Cubs drew first blood on Joe Tinker's home run.

For a while it looked as if Tinker's homer would be enough. But in the sixth, Buck Herzog reached base on Steinfeldt's error and scored on a single by Mike Donlin. The Cubs were retired quietly in the ninth. With one out, the Giants' Art Devlin singled but was forced out on Moose McCormick's grounder. Fred Merkle, fatefully starting at first base because regular Fred Tenney was ill, singled to right. Some accounts claim Merkle could have reached second on the hit, but with two out the risk was not worth it, and Merkle stayed at first. Al Bridwell rapped a single to center, scoring McCormick and sending Giants fans into seventh heaven. The hit also

Sam Crawford helped lead the Detroit Tigers to the World Series for three consecutive seasons, 1907–1909. Crawford batted .243 in three World Series (National Baseball Hall of Fame Library, Cooperstown, New York).

sent Merkle straight to the Giants clubhouse. Merkle had neglected to touch second. The deed had not gone unnoticed by Johnny Evers, who screamed for the ball. The throw from Circus Solly Hofman was wide of the mark and the game ball was lost in a mass of celebrating Giants fans. A ball—whether or not it was the game ball is subject to debate—was recovered despite the energetic efforts of Giants pitcher Iron Man McGinnity to keep the game ball from getting into the hands of Cubs players. Evers tagged second in an appeal to base umpire Bob Emslie. Emslie did not see the play and refused to make the call. Emslie asked his partner, Hank O'Day. O'Day said he had seen the play, granted Evers's appeal, and called Merkle out on a force. Because the crowd had taken over the field ... O'Day declared a tie game. John McGraw never blamed Merkle or anyone else for the blunder.[19]

But no matter how the Cubs won the pennant, they still had the best team of the decade with Tinker to Evers to Chance plus Three Finger Brown on the mound. After being swept last year, the Tigers wanted to gain some respect from the Cubs and the National League. It would take a lot more than just Crawford and Cobb to beat the Cubs. They needed production from some of the other players.

> The Tigers' infield was solid, if injury prone, throughout 1908. Claude Rossman anchored first, hitting .294. He was a superb bunter and, like Crawford, he would pull off plays with Cobb. Their favorite was a bunt and run…. Over at third base, team captain Bill Coughlin managed to play only 119 games. His frequent injuries were hard felt because he was a strong defender. Shortstop and second base were other problem areas due to injury. Detroit was fortunate to have one of the great characters of the game, Germany Schaefer, on the roster in 1908. Schaefer was a capable number two hitter in the lineup and managed a .259 mark in 1908. Versatility was his major asset. Because of injuries to others, he played 68 games at short, 58 at second, and 29 at third. Behind the plate, Charlie "Boss" Schmidt was the first stringer and played 121 games. He was noted for his physical strength and toughness. He had once boxed an exhibition with heavyweight champ Jack Johnson. Ed Summers's twenty-four wins paced the staff in his first year. Without him, Detroit's pitching would not have come close to keeping them in the chase."[20]

But, of course, the Cubs had Tinker, Evers and Chance as well as the same quartet of hurlers that dominated the Tigers in the 1907 series. Detroit looked poised finally to win its first-ever World Series game in the opener, leading 6–5 going into the ninth inning. The Cubs, however, rallied for five runs to draw first blood in the series, 10–6. Joe Jackson of the *Detroit Free Press* shared his observations:

> Victory slipped from the grasp of the Tigers in the first game of the second world's series in which they have figured just as it seemed almost certain that they had shaken off the hoodoo that pursued them in their first quest for the blue ribbon honors of baseball…. Coming into the ninth inning … Eddie Summers weakened, and having retired the first man, was found for six consecutive singles. As a result, five runs came over, turning it from apparent victory to a 10 to 6 defeat.[21]

Ed Reulbach held Crawford hitless while Cobb had two hits and scored twice. Crawford again went hitless in the second game and Orval Overall topped the Tigers, 6–1, to give the Cubs a 2–0 lead in the Series. The game was lost in an eerily similar fashion to the opener. Joe Jackson's take: "In one awful inning, sadly suggestive of the session in which the Tiges were trounced on Saturday, the second game of the 1908 world's series was lost by Detroit today. It was the eighth in which things happened, six runs on the same number of hits, being rolled up by the Cubs."[22]

Cobb managed just one hit in the game as Overall allowed one run on four hits to earn the complete-game victory. Meanwhile, the Cubs' six runs were scored by six different players and their seven hits were made also by seven different players.

The Tigers faced a must-win in the third game as no team had gone on to win the World Series after losing the first two games (and no one would until Brooklyn won its only World Series in 1955). The Tigers finally broke out of their hitting slump and tagged Jack Pfiester for eight runs on 11 hits. Crawford posted two of those hits and scored once while Cobb slapped four hits and scored a run.

> Detroit more than got back these three with a joyous five-run scoring riot in the sixth inning. It was to be twenty-six years before Tiger fans were to enjoy another similar World

Series inning. And it would have been more but for a beautiful Chicago double play, in which Artie Hofman doubled the great Cobb at the plate. The Tigers filled the bases with none out, when Pfiester walked Mullin, McIntyre slashed out a single, and Pfiester threw O'Leary's sacrifice bunt to third too late to force Mullin. By this time the Giant-Killer had a fine kettle of fish on his hands, and he didn't squirm out of it. Both Crawford and Cobb outfooted infield hits, each letting in a run, and the score was tied. But there was more fun in the offing! Rossman's steaming single drove in O'Leary and Crawford and sent Ty scampering to third. Still, with nobody out! Schaefer then lifted a fly to Hofman in center, and Cobb started home the moment the ball was caught. But Circus Solly threw a strike to the plate, and Kling pressed the ball on Ty for a double play as the Peach slid hard into the catcher. However, a fifth run came over when Ira Thomas poled a double, scoring Rossman. Just for good measure and to be on the safe side, the Tigers got two more off Pfiester in the eighth on Cobb's double, a perfect bunt by Rossman, an intentional pass to Thomas, Coughlin's sacrifice fly, and a single by that hitting pitcher, Mullin.[23]

Mullin held the Cubs hitters in check and the Tigers won 8–3 to stay alive in the series.

Detroit celebrated its first ever win in a World Series game, but it would be short-lived. Mordecai "Three Finger" Brown was waiting in the wings to get another chance at the Tigers on October 13. In his only start of the 1907 World Series, Brown had shut out the Tigers. It wasn't any different in 1908 as Brown baffled the Tigers hitters and won, 3–0. Crawford managed two hits, as did O'Leary, but no one else could scratch one out against Brown. The *Detroit Free Press* headline read "Mordecai Brown is invincible in the fourth big battle." Joe Jackson of the *Free Press* would go on to describe Brown's dominance: "History repeated in the fourth game of the world's series. Mordecai Brown the three-fingered twirler who, in his only start of the 1907 series, handed Detroit the single shut-out of that set, yesterday made his appearance in the first game that he has started this time. He set out the ciphers once more the result of the contest being almost the same as that in which he figured last year."[24]

Down 3–1 in the Series, things looked bleak at best. The Tigers knew it was over and managed just three hits (one by Crawford) against Overall in the fifth game. The fans knew it was over, too, as just 6,210 were on hand. Overall shut out the Tigers and the Cubs won, 2–0, to become the first team in baseball history to win back-to-back World Series championships. It was the same score the Cubs beat the Tigers by in the final game of the 1907 Series.

Crawford once again hit .238 for the Series with five hits in 21 at-bats and two runs scored. Cobb bounced back from his awful 1907 series to bat .368 with three runs scored. No other Tigers regular managed a .300 average in the Series. In fact, Crawford was second to Cobb. The offense that had propelled them to the World Series again sputtered with the championship on the line as the Tigers batted .209 collectively while allowing a .293 average to Chicago in the five games. First baseman and manager Frank Chance batted .421 with eight hits while three other Cubs were over .300 for the Series. "Frank Chance has a wonderful team, one of the greatest that ever played ball. I congratulate him and his followers. He has a team of game, heady ballplayers. Chicago won because the Cubs outplayed us. There are no regrets for me to offer. We were beaten and beaten fairly," Jennings said.[25]

For the second straight year, the Tigers were stuck with a bittersweet taste in their mouths. Two years in a row, they fought tooth and nail for 154 games to barely come away with a pennant before seeing their hopes of the first Detroit championship dwindle at the hands of Three Finger Brown and the Cubs.

Next year would be different, they vowed. And it was ... with strange similarities.

6. Another Empty Pennant

The Tigers had managed to win two consecutive pennants but flopped in the World Series. Could they become the first team to win three straight American League pennants? More importantly, could they get over the hump and become World Series champions?

The Tigers had their doubts. Detroit fans also had their doubts. They had every confidence that their team was one of the best ever assembled, but they had watched their mighty Tigers (or Jungleers as they were now sometimes called in the *Detroit Free Press*) fall flat on their faces against the mighty Chicago Cubs dynasty, which had won its second straight World Series after taking its third pennant in a row.

But 1909 was a new year. Ty Cobb and Sam Crawford were one year older and more experienced. They were also motivated not to come up empty a third time in a row. It was the most important season of their careers. Win a third pennant and they had another shot at glory. Miss the World Series and they might never get back there again. The team was made up of the same core, but added third baseman George Moriarty, who was a defensive boost. The Tigers had plenty of offense, led by Crawford and Cobb. Detroit also retained its great pitching with George Mullin and "Wild Bill" Donovan, though Ed Siever retired after just seven years in the majors.

Mullin opened the season with a one-hit shutout, beating the Chicago White Sox, 2–0, on April 14. He struck out five and walked one. It was a tremendous start for the Tigers, who would need another big season from Mullin. Crawford, however, didn't start so strong, going 0-for-4 against Frank Smith. Crawford quickly recovered with five hits in the next two days, leading Detroit to a sweep of the White Sox with 3–1 and 10–2 victories.

It was on to Cleveland, where the Jungleers took the first two games to start the season 5–0. On April 20, the great Cy Young stopped Detroit in its tracks with a 12–2 victory. Crawford was hitless in four trips to the plate and Cobb managed just a single off of the all-time wins leader.

There was more good news for Detroit. The owners, William Yawkey and Frank Navin, secured half the interest of Bennett Park, promising to build a bigger and better ball park for Tigers fans within the next couple of years at the corner of Michigan and Trumbull, which would remain the home of the Tigers through 1999. Fans were buzzing with excitement. They would have the best stadium in the league to match their best team in the league.

The first-place Tigers lost two of three to the White Sox to drop into second place at 6–3. Crawford pounded out three hits in the next two games as the Tigers beat Cleveland, 3–0 and 4–2, to return to first place. Cy Young was next on the hill for the Naps, on April

28, but the Tigers fared much better against him this time. Crawford led the charge, slapping two singles and a double to knock in two runs and score one. It was the best game of his career against Young and propelled the Tigers to an 8–1 win and a sweep over Cleveland.

Beating Young gave the Tigers a lot of momentum. In fact, they would remain in first place in the American League until the end of May, when the Philadelphia Athletics would charge to the top of the standings. The Tigers charged into May with a 10–3 record but were almost frozen on May 1, when snow twice delayed their game at home against the St. Louis Browns. Joe Jackson of the *Detroit Free Press* described the scene at Bennett Park: "There may have been more peculiar games played since the league was started, there may have been a May day on a Detroit ball field that was colder, that was more breezy, and that was marked by a heavier snowfall: there may even have been days on which good baseball seemed out of the question and in which the Tigers pulled off more good stuff against a handicap, behind their pitcher, all of these things may have been or may have happened: but there were 2,193 fans at Bennett Park yesterday who will never be convinced … that such conditions could possibly be the case." Despite the cold and snowy conditions, Crawford's bat was still on fire. He smashed the first home run of the season by a Detroit player to beat the Browns, 5–2.

The snow quickly turned to rain and Detroit had five games rained out in the next two weeks. Crawford scored the winning run after singling in the top of the tenth inning during a 3–1 victory at St. Louis on May 5.

After two travel days and two more rainouts, the Tigers did get their game in on May 11. They celebrated their 1908 pennant by raising the flag at Bennett Park before their game against New York. The Tigers, sparked by their pennant, went out and beat the Highlanders, 16–6, and remained in first place with a 15–5 record. Crawford belted his second home run of the season the following day as the Tigers routed the Highlanders, 11–4.

The Tigers then faced the Boston Red Sox, who had surged into second place. It was an important series for the Tigers, who didn't want to give up their lead. Sweep Boston and the Tigers would take control of the standings. Get swept and the Red Sox would tie them for first place. Neither scenario happened. The Red Sox took two of three from the Tigers and moved within a game of first place.

Detroit was in a tight spot. Not only had the Tigers let the Red Sox get within one game of first place, but they had to face the Philadelphia Athletics in a four-game set. The Tigers and Athletics had turned into the biggest rivalry in the American League. Detroit's hitters packed the most wallop, and the Athletics had the best pitching staff in the league.

The Tigers had to face future Hall of Famer Chief Bender in the opener on May 19. Bender stifled the Detroit hitters, allowing just six hits—one to Crawford—and striking out eight. He didn't walk anyone and Philadelphia won, 10–2.

It didn't get any easier in the next game when they faced future Hall of Fame lefty Eddie Plank—Crawford's nemesis. But this time, Wahoo Sam would have the upper hand. Crawford had a hit and a run scored as part of a three-run first inning that chased Plank from the game. The Tigers went on to win, 5–3.

Philadelphia struck back with an 8–4 win behind Jack Coombs, then ran Plank out to the mound again for the finale. Two days after being pulled in the first inning, Plank dominated the Tigers hitters. He allowed six hits—two to Crawford—while walking two and striking out four. To add insult to injury, Plank took out his frustrations at the plate, slapping a pair of hits. Even worse, "Gettysburg Eddie" dropped the Tigers out of first place. The Tigers were 18–11 but Philadelphia was 17–10 to lead by percentage points.

Crawford continued his .300 pace against the Washington Senators and led the Tigers right back into first place. He went 4-for-11 in the four-game set as Detroit took three of the games without having to face Walter Johnson. Detroit continued its roll by sweeping the Chicago White Sox in four games. Crawford belted six hits in the series.

Wahoo Sam was swinging the bat well as the Tigers rolled into Boston on June 2. He smacked two singles in a 6–5 loss in the opener but was the hero the following day. In the sixth inning, Crawford belted a two-run homer to lead the Tigers to a 5–3 victory. With one more game to go in Boston, Crawford again was the hero, this time in the field as well as at the plate. In the third inning, Boston's version of Sam Crawford—future Hall of Fame right fielder Harry Hooper—was up and hit one Crawford's way. "Crawford did the prettiest fielding of the visitors, making a star catch off Hooper in the third inning, taking a ball close to the ground at full speed, when it seemed sure to drop safely,"[1] the *Detroit Free Press* reported. At the plate, Crawford tallied three hits, including a double, as George Mullin shut out the Red Sox, 5–0. It was the third multi-hit game in a row for Crawford and his fifth in his last eight games.

Crawford cooled down in New York, going 2-for-14 in a three-game set with the High-landers. The Tigers took two of three from New York, which had moved into second place at 22–16. Detroit had a comfortable lead at 28–14 but needed those victories, especially the third game. George Mullin beat the Yankees, 2–1, to win his 11th straight decision.

The Tigers needed to keep the momentum going as they shifted to the nation's capital, but looming was the greatest pitcher in baseball history, Walter Johnson. The Big Train promptly shut out the Tigers, 1–0, spoiling a masterful performance by Ed Killian. Johnson also continued his struggles against Crawford, who pounded two hits. The Senators took the second game, 6–2, followed by an off day. While the Tigers were relaxing in Washington on June 13, they were given quite a scare when Mullin, fresh off his 11th straight win, was hospitalized after drinking water from the Potomac River made him sick.

The rain wasn't helping the Potomac or a sick Mullin, but it helped the Tigers eke out a 1–0 victory in five innings. It was the 30th victory of the season for the Jungleers (with 16 losses). The Senators took three of four when Johnson struck out eight to beat the Tigers, 2–1. Again Crawford had two hits off The Big Train, but again Johnson retired the rest of the Tigers lineup with relative ease.

The Tigers got some good news when Mullin was cleared to start as the Tigers moved to Philadelphia. Mullin battled back and forth with Chief Bender. Crawford continued his strong hitting against the best pitchers in the game with two hits off Bender. But in the end, Bender earned the 5–4 victory and ended Mullin's win streak at 11.

While the Tigers were comfortably in first place, Philadelphia had moved into second place. Detroit needed to bounce back and not let the end of Mullin's win streak affect them. But looming on the mound was Eddie Plank, the third-winningest left-handed pitcher in baseball history, not to mention Crawford's personal nemesis. Crawford's hot hitting was cooled as he went hitless against Plank, but the rest of the Tigers pounced on him and beat the future Hall of Famer, 4–1, as Cobb tagged him for two hits. Detroit, obviously run down from facing three future Hall of Fame pitchers in a row, lost 3–1 to Harry Krause.

Crawford again went hitless and the Athletics climbed back into the race. The American League standings as of June 18:

Team	W	L	Percentage
Detroit	31	19	.620
Philadelphia	28	20	.583

After ending their 15-game road trip in disappointing fashion, the Tigers were more than happy to return to Bennett Park. First up was a makeup game with the Chicago White Sox, and Crawford snapped out of his hitting slump in a big way. "Crawford came to bat in the seventh inning, with his team a run behind … and sandwiched a very healthy triple between two full grown errors. The results were a pair of tallies," Joe Jackson of the *Detroit Free Press* wrote. Crawford's triple tied the game and he scored the winning run to beat the White Sox, 5–4.

The St. Louis Browns were next to face Detroit. The teams would get very familiar with each other over the course of eight games, the first three in St. Louis, the others in Detroit. The Browns were a formidable contender last season, but the Tigers had their number in 1909, unbelievably sweeping St. Louis in all eight games—including two against future Hall of Famer Rube Waddell. Crawford posted 14 hits and scored ten runs to lead the offensive attack. Crawford's best game of the year came in the fifth game. He slammed three doubles and a single and scored twice as the Tigers won, 8–1. Between Crawford finding his stroke and the eight-game sweep, the Tigers improved to 40–19.

It was back on the road to face the White Sox, and the Tigers entered Chicago by winning their tenth game in a row on June 27. The White Sox took the second game of the doubleheader and put Bill Burns on the mound for the series finale. He kept the Tigers in check, allowing no runs in the first eight innings. In the ninth inning, Crawford doubled and scored on a single by Claude Rossman to tie the game, 1–1. Red Killifer doubled and scored the winning run in the tenth inning. The Tigers added a run and beat Walsh and the White Sox, 3–1.

The roll continued for the Tigers as they knocked off Cleveland and Cy Young, 3–2. In the second game, however, future Hall of Famer Addie Joss pitched a four-hitter and beat the Tigers, 7–1. Crawford was just 2-for-10 against the trio of future Hall of Famers the Tigers faced in a row. But he brought the lumber the following day, smashing a home run, a triple and a single to go 3-for-3 with two runs scored, leading the Tigers to a 9–3 victory. Two days later Young rebounded to beat the Tigers, 4–1, giving Cleveland two wins in the five-game set.

Crawford faced former teammate Rube Waddell next in St. Louis and sparked the game-winning rally in the eighth inning with an RBI single on the Fourth of July. He knocked in Matty McIntyre to tie the game, 1–1, and scored the winning run on Cobb's triple. After losing, 3–1, to the Browns the next day, the Tigers faced Cleveland again, and Cy Young threw a complete-game shutout, beating Detroit, 6–0. Joss came back to beat the Tigers the following day, 4–3, and the Tigers fell to 46–25, though still in first place.

Despite losing three consecutive games, the Tigers still had a comfortable lead and could keep it that way with a good showing against the second-place Philadelphia Athletics, who were in town for a four-game series. The Tigers lost the opener, 3–1, to Krause, then were shut out, 2–0, by Plank in the second game. Crawford slammed three hits, including a double, and scored twice against Chief Bender as the Tigers roared back to win 9–5 in the third game. Krause got another win against Detroit, this time 7–1, and the Athletics took the series three games to one to close in on Detroit. The standings through July 11:

Team	W	L	Percentage
Detroit	47	28	.627
Philadelphia	45	27	.625

The Tigers had an off-day July 12 but gained some ground when Joss threw a ten-inning shutout to beat Philadelphia, 1–0. Meanwhile, the Tigers shut out the Senators, 3–0, the next day, then beat the great Walter Johnson, 9–5, in the first game of a doubleheader and won the second game, 7–0, to sweep Washington.

Crawford had been quiet the past few games and took his aggressions out on New York pitching with two singles, a double and a run scored in a 4–3 Detroit victory. The Athletics lost that day and Boston won to surge into second place. The July 18 standings:

Team	W	L	Percentage
Detroit	52	28	.650
Boston	48	34	.585
Philadelphia	46	33	.582

The Yankees won the next two games before Summers threw a complete-game shutout in the final game of the series.

In Detroit the surprising Red Sox, the upstart team, challenged Detroit for first place. The Tigers quickly dropped Boston back into third place by sweeping both games of a doubleheader, including a 5–2 win over Smoky Joe Wood in the opener. Detroit improved to 57–30 with a 12-inning win the following day, sparked by two Crawford hits. Wahoo Sam continued his clubbing with three hits in the finale, but he was the only Tiger to get his bat going and Detroit lost, 4–0. Mullin allowed all four runs in the first inning but settled down to pitch a masterful game. But Cobb and a slew of Tigers went hitless and couldn't bring Crawford in.

Detroit visited Cleveland for another two-game set beginning on July 27. The Tigers, showing they were the dominant team in the league, knocked off Joss, 3–1, and beat Young, 5–4. Then the Tigers had a meltdown. The Highlanders then took three of four games to halt the Tigers' momentum. The standings through July 31:

Team	W	L	Percentage
Detroit	60	34	.638
Philadelphia	56	38	.596

After an off-day, all of baseball took August 2 off for the funeral of National League President Harry Pulliam. Detroit played back-to-back doubleheaders with the Red Sox and lost three of the four games despite eight hits from Crawford. Detroit had wasted Crawford's big games and wouldn't get much help from Wahoo Sam in the next two weeks. Crawford went into a slump and managed just one multi-hit effort in his next 15 games.

With Crawford injuring his leg and not hitting well, Detroit dropped three of four to Philadelphia, including two wins by Eddie Plank. Plank pitched a masterpiece in the finale, beating the Tigers, 3–1, and creating a logjam atop the American League standings August 10:

Team	W	L	Percentage
Detroit	62	40	.608
Philadelphia	62	40	.608
Boston	61	44	.581

It got worse before it got better for the Tigers. Detroit dropped its fourth game in a row to Washington but bounced back to beat Walter Johnson, 6–1. Detroit manager Hughie Jennings flipped Cobb and Crawford in the lineup to have Cobb batting third and Crawford fourth, but both went hitless against The Big Train. The win kept the Tigers tied with Philadelphia at 63–41.

Crawford's lame leg, Cobb's stone-bruised foot, and an assortment of injuries to McIntyre, the Tigers on August 14 yielded first place to the Athletics, the first time they had been out of the lead all season. Meanwhile Jennings, thoroughly dissatisfied with his infield, had undertaken to rebuild it at the same time that he tried to keep his team in contention for a third straight pennant. First the Tiger manager traded the popular but badly slumping Schaefer to tail end Washington for Jim Delahanty, a good hitter, a capable second baseman, and one of five Delahanty brothers to play in the majors. After experimenting with [George] Moriarty at first base, Jennings then put him back on third and dealt the wild-throwing and chronically discontented Rossman to St. Louis for Tom Jones, a solid veteran who was not much at bat but a steady fielder. As Crawford was taking a fourth ball, Cobb unaccountably took off for third. Paddy Livingston's throw to third-baseman Frank Baker had him easily. When Cobb hook-slid to his left, Baker reached over the bag and tagged him with the ball in his bare hand. Cobb's right foot grazed Baker's forearm and opened a small cut. Baker and the rest of the Athletics stormed around the umpires, claiming that Cobb should be ejected for deliberately spiking the third baseman. Less than mortally wounded, Baker had a bandage wrapped around his arm and remained in the game. The next day Donovan beat Eddie Plank 4–3 before another big weekday crowd, with Cobb getting two hits and a run batted in. On the 26th Detroit made it a sweep, Mullin shutting out the Athletics 6–0 for his twenty-second win. Crawford and Cobb, having switched places in the batting order [with Crawford now in cleanup], each had two hits; and Cobb again bedeviled Collins, this time scoring when he drew the second baseman's wild throw home. In the aftermath of the Baker spiking, Connie Mack lost his composure for one of the few times in his life. Calling Cobb the dirtiest player in baseball history, he threatened to take up the issue of Cobb's tactics with the American League owners. President Ban Johnson, exhibiting his frequent impetuosity, warned that Cobb "must stop this sort of playing or he will have to quit the game."[2]

After two more wins, the Tigers and Athletics were still tied at 65–41. Detroit fell out of first place by percentage points the next day when Philadelphia won and the Tigers were rained out. Both teams lost the next game and the Athletics were still ahead. Playing the Chicago White Sox, the Tigers were shut out by future Hall of Famer Ed Walsh on August 18 and dropped into third place:

Team	W	L	Percentage
Philadelphia	67	42	.615
Boston	67	44	.604
Detroit	65	43	.602

This loss was devastating to the Tigers, who were in shock that they could be so far ahead of the Athletics and Red Sox for most of the season, but still be vulnerable to both teams this late into August. The Tigers won their next three games, including a 3–1 victory over Walter Johnson, but so did the Athletics. Detroit needed something to spark the team as it headed into the home stretch of the season. If they were going to claim a third straight pennant, they would need Crawford to snap out of his skid and be the dominating run producer he had always been.

Crawford knew he needed to pick up his game and responded the next day (August 23) with a banner day. He pounded out four hits and the Tigers beat Washington, 11–6. He singled and scored in the fourth inning, doubled in a run and scored in the fifth, doubled in the seventh and singled in the eighth.

The Tigers had been waiting for this offensive display from Crawford. They had also been waiting to meet Philadelphia head-to-head again to take the pennant race into their own hands. In the first game, on August 24, the Tigers trailed 5–3 going into the bottom of the seventh inning. Oscar Stanage led off with a grounder to third base and made it all the way to second as Frank "Home Run" Baker's wild throw eluded first baseman Harry Davis. Stanage was thrown out after a bad bunt by pitcher Eddie Summers, but Davy Jones bunted Summers to second. Shortstop Donie Bush walked and Ty Cobb knocked in both runners with a double. Crawford was up next, reached first base on an infield single, and took second on a bad throw that scored Cobb. Crawford scored on a single by Jim Delahanty. It was the fourth run of the inning and gave the Tigers a 7–5 lead. The Athletics scored one run in the top of the ninth inning but it wasn't enough to avoid a 7–6 Tigers win. The Tigers had returned to first place, or at least a tie for first place:

Team	W	L	Percentage
Detroit	71	43	.623
Philadelphia	71	43	.623

That seventh inning was the pivotal point in the season. It put Detroit back in first place and spared a three-game sweep by the Athletics that kept the Tigers in first place the rest of the season. Detroit beat Eddie Plank, 4–3, in the second game and won the series finale, 6–0, on a shutout by George Mullin. Of course, Mullin couldn't do it alone. Crawford posted another multi-hit game with two singles off Chief Bender.

The Athletics left town and the Tigers continued to hit. Crawford and Cobb clouted home runs off Jack Chesbro of the New York Highlanders, giving the Tigers their third consecutive victory against future Hall of Famers. Wahoo Sam also laced two singles and scored twice. Crawford went 3-for-6 in the final two games and the Tigers completed the sweep of New York with 2–1 and 7–3 victories.

Detroit was on a roll, and the Boston Red Sox would soon find that out just like the rest of the American League had. The Red Sox were in third place and not out of the pennant race yet. The Tigers knew it and promptly put them out of their misery with a three-game sweep. Crawford tripled home two runs in the first inning as the Tigers jumped out to a 5–0 lead and hung on for a 7–4 win. Crawford scored three runs in the series and Detroit pushed its record to 79–43. Amazingly, the Tigers had gone from reeling to reeling off 14 consecutive victories.

Even the best winning streaks have to come to an end sometime. Detroit's 14-game streak ended when Cleveland swept the Tigers in a doubleheader on September 4. Cy Young struck out three in a 4–3 Cleveland victory in the afternoon game. That night, Cobb continued his habit of getting in fights in Cleveland. It was the second straight year the "Georgia Peach" had a major physical altercation in Cleveland.

On September 4 in Cleveland, at 2 o'clock in the morning, Cobb got in a fight with George Standsfield, the black watchman at the Hotel Euclid. The watchman had a club and Cobb pulled a knife. Both men were bloodied in the fight. Cobb bandaged himself and played all 18 innings of a doubleheader that afternoon. Fans and players were aghast at seeing Cobb play with blood seeping from the bandages about his face and head. A warrant was issued for Cobb's arrest for aggravated assault and intent to kill. In the morning the police went to arrest him. They waited outside by the car the Tigers were supposed to leave in, but Hughie sneaked Cobb out a back service entrance and through side streets to the train station, where the Tigers left for St. Louis. Cobb avoided Ohio the rest of the season and during the World Series. He did a lot of train-hopping through Canada. During one trip between Pittsburgh and Detroit during the World Series, an uncle drove him through Ohio, while Cobb hid in the back seat under a blanket.[3]

It was a momentary setback for the Tigers, who roared back to sweep the St. Louis Browns the next three games. Next they hosted Cleveland in a five-game set. Crawford tagged Addie Joss for two hits in a 6–4 Detroit victory in the opener, despite Joss helping his own cause with a home run. The Naps took the next game, 7–4, before the Tigers closed

Sam Crawford, right, talks with teammate Ty Cobb, left, and Cleveland outfielder Joe Jackson, center, prior to a game. In 1911, Cobb (.420), Jackson (.408) and Crawford (.378) had the top three batting averages in the American League (National Baseball Hall of Fame Library, Cooperstown, New York).

the series with three victories. The Tigers took two of three from the Browns thanks to Crawford's five hits and prepared for their last big series of the season.

The Tigers traveled to Philadelphia for a four-game series with the second-place Athletics. Win the series and they could all but clinch the pennant. Get swept and it could go down to the wire. The Tigers had everything to lose and the A's had everything to gain. It was a close series and no game would be decided by more than two runs.

In the opener on September 16, the Tigers trailed 2–1 in the ninth inning. They mounted a rally that loaded the bases for Cobb, arguably the best hitter in baseball history. With a full count, Cobb chased a high pitch from Eddie Plank and struck out to end the game. Crawford scored the only run of the game for the Tigers after walking in the sixth inning.

Detroit bounced back to win the second game, 5–3, over Krause to recapture a four-game lead in the standings. Crawford had an RBI groundout in the third inning, but it was Cobb who was determined to make up for striking out with the game on the line the day before. The "Georgia Peach" smacked two hits and knocked in a pair of runs to pace the Detroit offense.

That same offense was stymied in the third game by Chief Bender. The future Hall of Fame right-hander didn't allow any Tiger past second base and shut out the Jungleers, 2–0. Crawford found his hitting stroke in the series finale with two hits and an RBI, but the Tigers managed just four other hits collectively and Eddie Plank beat them for the second time in the series, 4–3. Philadelphia had taken three of the four games in the series to close in on Detroit in the standings:

Team	W	L	Percentage
Detroit	89	50	.640
Philadelphia	87	52	.626

With 11 games to go, anything still could happen. The Tigers, who came into the series confident, were given a harsh dose of reality that the season wasn't over yet. The Tigers needed to move on quickly and not dwell on the poor showing against the Athletics. Detroit began a series in Washington on September 24 and won three of the four games, with the lone loss coming in a 2–0 loss to Walter Johnson—one of his record 110 shutouts. The Tigers kept their momentum going as they took three of four in New York.

The Tigers swept Boston in a doubleheader on September 29 with Ed Killian earning both victories—both complete games, giving Detroit at least a tie for the pennant. Detroit clinched the pennant the following day on an unusual circumstance. While the Tigers were winning, Philadelphia was struggling to keep up. The Tigers dropped the game against Boston on September 30 but won the pennant when Philadelphia lost to remain out of reach of Detroit's 97–53 record.

Detroit finished the season 98–54 and could breathe a sigh of relief at winning its third consecutive pennant. Meanwhile, the Cubs won more than 100 games again but were beat out by the Pittsburgh Pirates, who finished 110–42 to take the National League pennant, while outscoring their opponents 701–448 throughout the season. The Tigers were looking forward to facing another opponent in the Fall Classic and were hoping for a better showing than their sweep in 1907 and losing in five games in 1908 at the hands of the Cubs.

The World Series was only five years old in 1909 and it had never seen anything like what was waiting when the Tigers and Pirates faced off. The two greatest players in the game would be facing each other in the World Series for the first time. Cobb, who had won another batting title, the triple crown, and established himself, by far, as the greatest player in the American League, was about to go head-to-head with Honus Wagner, the greatest player in National League history. Both legends wanted to win the World Series and wanted to show who really was the best.

Baseball would see this kind of individual matchup only a handful of times: with Babe Ruth and Rogers Hornsby in 1924, Stan Musial and Ted Williams in 1946, Mickey Mantle and Hank Aaron in 1957 and 1958 and Mantle against Willie Mays in 1962. But it all started with Wagner and Cobb. Wagner also had a sidekick headed for the Hall of Fame in Pittsburgh outfielder Fred Clarke, who was also the manager. Clarke would figure prominently in the scoring as would Cobb's wing man Crawford, who wanted to see Wagner and Cobb meet head-to-head as much as the fans, as he told Lawrence Ritter in *The Glory of Their Times*:

> I must say, though, that the greatest all-around player I ever saw was in the National League. I played against him for four years, from 1899 through 1902, when I was with Cincinnati and he was first with Louisville and then with Pittsburgh. People always ask me about Ty Cobb, you know: "You played in the outfield next to Cobb for all those years. Don't you agree that he was the greatest player who ever lived?" Cobb was great, there's no doubt about that; one of the greatest. But not the greatest. In my opinion, the greatest all-around player who ever lived was Honus Wagner.
>
> Cobb could only play the outfield, and even there his arm wasn't anything extra special. But Honus Wagner could play any position. And, of course, you know he led the league in batting eight times.
>
> Don't get me wrong. I'm not running Cobb down. He was terrific, no doubt about it. After all, he stole almost 900 bases and had a batting average of .367 over 24 years in the Big Leagues. You can't knock that. I remember one year I hit .378—in 1911, I think it was— and I didn't come anywhere close to leading the league: Joe Jackson hit .408 and Cobb hit .420. I mean, that's mighty rugged competition.
>
> It was that Cobb was so fast in thinking. He didn't outhit the opposition and he didn't outrun them. He outthought them!
>
> A lot of times Cobb would be on third base and I'd draw a base on balls, and as I started to go down to first I'd sort of half glance at Cobb, at third. He'd make a slight move that told me he wanted me to keep going—not to stop at first, but to keep going to second. Well, I'd trot two-thirds of the way to first and then suddenly, without warning, I'd speed up and go across first as fast as I could and tear out for second. He's on third, see. They're watching him, and suddenly there I go, and they don't know what the devil to do.
>
> If they try to stop me, Cobb'll take off for home. Sometimes they'd catch him, and sometimes they'd catch me, and sometimes they wouldn't get either of us. But most of the time they were too paralyzed to do anything, and I'd wind up at second on a base on balls. Boy, did that ever create excitement. For the crowd, you know; the fans were always wondering what might happen next.[4]

Cobb worked as hard to get to Pittsburgh as he did at the plate in the Series. Because of his earlier incident and pending charges in Cleveland, officers were on the lookout for Cobb at the train stations. He was forced to bypass Ohio altogether.

> "The World Series got under way in the Pittsburgh park on October 7. Cobb arrived by an out-of-the-way route. While the rest of the team came through Cleveland on the Lake Shore railroad, he and his wife traveled across Ontario to Buffalo and then south to Pitts-

burgh on the Michigan Central and Pennsylvania lines, so that Cobb could avoid being arrested in Cleveland, where the authorities had secured an indictment for felonious assault in the Stansfield matter. For the rest of his series travels Cobb had to continue to bypass Ohio."[5]

The series didn't start out well for Cobb and the Tigers as Babe Adams beat them, 4–1, in the first game in Pittsburgh. Cobb went hitless while Wagner and Crawford each tallied a single. Clarke was the offensive star of the game, clouting a home run off George Mullin.

Detroit quickly evened the series with a 7–2 victory behind "Wild Bill" Donovan in Game 2. Every Tiger except Donovan had at least one hit (Crawford doubled) and jumped on Howie Camnitz for two runs in the second inning and three in the third. While Wagner managed only one hit to match Cobb, the intensity of the individual rivalry remained heated. "Down here they insist on being interested in the duel between the rival slugging kings, Cobb and Wagner, as they are in the game's result," Joe Jackson of the *Detroit Free Press* wrote. "Today Ty got one clean hit and lost another through a great one-hand stop by Bill Abstein behind first base. His leading achievement was the theft of home, in the third inning."[6]

The Tigers could take their first-ever lead in a World Series with a victory in Game 3, but it looked dim after Detroit starter Eddie Summers was tagged for five runs in the first inning. "It was all over, to all intents and purposes—the first game of the World's series that Detroit fans were privileged to view—before the Tigers ever got the chance to bat. Five large tallies, chalked up to Pittsburgh's credit in the opening inning, really decided the outcome,"[7] Joe Jackson wrote. Detroit got their bats going but could never make up the deficit and lost, 8–6. Crawford went 0-for-5 in the game while Cobb had a single and a double. Wagner, on the other hand, totally dominated the game with a 3-for-5 performance and two RBI.

Detroit could have folded right there, but knew that all it would take to even the series was some timely hitting and a dominating performance on the mound. George Mullin was up to the task, shutting out the Pirates, 5–0, on five hits to even the Series, 2–2. As for Game 5,

> Crawford finally showed the Pirates what made him one of the best in the game and worthy to be considered a sidekick of Cobb. "Wahoo Sam" rocked Pittsburgh starter Babe Adams for a home run, single, double and two runs scored. Detroit tied it up in the sixth when the Cobb-Crawford combination functioned in American League fashion. Cobb slapped a single to right, and came all the way home on Wahoo Sam's steaming double to center. Then Honus Wagner threw Delahanty's grounder to the grandstand, and the barber galloped home with the tying run. In the first half of the eighth, Sam Crawford hit the longest ball of the Series, a terrific home-run clout deep into the center-field bleachers.[8]

But Wagner's sidekick Clarke had some power in him too and smashed a home run in the seventh inning to spark a four-run frame as the Pirates won, 8–4. Summers took another loss after coming back to pitch on two days' rest, though he only pitched one-third of an inning in his original start.

The Pirates led the Series, 3–2, and were one win from winning their first World Series title. Manager Clarke went for the kill with Vic Willis on the mound. Cobb and Crawford each doubled, but it was Crawford's defense that saved the game and the Series. Playing first base, "Wahoo Sam" threw out Abstein at the plate in the ninth inning and the Tigers hung on to win, 5–4. "There have been exciting games at Bennett Park this season ere this. But there has been none that stirred spectators more. It was a contest that, like those that have gone before, well served to demonstrate how well matched are the two contenders for this year's world's title," Joe Jackson wrote.[9]

Both teams were well matched. Both had great pitching with a powerful one-two punch on offense and a great supporting cast. And both had managed to win three of the first six games of the World Series. With all the drama in the first six games of the Series, the seventh game was very disappointing, except to the Pirates. Both managers sent out their aces. Jennings went with Donovan while Clarke countered with Adams. Though Donovan had pitched a complete game in Game 2, he was weak from a bout with malaria and had started only 17 games in the regular season. Donovan lived up to his "Wild Bill" nickname. After hitting the first batter with a pitch, he proceeded to walk six batters in the first two innings. After three innings, Donovan was gone and Adams was holding a 2–0 lead. Jennings had fresh arms on the bench, but brought Mullin back. He was spent and it showed. The Pirates got to him for five more runs and won easily, 8–0.[10]

> The Pittsburgh Press was the first to pounce on Hughie for starting Donovan. "Manager Hughey Jennings made a big mistake when he decided on the veteran Donovan to oppose Adams. Donovan made good his sobriquet of 'Wild Bill' before the first inning was over." Adams proved to be tougher than Donovan, holding Cobb and Crawford hitless and pitching a six-hit shutout and bringing Pittsburgh its first championship with an 8–0 rout. The crowds at the seven games set a new Series attendance record and put $1,274.76 in each Tiger's pocket…. So Navin was willing to settle with Cobb for a three-year contract at $9,000 per year. Only Honus Wagner, a thirteen-year veteran who had been a top star long before Cobb began playing pro ball, would be making more money in 1910…. Then it was back to Cleveland, where Navin's attorneys had plea-bargained the charge against Cobb down to assault and battery. On November 22, Cobb pleaded guilty to the lesser charge and was fined $100 and costs."[11]

Joe Jackson wrote, "After three efforts to clinch the world's championship, with this season offering a better opening than either of the two that have preceded it, the Tigers remain in the same position that they have occupied since Jennings came here, and since they became habitual league pennant winners."[12]

It had been three pennants in a row for the Tigers and three major disappointments in the World Series, the most difficult coming with the most recent Series where they fought back to tie the Pirates three times but had nothing go their way in the seventh game.

"We were beaten," Hughie Jennings said. "But I feel my team is, nevertheless, worthy of credit for its game fight. I blame our defeat on the weather conditions more than anything else. Had it been warm in any of the last four days Bill Donovan would surely have won his game. He insisted on pitching every day, even though it was cold, but it was evident after he had gone a few innings that he could not warm up to his work. Mullin did great work, but a man, even though he is big and strong, cannot expect to work every day and that was why I was willing to pitch Donovan today, for I felt confident George could not deliver and this was not a game for one of the youngsters." Baseball had never seen anything like the 1909 World Series. Attendance was 145,807. Winners' shares were $1,825.22. The Tigers, as losers, got $1,274.76 each. Navin was furious with Jennings for how he handled the pitchers in the Series, and was going to insist on no raise for him in 1910.[13]

Detroit fans had begun to expect a World Series appearance out of the Tigers. The players too had become accustomed to winning and believed they would get another shot at a World Series title again in 1910. Little did they know that the Tigers would not appear in a World Series again until 1934. Crawford would never again be on a pennant winner, which was difficult to believe with the talent the Tigers had. He finished his World Series career with a .243 average in 17 games. He rapped out 17 hits in 70 at-bats with one home run, seven runs scored, a stolen base, and eight runs batted in. Though Crawford would never again reach the World Series, his career was full of seasons where the Tigers were on the brink of another pennant. That drama drove Crawford to many more dominant seasons as he led the Tigers search for another Fall Classic.

7. Aftermath of a Dynasty

Detroit had gone further than any other team had ever gone without winning the World Series in 1909. In the first Series in history to go seven games, the Tigers became the first team to reach the seventh game and lose. Adding insult to injury was the fact that the Tigers were the first American League team to reach three consecutive World Series—and ended up losing all three. The Tigers could continue their run of firsts if they could win a fourth straight pennant. While it was a lofty goal, Detroit had won three pennants in a row and still had Crawford, Cobb and the same nucleus that had proven to be the best team in the American League year after year. They expected to win and expected Crawford and Cobb to lead them to victory.

The 1910 season started in that direction beginning with Opening Day. Detroit fans expected big things from their team and set an Opening Day attendance record of 14,703. Crawford and Cobb picked up right where they left off from 1909. With Cleveland in town, the Tigers faced one of the best pitchers in the game, Addie Joss, who finished his career with the second-lowest ERA in baseball history. Joss wasn't as close to mid-season form as the Detroit sluggers, however. Crawford pounded out three singles and a double. He knocked in three runs and scored one. Meanwhile, Cobb slapped two hits and scored three runs, and the Tigers jumped on Joss for seven runs. Unfortunately, the Naps torched Detroit starter George Mullin and beat the Tigers, 9–7, in 10 innings. In many ways, it was a fitting start to 1910. It was a sign that winning was not going to be as easy as it had been the past three years. Joss took his frustration out on the Chicago White Sox in his next start, throwing a no-hitter on April 20.

Detroit dropped the first two games to Cleveland, then went on a five-game win streak that included a 5–0 victory over the Naps in their first game in Cleveland's new ballpark on April 21—the same day the most famous writer in American history, Mark Twain, died. Crawford managed two hits, a stolen base and a run scored in the victory. Crawford continued his strong batting in the second game of the series, slamming two triples and a single. He knocked in a pair of runs and scored one himself. Detroit swept Cleveland with a 5–0 shutout over Willie Mitchell two days later. Crawford had eight hits during the five-game win streak, including two more against Mitchell.

The Tigers lost the opener in St. Louis, 6–5, in 12 innings on April 25, before winning the next three convincingly, 7–1, 7–1 and 5–0. Crawford managed just three hits in the series, but two came in the finale on April 29, and the Tigers reached first place with an 8–3 record (.727). Detroit remained in first the following day despite being shut out by Chicago's Doc White, 1–0. In the second game of the series, future Hall of Famer Ed Walsh beat the Tigers, 4–3, in 15 innings. The spitball artist struck out 13 and walked just one, sending the Tigers into second place. Detroit beat the White Sox, 3–0, the following game but still were in second place by percentage points.

The Tigers returned to the top of the American League standings (10–5) with a 4–0 shutout over the White Sox on May 4. Crawford pounded White for a single, a double and a run scored to lead the Tigers' offensive attack. George Mullin pitched masterfully for Detroit, but it was the defense which overshadowed both Crawford's and Mullin's performances. Here is how the *Detroit Free Press* described the play:

> Overshadowing all other features of the game, both as a spectacular performance and because of its important bearing on the game, was the hair raising triple play that Hack Simmons started in the second inning. Detroit had two runs to the good, and Chicago seemed on the way to overtaking this when Dougherty, first batter of the second inning, made first on Delahanty's muff of his fly, and advanced to second on Willis Cole's single. Billy Purtell had two strikes on him when he met one. He smashed it towards right, and there were visions of a run over and another man on third. But Simmons was right in the path of the ball. He grabbed it, thereby retiring the batter. He touched the sack, and thus doubled Cole. Both runners had started with the crack of the bat, and Simmons thus had plenty of time to run and throw to little Bush, who was covering second and yelling for the ball. It beat Dougherty back, and the side was wiped out and a promising inning ended almost in a twinkle. This feat about decided the outcome.[1]

The Tigers beat Ed Walsh the following day, 5–3, but lost the next two to the White Sox, falling out of first place. Though just one game behind the Philadelphia Athletics, Detroit would never return to the top of the American League standings in 1910. Crawford did his best to keep the Tigers going, rattling off three straight multi-hit games. The Tigers beat St. Louis in a makeup game, then beat the Highlanders, 5–3, in ten innings in the first of a four-game series. Crawford doubled and scored the winning run in the tenth inning on a double by Delahanty. He also made a home run-saving catch. The Tigers lost the next two, then won two, then lost two to the Boston Red Sox.

Detroit needed consistency and one way they could get it was to finally return to Bennett Park. Crawford powered the Tigers to a 14–2 stomping of the first-place Philadelphia Athletics in the opener. He tallied two singles and scored a run against Harry Krause. But with the Tigers struggling with inconsistencies, the last person they wanted to see take the mound was Crawford's nemesis Eddie Plank. "Gettysburg Eddie" held Crawford hitless and beat the Tigers 5–3 on May 20. He allowed two earned runs, while scattering 10 hits, struck out six and walked two. The Tigers lost to the Athletics again 7–4 and found themselves in fourth place (16–13), well behind the A's (20–5). Detroit lashed back with a 5–3 win over future Hall of Famer "Chief" Bender. The inconsistencies continued as the Tigers faced Washington. The Tigers lost the first 3–2 in a rain-shortened, six-inning game, then were shutout 2–0 the following day. The Tigers won the next day but faced legendary Walter Johnson in the finale. "The Big Train" struck out six and walked one while allowing one run and two hits. Crawford only managed one single in the four-game series.

Detroit was home on May 28 to play Chicago in a makeup game and won 9–1. The Tigers then swept St. Louis in four games to move up to third place with a 23–16 record. Meanwhile, Philadelphia was dominating the American League at 26–9. Guess who came to town next? The Athletics. And guess who was on the mound in the opener? Eddie Plank. But the Tigers were on a roll at home and jumped on Plank for five runs in the first inning, chasing him from the game. Crawford tripled during the rally and scored. The Tigers won the next day, June 4, 10–7. Philadelphia manager Connie Mack decided to take a chance and pitch Plank again on just two days of rest. Of course, Plank only made it through one inning two days earlier. Plank pitched well, allowing just two runs on eight hits, but the Athletics couldn't get their bats going and the Tigers won 2–0. Meanwhile, the Highlanders won and took over first place. It was only a brief takeover, but the Athletics were happy to get out of Detroit after being swept by the surging Tigers.

Washington was next to come to town and Detroit continued to dominate, winning the first three games of the series 4–1, 4–2 and 5–1. Crawford had a hit in each game and though he was slumping, it didn't matter because the Tigers were winning. Detroit had rattled off 11 consecutive victories since losing to Johnson on May 27 in Washington. "The Big Train" was on the mound again in the series finale at Bennett Park on June 9. Fitting that the streak started after Johnson and would end with Johnson. He struck out eight Tigers while walking just one, scattering six hits and allowing just one run in a 7–1 Senators victory.

The Tigers remained in third place and hosted the first-place Highlanders next. Crawford hit a sacrifice fly to lead the Tigers to a 4–3 victory in ten innings on June 10. The next day, Crawford slammed a home run in the sixth inning off Hippo Vaughn, but the Tigers lost, 4–3. Coming that close to a victory frustrated the Tigers. They knew they needed to take care of the Highlanders and Athletics every chance they got if they were going to remain in the pennant race. Detroit took out their frustrations on Jack Warhop, batting around in the sixth inning the next day and beating the Highlanders, 8–3. Crawford went hitless in the game. He was in the middle of a mid-season slump that saw him go 11 games without a multi-hit game. He managed a single in Detroit's 5–1 win over New York in the series finale. The Tigers were 32–18 after winning the series but still in third place behind Philadelphia and New York.

Boston visited Bennett Park on June 15 for a five-game series. The Tigers won three of the five games, but more importantly, Crawford broke out of his hitting slump with ten hits in the series. He knew it would only be a matter of time. Most players have one or two stretches in a season where they struggle for a week. When the Highlanders left Detroit, they had a momentary lapse and handed over second place to the Tigers on June 23. Detroit beat St. Louis, 10–4, that day behind two hits and a run from Crawford. But the Tigers lost five of seven games to the Browns and were back in third place.

The Tigers needed some inspiration. Manager Hughie Jennings hoped it would come on June 28 when the Tigers hoisted their 1909 pennant. It didn't work. Crawford doubled and scored twice but Chicago's Ed Walsh beat the Tigers 8–5. Detroit won the next game but then lost nine of their next 12 games. On July 8, first-place Philadelphia came to Detroit and beat the Tigers, 4–3, to send them into fourth place (41–32). Eddie Plank shut out the Tigers on five hits the following day. Philadelphia swept the Tigers in four games and left Detroit with a 49–23 record and a six-game lead.

Crawford's heroics returned July 13 against Washington. The Tigers were in a battle with Walter Johnson and the Senators. Behind 6–5 in the bottom of the ninth inning, Crawford slammed a triple off "The Big Train" that knocked in the tying and winning runs. A few days later in New York, Crawford played first base and went 1-for-4. Back in right field, his comfort zone, the next day, he cracked a pair of hits and helped the Tigers win, 6–2. For three weeks, the Tigers remained in fourth place. On July 29, Eddie Summers outdueled Ed Walsh, 1–0, allowing just one hit. Cobb slapped three hits and scored the only run of the game. It was the third straight shutout for Detroit pitching. "Wild Bill" Donovan and George Mullin both pitched shutouts before Summers. It capped 30 consecutive scoreless innings by Detroit pitching, which tied the American League record held by Washington. (In the National League, the Pirates had won six shutouts in a row.) But for all the heroics on the mound, the Tigers were still in fourth place. They wouldn't stay there very long.

On August 5, the Tigers started a four-game series with New York and swept the Highlanders to pass them for third place (Boston was in second behind Philadelphia). Fittingly, the Athletics and Eddie Plank invaded Bennett Park the next day. Plank threw a complete game and allowed just one run on five hits—two by Crawford. Three days later, Plank again beat the Tigers, 7–4.

Detroit went 7–7 the next 14 games, including a loss to Walter Johnson, and dropped back into fourth place. Lost in the inconsistencies, Crawford had two of his best games of the season back-to-back. On August 20, he slapped three hits and scored twice in a 9–0 win over Boston. The following day, Crawford belted a single, double and two triples against Warhop in New York and the Tigers won, 8–5.

The Tigers weren't happy to be back in fourth place and took it out on Plank the next day, August 29. Detroit scored five runs in the first three innings to chase Plank. Two days later, the Tigers beat Chief Bender and started a six-game win streak. After two losses to Cleveland, Detroit ran off four consecutive victories again and five of their next six. Plank, anxious for revenge after his last outing against Detroit, stopped the Tigers' streak with a 7–1 victory. He allowed four hits, none to Crawford. But the Tigers continued to win and moved into second place, passing New York with an 80–60 record on September 20. Even more remarkable was the fact that Detroit was doing this without the hitting of Crawford who was 4 for his last 38. One was a game-winning double against the Indians on September 9. The Tigers lost all three games to the Highlanders and dropped back into third place, where they would stay the rest of the season. They finished 86–68, behind Philadelphia (102–48) and New York (88–63).

Crawford finally began hitting again, but it was too late. He finished the season 19-for-34, including six multi-hit games in the last eight. The *Detroit Free Press* summed up the disappointing finish for Crawford and the Tigers after Detroit's 3–1 victory over St. Louis on October 1. Crawford won the game with an RBI double in the bottom of the eighth inning. The *Free Press*'s headline read: "Samuel, 'the Man Who Can't Hit in Pinches,' Drives in Winning Run for Tigers."[2] It was a blow to Crawford, who was the first player to lead both leagues in home runs. He also had a great year in 1910, struggled just at the end. He led the American League with 120 runs batted in and 19 triples. However, he batted just .289 after finishing the 1909 season at .314. That is still a more than respectable average, but Crawford had higher standards for himself. It was the only season as a full-time player he failed to bat at least .295. He also knew that if he had finished the year a little stronger, he would have batted .300. The *Free Press*, like Crawford, felt frustrated, as most Detroit fans did. They loved "Wahoo Sam," but were disappointed in the Tigers' fall from the top of the American League, which they had dominated for three years. Crawford showed at the end of the season that he could still hit, and he would continue to hit for seven more years.

He went south to get his stroke back. The Tigers played a series of exhibition games in Cuba against the Leland Giants, an all-black team.

> Following the conclusion of the Giants' games, several Leland players including [John Henry] Lloyd, Charlie "Home Run" Johnson, [Bruce] Petway and [Pete] Hill, remained on the island [Cuba] to participate in a series with the Detroit Tigers. After sweeping three straight American League pennants, the Tigers had come in third behind the Athletics and the Highlanders. Hugh Jennings' offense was triggered by Ty Cobb, who had just won his fourth consecutive batting crown with a .385 mark and had stole 65 bases, along with fellow outfielder Sam Crawford, whose 120 runs batted in had led the league. After splitting earlier contests, the Tigers won all but one of the five games that Cobb participated in. The great star batted .368 but suffered the indignity by twice being thrown out by Petway while attempting to steal second base. He was equally appalled by the fact that three Leland players who appeared in six games outhit him: Lloyd batted .500, Johnson .412, and Petway .389. Evidently, Cobb swore that he wouldn't allow himself to be embarrassed in such a manner again, henceforth refusing to join in barnstorming affairs involving black ballplayers.[3]

Whatever adjustments he made while playing in Cuba, "Wahoo Sam" returned to his old form, and that was good news for Detroit.

After slumping during the stretch run of the 1910 season, Crawford had something to prove to the Detroit fans and to himself in 1911. On opening day, April 13, the Tigers faced future Hall of Famer Ed Walsh, who had owned the Tigers in 1910. Crawford jumped on the spitballer for a single, double and triple, while scoring one run. Cobb added a home run off Walsh and George Mullin beat Chicago, 4–2. E. A. Batchelor of the *Detroit Free Press* wrote: "[If Cobb only had] a little co-operation with Wahoo Sam in the lumber industry it would have sent the Detroit total to double figures."[4]

Crawford slammed three hits again the following day in a 6–0 win. After going hitless in the third game, he slapped three more hits against Hi West in the opener with the Cleveland Naps on April 16. The second game of the series was postponed so the Cleveland players could attend the funeral of their teammate, Addie Joss, in Toledo. The ace starting pitcher died of meningitis after nine years in the majors, and his teammates threatened to strike if they were unable to attend. Several Tigers also attended. "I admired Joss as a man and a ballplayer," Tigers manager Hughie Jennings said.[5] Crawford and the rest of the players agreed. Though ten years of service was required for election to the Hall of Fame, an exception was finally made for Joss in 1978 and he took his rightful place in Cooperstown with 160 wins in nine seasons and a 1.89 ERA (second all-time).

The Tigers won the next day, 5–1, then traveled to Chicago to start their first road trip of the season on April 20. Detroit again beat Ed Walsh, 6–3, and completed a 6–0 start to the season. Crawford managed a hit in 11 of the first 12 games, helping the Tigers to an 11–1 record. On April 30, Crawford had his fifth three-hit game of the young season and led the Tigers to a 5–4 victory over Cleveland. Detroit continued its roll with a 14–5 win the next day and continued the win streak for nine games, capped by a 10–0 stomping of Jack Warhop and the Highlanders. Crawford had yet another three-hit game and scored two runs. Detroit was in first place at 21–2, well ahead of the Boston Red Sox (11–9). Detroit lost the next two games to the Highlanders, but won six of the next seven games. Second place changed from Boston to Chicago and then to Philadelphia, who invaded Detroit on

May 18. The Tigers won the first two games, 9–4 and 9–8, then lost a 14–12 slugfest, dropping to 27–6 and propelling the Athletics into second place at 16–12.

Detroit continued to stay well ahead of the pack through June, thanks in large part to Wahoo Sam Crawford. From May 6 to June 3, Crawford went 43-for-102 at the plate for an astounding .421 average, including 15 multi-hit games. But on June 7, the Tigers lost to the Athletics 4–3 and would drop six of eight games. The Tigers were still in first place at 37–18, but the Athletics were 33–18 and playing good baseball, somehow hanging close. Back home, Crawford pounded out three multi-hit games to propel the Tigers to four straight wins. On June 18, the Tigers trailed 13–1 in the fifth inning before Crawford sparked a comeback for the ages. Wahoo Sam slammed an RBI double and triple and the Tigers scored eight runs in the last two innings to win, 16–15. After splitting the following four, however, Detroit (43–20) was barely ahead of the surging Athletics (39–20).

Connie Mack had his team on a mission. The Tigers weren't exactly slumping. They had gone 9–6 in the last 15 games through July 2 and were 46–22, compared with Philadelphia's 43–22. The Tigers were off July 3 and split a doubleheader with Chicago on July 4, losing the first, 7–3, to Ed Walsh and winning the second, 11–10. Meanwhile, Philadelphia swept two consecutive doubleheaders and was stunningly in first place at 47–22 (.689), while the Tigers were 47–23 (.676). Detroit slammed Chicago, 8–1, on July 5 to return to first place, coupled with a Philadelphia defeat. The Tigers kept their lead—barely. They won four in a row. Then Crawford pounded the Senators for four hits, including a double and a home run on July 9, but Detroit lost to Washington, 7–6. The following day Crawford tripled home a run and scored in the sixth inning to give the Tigers a 4–3 win and improve to 51–24 (.680) while the A's were 49–25 (.662).

A showdown with the Athletics loomed on July 11. Philadelphia visited Bennett Park for a four-game series with 1½ games separating the Tigers and A's. But it wasn't as climactic as anticipated. Detroit defended its home ballpark and took a stronger hold on first place. After winning 14–8 in the opener, Crawford clubbed a home run and had three hits in a 9–0 rout in the second game. Detroit had 8–7 and 6–1 victories, but ended the series with an 8–6 loss. The pennant looked even closer when the Tigers swept the Red Sox, highlighted by Crawford's four-hit performance in the third game. He slammed a double, triple and knocked in all three runs in a 3–2 win over Ray Collins. The Tigers pushed their win streak to nine as New York came to town. Detroit's hard work was easily erased as the Highlanders swept the Tigers in four games to close the homestand. Crawford was the only Tiger who hit in the series, slapping nine hits in 18 at-bats (.500).

It wasn't how the Tigers wanted, or expected, to leave town. Now a 23-game road trip came at an inopportune time for the Tigers, who, though still in first place, were down after being swept. At first, they responded by taking two of three from the Senators, including a 7–1 rout of Walter Johnson, who struck out eight but allowed seven hits. Crawford managed one of those hits against his old friend and scored twice.

Crawford traveled to Cleveland for another friend July 24. The Naps staged a game against an All-Star team to raise money for the family of Addie Joss, who had died of meningitis. It wasn't easy to plan in the middle of the season, but it was important to the players. The idea lacked steam, however, until Young and several of Joss's other friends pushed the proposal. With Ban Johnson's approval, the game was schedule for July 24, 1911, and when it was held, nine future Hall of Famers took the field—Frank Baker, Ty Cobb, Eddie Collins, Sam Crawford, Walter Johnson, Larry Lajoie, Tris Speaker, Bobby Wallace, and Cy Young. Also in action were such stars as Hal Chase, Russ Ford, Joe Jackson, Gabby Street, and Joe Wood.[6] It was an important cause, but the most important series of the season for the Tigers began July 28 in Philadelphia. The Athletics were still a close second in the standings and were still brooding over being swept in Detroit two weeks earlier. The Tigers hadn't seen much of Philadelphia's best pitchers in that series, though they beat Jack Coombs twice. They would at Shibe Park, beginning with a doubleheader on July 28. Chief Bender opened the series with a 1–0 shutout in 11 innings, while Coombs won the second game, 6–5. Ace Eddie Plank was on the mound in the third game and was at the top of his game. Crawford was, too. Wahoo Sam had a single, doubled in a run and scored against Gettysburg Eddie. Plank kept the other Tigers at bay (Cobb went 1-for-4 and scored a run) and beat Detroit, 11–3. The Tigers salvaged the last two games of the series, winning 6–3 in ten innings, then pounding Coombs for nine runs in two innings in a 13–6 victory on August 1. The Tigers had shown their weaknesses and their lead had slimmed. Detroit was 63–32 (.663) while the Athletics were right on their heels at 60–34 (.638).

The Tigers moved to Boston, where they lost the first four games of a five-game set. The last loss, on August 4, proved costly. While Detroit had lost four straight, Philadelphia won three in a row to improve to 63–34 (.649) and take over first place from the Tigers, who dropped to 63–36 (.636). Astonishingly, with a race that close for much of the season, the Tigers would never return to first place in 1911. The Athletics steadily built momentum after the Tigers opened the season 27–6. They got some help down the stretch from other teams, of course. On August 14, Ed Walsh shut the Tigers out, 2–0, while pitching a one-hitter. Meanwhile, the lowly Highlanders beat the Tigers 15 times in 1911. The Tigers collapsed after the series in Philadelphia, going 17–15 in the next 22 games. On August 27, the Tigers hosted the Athletics at Bennett Park. They took two of three, with the lone exception being another dominating performance from Plank in a 12–3 victory. But the Tigers' collapse was too great. After winning the final home series against Philadelphia, the Tigers were 74–48 (.607) while the Athletics were comfortably ahead at 77–42 (.647).

Detroit ended the season on a 23-game road trip still within reach of the Athletics, but needing a lot of help from other teams. Neither happened. The Athletics kept on winning and the Tigers couldn't put together a streak, going 10–13 on the road trip. Fittingly, with their backs against the wall, the Tigers were again at Shibe Park in Philadelphia on September 23. Harry Krause and the A's won the first game, 14–3, despite two hits by Crawford. With the victory, the A's could clinch the pennant by beating the Tigers the following day. Crawford did everything in his power not to let that happen. He posted three hits, scored twice and knocked in a run, while Mullin kept the Philadelphia hitters at bay in Detroit's 6–3 win. Coombs was back on the hill September 26 in the series finale. He, too, had trouble with Crawford, who slammed a home run into the right-field stands in the ninth inning. He also singled and scored in the fourth inning as Detroit tied the game 3–3. But Frank "Home Run" Baker pounded two home runs, one against Willett, one against Ralph Works, and the Athletics scored eight more runs to win 11–5 and capture their second consecutive American League pennant.

Final American League standings of 1911:

Team	W	L	Percentage
Philadelphia	101	50	.669
Detroit	89	65	.578
Cleveland	80	73	.523

It was tough for the Tigers to swallow, especially Crawford, who after struggling down the stretch in 1910, hit well for the duration of the 1911 season. In 1910, he led the league with 120 RBI, but his average dropped to .289. In 1911, he had perhaps his best season in the majors. He batted .378, a career high which was third in the league behind Cobb and Shoeless Joe Jackson, who each topped .400 that season. Crawford also tallied a career-high 109 runs and 217 hits. He slammed 36 doubles, 14 triples, and seven home runs, and knocked in 115 runs. But he was again overshadowed by his teammate, Cobb, who turned in the greatest season of his career. He led the American League in runs (147), hits (248, the most of his career), doubles (47), triples (24), RBI (127), stolen bases (83), and of course, batting average at .420, the highest of his career. Crawford would continue hitting the same way in 1912, just not in the same place.

8. Michigan and Trumbull

Baseball was becoming more popular every year. Many of the early ballparks were built predominately with wood and were not spacious enough to hold the overflowing crowds. In the first part of the 20th century, it was a common occurrence to have spectators standing in the outfield, roped off from the playing field. Detroit owner Frank Navin saw an opportunity to draw more fans to see his perennial contenders. So the Tigers joined the steel and concrete era and opened Navin Field (later called Briggs Stadium, then Tiger Stadium) on April 20, 1912. It was a Detroit landmark that would remain an important part of the city and the Tigers through 1999.

The Tigers were hoping the new stadium would spark them back to the American League pennant after missing out the last two years. It just so happened that the Boston Red Sox were thinking the same thing about their opening of Fenway Park that same year. With the Boston pitching and Detroit hitting, it wasn't a surprise that one of the two new parks would be in the World Series. But which one?

A crowd of 26,000 helped dedicate Navin Field and watched a thriller of an opening game against Cleveland. The *Detroit Free Press* described the scene: "Every seat was taken and thousands stood around the borders of the outfield, necessitating ground rules which limited the length of any hit to two bases. The assemblage was just as enthusiastic as it was big, too, and there were abundant opportunities for shouting, as the game was one of those desperately-fought affairs in which each side has numerous chances to win and peril often is averted only by splendid fielding or nervy pitching or both."[1]

The scoring began in the first inning for the Tigers as Ty Cobb and Sam Crawford executed a double steal—twice. After each singling off Van Gregg. Cobb stole third while Crawford took second, then stole home on a high pitch from Gregg as Crawford scampered to third. Neither was through contributing to the Tigers offense. Cobb scored again after singling, but it was Crawford who was the real star of Opening Day: "In weight of slugging that king of main-strength club artists, Sam Crawford was the day's best bet. Two singles and a double, which would have been a triple at least and probably a homer but for the restricting ground rules, were Sam's contributions to the crowd's happiness,"[2] E. A. Batchelor of the *Detroit Free Press* wrote.

As good as Crawford hit, George Mullin pitched even better, especially in a pinch. He left 12 Cleveland runners on base after pitching out of numerous jams. Fittingly, Mullin knocked in Donie Bush with the winning run in the bottom of the 11th inning to give the Tigers a 6–5 victory, the first of many at Navin Field.

It was a promising start for a team that had such a disappointing finish to the 1911 season and began the 1912 season 4–3. The promising start didn't last long, however. The Tigers were shut out, 4–0, the following day and lost four straight games and six of the next seven. Detroit needed to end April on a high note. Crawford and Cobb saw to it, personally. Crawford pounded three hits to help the Tigers tie the Chicago White Sox, 3–3, after nine innings. In the tenth, however, it was Cobb's base running that won the game. Cobb singled with one out. Crawford followed with a line drive to center field, and that's when Cobb's fury on the base paths began, as described by the *Detroit Free Press*:

> Ty turned to second and paused just long enough to convince Ping Bodie, who fielded Sam's drive cleanly, that he intended to stop there to wait further developments. The moment that the Sox center gardener made up his mind that the Georgian was going to do one thing. Ty did another, dashing for third as hard as the gods of baseball would let him. It took "Ping" a fraction of a second to get over his surprise at this apparent attempt at self-destruction but he gathered himself together and made a fast throw to third base. The ball came to Tannehill on a short hop, struck him in the chest and bounded a few feet away. Instantly, Ty took in the situation, saw the ball lying almost on the base line and slid feet first into it, deliberately it seemed. The sphere rolled to the Detroit bench, and Tyrus dashed home with the winning run.[3]

The Tigers traveled to the East Coast for the first time on May 7 to face the Boston Red Sox. "Smokey Joe" Wood beat Detroit, 5–4, in the Tigers' first trip to the new Fenway Park. Mike Sowell, author of *The Pitch That Killed*, writes that "when Detroit slugger Wahoo Sam Crawford first saw the (right field) screen, he defiantly proclaimed: 'So that's Barney's (Ernest Barnard) dream. I'll show him.'"[4] Crawford drove a ball over the fence in one of his first appearances in the remodeled park. Charley Hall won, 7–4, the following day. The Tigers were 9–13 and the wheels were threatening to come off. They needed Wahoo Sam. Crawford stepped up in a big way, slamming a home run in the ninth inning to beat Buck O'Brien and the Red Sox in the finale on May 10. The following day, it was off to the Big Apple where Crawford didn't let up. He pounded Hippo Vaughn for three hits and scored twice in a 9–5 victory. But the drama was just beginning in New York.

Ty Cobb was frustrated with the way the season was going. Not that he needed a reason to act more paranoid and destructive. On May 15, during an 8–4 victory over the Yankees, Cobb was berated by insults from a fan. In the fourth inning, it became too much for the Georgia Peach. Cobb rushed into the stands and started beating the heckler. "It long has been a recognized fact in baseball that Ty Cobb is a great hitter, but until this afternoon, it was not known that his hitting ability extended beyond the batter's box,"[5] E. A. Batchelor of the *Detroit Free Press* wrote.

American League President Ban Johnson suspended Cobb indefinitely. The Tigers were rained out the next day, then beat Philadelphia 6–3 to reach .500 (14–14). Even though most of the Detroit players didn't get along with Cobb, none wanted to play without him. The Tigers protested the game on May 18—the first player strike in baseball history. No regular played and management struggled to find enough replacement players to have a game at Philadelphia's Shibe Park. Replacements were found and promptly lost, 24–2, to the Athletics.

> Johnson was not pleased with the protest or the way the Tigers shamed baseball by running a team of scrubs onto the field for a major league game. "I am amazed at the attitude of player Cobb and his teammates toward the American League, which, while insistent on good order on the field and strict compliance with the rules of the game, has always

extended consideration to and provided protection for its players…. Player Cobb was indefinitely suspended…. Cobb's suspension stands until the case can be investigated," Johnson said. "An American League player who is taunted or abused by a patron has only to appeal to the umpire for protection against attacks from the grandstand or the bleachers to have the objectionable party evicted from the grounds." Manager Hughie Jennings was forced to run a poor team on the field when Johnson responded by suspending the entire Detroit club. "Detroit will be represented by a ball club before the middle of the week," Johnson said. "Cobb's suspension is a secondary consideration now. We will have to see that the Detroit club is able to put a satisfactory team in the field before we take any action in the Cobb case at all." The Tiger players were also in deep with owner Frank Navin. The signers of the Tiger "declaration of independence" now stand suspended automatically. When they refused to play on Saturday they broke their contracts with the Detroit club, and according to the league rules, they placed themselves beyond the pale by this act.[6]

Cobb was happy with the grief he had caused Johnson but did not want his teammates to suffer. He pleaded with them to end the protest and return to the field. He also agreed to serve the rest of his suspension without incident. "I am willing to endure my suspension for whatever further period Mr. Johnson may think it necessary to keep me out of the game," he told the *Detroit Free Press* on May 21. "I did not ask the men to strike, but when they did so on my account of course I supported them. Now that the only way out of the trouble seems to be for me to remain under the ban, I will submit to the end that Mr. Navin may suffer no further embarrassment. My original contention that I was unjustly treated by being suspended without a hearing and for an act that was provoked by fiendish persecution still stands. I thought I was right and still think so, but for the sake of peace will take my medicine. I hope that Mr. Johnson will vindicate me when he learns all the facts in the case."

The Tigers returned to the field on May 21. George Mullin, well rested, shut out Walter Johnson and Washington, 2–0, and the Tigers improved to 15–15. Ty Cobb returned to the lineup on May 26 and slapped two hits in a 6–2 win over the Chicago White Sox. Detroit won five of its first eight games after the protest and improved to 19–18, their first winning mark since April 18 when they were 4–3. The Tigers then took three of four from New York and rose to third place before taking another tumble. They split a four-game set with the Red Sox, then lost the first three to the Washington Senators. In the final game, Detroit again faced Johnson, who was looking for a little payback. He allowed the Tigers just three hits and struck out five on his way to a 5–1 victory to complete Washington's sweep of the Tigers, who were back below .500 at 25–27.

It was a dangerous time for the Tigers, who risked a tailspin that could ruin the entire season. After facing Johnson, the last team Detroit wanted to see was the Philadelphia Athletics and their brilliant pitching staff. Of course, Philadelphia was the next team to visit Navin Field, and Connie Mack sent his ace, Eddie Plank, to the hill. The Tigers had struggled to hit the fireballing Johnson and now faced Plank, the first "crafty left-hander" in baseball history. Plank didn't fare quite as well as Johnson, but scattered eight hits to beat the Tigers, 4–3. Crawford managed one hit and scored one of the Tigers' three runs. Detroit was against the ropes and had to face Chief Bender—their third future Hall of Fame opponent in a row. Bender pitched well, but the Tigers, led by Cobb's three-hit performance, eked out a 4–3 victory. Philadelphia's Jack Coombs beat the Tigers 6–1 on June 15. Detroit went 5–7 in its next 12 games and there was a lot of talk about firing Hughie

Jennings as manager. E. A. Batchelor of the *Detroit Free Press* wrote an article claiming that if Detroit didn't make a better showing that Jennings's head would be demanded by the owners. Five days later, Ed Walsh of the White Sox shut the Tigers out, 12–0.

July was a new month and Crawford had been quiet for much of the season, but he was about to snap out of his funk and lead the Tigers in search of a winning record. On July 1, Crawford pounded a single and a double to lead the Tigers to an 8–2 win over Cleveland. It was the first of four straight multi-hit games for Wahoo Sam, something he had not done all season. He helped the Tigers win five of six. On July 4, he led the Tigers to a 9–3 win over St. Louis in the first game of a doubleheader. He managed just one single in the next game, but it wasn't needed. George Mullin threw a no-hitter against the Browns and Detroit won, 7–0.

Crawford wasn't finished. When the Tigers traveled to New York on July 9, he slapped three hits, scored twice and led the Tigers to a 6–2 victory, following with another three-hit performance in an 11–3 win the next day. The Tigers improved to 39–39 and move up to fifth place. It capped an 11-game stretch during which Crawford hit .523 with 23 hits in 44 at-bats and scored 13 runs. More importantly, the Tigers won eight of the 11 games.

Unfortunately in 1912, however, the Tigers could never put together a long enough streak. Detroit lost four of five games at Boston and then split a six-game set with the Athletics, dropping to 43–46. When one person had a good game, the rest of the Tigers didn't. It was the story of the season. On July 22, Crawford ripped two doubles off Walter Johnson, but The Big Train struck out ten and went on to win, 5–3. Three days later, the Tigers faced Johnson again, and again Crawford slapped two hits, but Johnson managed to hang on for a 7–5 victory in the finale in the nation's capital. As seemed to be the trend in 1912, the Tigers faced ace Eddie Plank in the next game, for the third time in less than two weeks, on July 27. Once again, it proved difficult to hit the crafty left-hander after dealing with The Big Train. Plank wasn't at his best, but held Crawford hitless and hung on to win, 9–5. The Tigers beat Jack Coombs the next day, then took it to Carroll "Boardwalk" Brown in the third game. Crawford powered three hits and scored twice. The Tigers trailed the Athletics 7–6 in the seventh inning and threatened but Connie Mack sent Plank out in relief and he closed the door on the Tigers the final 2⅓ innings.

Crawford had hit well for more than a month but had little to show for it except an increase in his own batting average. But he wasn't playing for his own stats. He wanted to win. In the finale with Philadelphia, he finally came up in a pressure situation. With the bases loaded and Detroit down by a run, Crawford belted a triple to clear the bases and lead the Tigers to a 7–6 victory over the Athletics. "When it came to real hitting, however, Sam Crawford carried off the honors with one thump that was worth the Tigers' other 10 and the Athletics' 13 together for all around enthusiasm and nerve. This welt was a triple smitten against the front of the right field bleacher in the third inning with the bases bulging with waiting Tigers,"[7] E. A. Batchelor wrote.

Washington invaded Detroit next and split the first two games. The Tigers then won five in a row to go above .500 for just the third time all season at 53–52 on August 7. Next Boston came to town and outfielders Tris Speaker and Harry Hooper did their damage. The future Hall of Famers each belted two hits and scored a run to lead the Red Sox to a 5–0 victory, as the Tigers couldn't get anything going against Ray Collins. Speaker and Hooper played center and right field, respectively. They were both stars and helped the

Red Sox win several pennants. The Speaker-Hooper duo got the best of Cobb and Crawford as the Red Sox went on to win three of the four games at Navin Field.

Of course it was hard for the Detroit duo to keep up when only one of them played. After the first game of the series, Cobb was assaulted while on his way home and was stabbed in the back with a knife. "Downtown Detroit was thrown into a paroxysm of excitement ... by a report that Ty Cobb, the greatest ball player of all time, had been assaulted by three thugs late Sunday night and was in a serious condition from stab wounds. Shrill-voiced newsboys bawled forth the tidings that 'Ty Cobb has been stabbed and is dying' and for an hour or so business practically was at a standstill. The murder of a president ... scarcely could have upset things more than did the tidings,"[8] the *Detroit Free Press* reported.

Cobb missed four games, came back to go 2-for-3 at New York, but then was forced to sit out the next game because of the pain. Crawford did what he could to fill the void left by Cobb's absence and his struggles when he returned to the lineup. Crawford led the Tigers to a 6–3 win over the Highlanders, who would change their name to the Yankees after the season, with two hits and an RBI. The next day, he torched George McConnell for four hits, including a triple, and scored twice. McConnell, though, kept every other Tiger in check and hung on to win, 5–4, helping the Highlanders take four of the five games. The Tigers lost seven in a row and dropped to 55–63, still in fifth place, despite Crawford hitting .444 during the skid. Without Cobb in the lineup, or at his best, the Tigers didn't have a chance. Detroit dropped 11 of 12 games and wouldn't get out of the second division. Crawford continued to hit even when the Tigers didn't. He went 11-for-21 in the first four games of September. He went hitless the following game, then went 6-for-12.

The Tigers were well out of the pennant chase and had to take joy in the little things. Like on September 20, when the Tigers faced first-place Boston. Crawford managed one hit off Smoky Joe Wood but made his mark by doubling off Tris Speaker at second base after making a fine catch. Cobb scored a pair of runs and the Tigers beat Wood, 6–4. It was more than just a win. It snapped Wood's American League record of 16 consecutive victories. Walter Johnson had set the mark earlier in 1912 and the Tigers denied Wood the chance of breaking the mark, which still stands. "I've never seen anything like Smoky Joe Wood in 1912," Harry Hooper said. "He won 34 games that year, 10 of them shutouts, and 16 of those wins were in a row. It so happened that that was the same year Walter Johnson *also* won 16 in a row."[9] Four days later, the Red Sox clinched the pennant in the new Fenway Park. The Tigers finished 69–83 in a distant and disappointing sixth place. Not the opening of Navin Field that they were hoping for.

After batting .378 in 1911, Crawford finished 1912 with another stellar season. He batted .325 with 189 hits, 81 runs scored, 21 triples and 109 runs batted in. Cobb batted .409 to take the batting title despite missing 14 games with his suspension and stabbing. Cobb would miss many more games in 1913.

The Detroit Tigers were coming off the most disappointing season in their history, finishing in lowly sixth place. They had off-field problems with Ty Cobb, and manager Hughie Jennings couldn't get any production from anyone other than Cobb and Sam Crawford. The off-field problems with Cobb were by no means a thing of the past. In fact, they started before the 1913 season when Cobb held out for a bigger contract. The Georgia Peach had won six consecutive batting titles and felt that he deserved the biggest contract in the

American League. Cobb wanted $15,000 a year, which sounds like peanuts compared with the salaries in today's game. Detroit owner Frank Navin did not agree, especially since the Tigers' poor previous season affected attendance and revenue.

"Tyrus R. Cobb, baseball's brightest star and most conspicuous holdout, seems to be butting his head into a stone wall in his argument with Frank J. Navin, president of the Detroit Baseball company," E. A. Batchelor of the *Detroit Free Press* wrote. "Mr. Navin today reiterated his determination to remain firm in his stand on the matter and said it in a manner that those who know him best believe to be final." Navin was clear on his position. "We need him badly and his absence is costing me money every day. But even if it takes my last dollar I am going to run my ball club," Navin told Batchelor. "Then when I am broke somebody else can take hold and run it better. I wrote Cobb tendering him the same contract that he was playing under last year, explaining when I did so that I was merely complying with the form which requires that all players be given contracts before Feb. 4 or become automatically free agents, and intimating that I was willing to give him an increase that would make him the highest salaried player who ever wore a uniform. Before leaving Detroit last fall, he said that he wanted $15,000 a year and a three or four year contract. I informed him that it was a waste of time to talk in such terms."[10]

Cobb, however, believed he was not the highest-paid player in the game and that Navin was giving him the runaround, telling him that it was his attitude and not the money, then sometimes saying it was all about money. "Mr. Navin's opening statement in which he says that discipline and not money is the important question at issue between us is enough to queer his whole vicious attack upon me," said Cobb, who settled for $11,333. "It seems that Navin has shifted around in his position. For several weeks past it has been a matter of money, of not being able to pay what I ask. In this connection I wish to deny the statement that I am the best paid ball player in the world. It is rather laughable to read Mr. Navin's statement regarding the discipline question."[11]

The Tigers were forced to open the season without Cobb. It wasn't a particularly good situation for a team which had sunk to sixth place and now had to play without its best player. Crawford started the season just 8-for-35, after signing for $5,000 in the off-season after a brief holdout, and the Tigers began the season 5–9. The Tigers needed a boost. Cobb provided it by returning to the lineup April 29. Having his intensity on the field seemed to rub off on everyone. "Best of all," Batchelor wrote, "Ty Cobb, whose oft-postponed appearance in the role of the returned prodigal really happened this time, looked like his old self."[12] Cobb was just 1-for-4 against the Chicago White Sox but managed to energize the crowd when he made it from first to third on a groundout. Meanwhile, Cobb's return brought out the best in Crawford, who batted third in the lineup—one spot ahead of Cobb—on this day. He took advantage of the position and slammed three hits, scored a run and knocked in a pair. The electricity increased when the 4–4 game was sent to extra innings. In the 12th inning, the White Sox scored two runs to take a 6–4 lead. Detroit stormed right back in the bottom of the inning to score one. Cobb reached on an error, but went first-to-third on Ossie Vitt's groundout. Crawford was up next and smashed a long drive to center which looked like the game-winner. Then the high winds blowing in at Navin Field knocked Crawford's blast down, it was caught by Chicago's Wally Mattick and the White Sox held on to win, 6–5.

The Tigers lost five in a row to the White Sox to fall to 5–14 before Crawford's double and triple helped beat the Sox, 2–1, on May 4 to snap the skid. Jennings had some kinks to work out. The biggest was the hole at first base. Ever since the Tigers had let go of Claude Rossman in 1909, there hadn't been a solid presence at first base in Detroit. The Tigers had plenty of outfielders, however, and Jennings decided to try Crawford at first again. It would make room for a promising young outfielder named Hughie High. Crawford initially balked at the idea, and Jennings was going to put Bobby Veach there but pushed Crawford on the idea of playing first. After playing 15 years in the majors, Crawford was not as fast as he used to be, so he finally relented. "Sam Crawford changed his mind about that first basing job and will be seen on the initial sack in the opening game of the New York series," Batchelor wrote. "Sammy doesn't want the infield position a bit, and would much prefer remaining in right field, where he is thoroughly at home and fears no play that could possibly come up. However, he realizes that there is pressing need of making room for Hughie High to become a regular member of the cast and for that reason he has put aside his own preferences and will do the best he can to hold down the initial. With a little practice, Crawford will be a capable baseman though he may never be a fielding star in that position. From time to time, he has filled in there when the Tigers were badly crippled and he always has been able to get away in fair style."[13] It didn't make much of a difference. The Tigers lost three of four to the last-place Yankees and dropped to 7–17, ahead of only those same Yankees.

Despite the struggles, the Tigers were still able to draw a big crowd from time to time. On May 18, Detroit hosted the Washington Senators and a record 24,455 attended the game to watch the great Walter Johnson battle Carl Zamloch on the mound. Johnson had just seen his record 56-inning scoreless streak come to an end in his last start against St. Louis on May 14. The game lived up to the billing as Johnson beat the Tigers, 2–1, with Detroit errors leading to both Washington runs. Cobb made one of those errors but made up for it by stealing home, another crowd pleaser. Crawford managed one of the six hits off The Big Train. He had one of his better games the following day against Philadelphia, rapping out a single and a double and scoring three runs in a 9–3 victory. The Tigers were still just 11–21. They split the next two with the Athletics. The Tigers went 6–5 the next 11 games before facing Plank again on June 3. Plank again beat the Tigers, this time 7–3 as he struck out seven and allowed five hits. Crawford tripled home a run and scored twice against Plank. It was the start of a four-game sweep by the Athletics in which they also pounded Detroit pitching for 14, ten and eight runs. Crawford had six hits and scored four runs in the series, but he was the only Tiger doing any damage.

Washington was next on the road trip and Crawford belted a home run in the opener to lead the Tigers to an 11–1 victory on June 6. The Tigers won, 6–4, the next day behind a pair of hits from Crawford, then fell to Johnson, 3–0, one of The Big Train's record 110 shutouts, in the third game. Crawford smashed another home run in the finale and the Tigers won, 11–0. Taking three from the Senators and losing one to Johnson was what every team in the American League could hope for out of a trip to the nation's capital. But the Tigers couldn't build any momentum out of it. Detroit lost 11 of the next 17 despite Crawford's strong hitting. He smashed a three-run homer in the seventh inning off St. Louis starter Roy Mitchell to beat the Browns, 5–2. Detroit skidded to 29–48 and fell back to seventh place. Five games later, Johnson shut the Tigers out again, 9–0, and the Tigers were 31–51. Crawford's best game of the season came on July 14 when he tagged Chief Bender for four hits. He slapped two singles, a double and a triple and knocked in a season-high five runs in a 9–8 Tigers victory. Crawford had two hits again the next day, but Plank shut the Tigers out, 7–0, and sent the Tigers to 35–54.

It never got better for the Tigers in 1913, although they did beat Eddie Plank twice, and Detroit finished in sixth place again with a 66–87 record. Plank and the Athletics got the last laugh and won the pennant at 96–57. Crawford hit .317 and led the American League with 23 triples. In addition, he scored 78 runs, knocked in 83 and had 193 hits, the second-highest total of his career. Cobb won his seventh straight batting title though playing just 122 games because of the holdout and a mid-season injury, batting .390, finishing well ahead of Shoeless Joe Jackson. Obviously pitching was a problem for the Tigers, who without Crawford and Cobb wouldn't have hit well either. Another disappointing season had the Tigers yearning for a new year. They hoped it would be a rebound year and Cobb would play the entire season. Neither would be in the cards.

Trips and Turbulence

The winter of 1913–1914 was a busy and turbulent time for baseball. A world tour was in the works and the rise of a third league threatened both the National League and the American League. It was a turbulent time for Sam Crawford and the Tigers, too. Crawford was a 15-year veteran, now 33 years old, and didn't know how much more baseball he had left in the tank. The Tigers were a far cry from the team that had won three straight American League flags, 1907–1909.

Wahoo Sam Crawford decided to play more baseball in the off-season. He teamed with Shoeless Joe Jackson to play in an exhibition series in New Orleans.

> Joe spent most of the winter home in Greenville, but he and Katie journeyed to New Orleans in late October. Joe and Sam Crawford, the hard-hitting right fielder of the Detroit Tigers, were the star attractions in a series of weekend exhibition games. Joe and Crawford recruited players from other major league teams and from local minor leagues. They made a simple financial arrangement in which the players themselves sold the tickets and the refreshments, then divided the proceeds at the end of the game. There wasn't a lot of money involved; after paying the expenses and splitting the receipts among all the players, Joe's share was usually somewhere between $1-$7 per game.[14]

It wasn't the last barnstorming experience for Crawford. In fact, his baseball expeditions were just beginning. Back in 1888, Albert Goodwill Spalding led a group of baseball stars on a round-the-world tour to promote the game and try to prove that baseball was 100 percent American, not derived from any game in England or any other country. In 1913, Chicago White Sox owner Charles Comiskey and New York Giants manager John McGraw put together a baseball tour to try once again to promote the game worldwide. The tour featured the "World Champion" Giants and a team of American League All-Stars. The tour went across the country before going abroad to several countries. Sam Crawford was one of the American League stars that Comiskey recruited, naturally. He was still the premier slugger in the game and one of the best-known players in the league. "Ty Cobb and Napoleon Lajoie demurred, but Speaker and Wahoo Sam Crawford accepted, as did Herman 'Germany' Schaefer of the Senators."[15]

Before the tour finalized, a huge cloud hung over the game. A group of businessmen had started a new league and began to lure some of the major league stars to sign. It was called the Federal League and threatened the game just as the Players' League had in 1890. "Sam was a member of the Comiskey-McGraw 'Round-the-World' tour of the winter of 1913–14. Federal League promoters met the ball players at the dock in New York; they snatched Otto Knabe and Mickey Doolan of the Phillies; got Tris Speaker a 100 per cent raise, and big salary boosts for Buck Weaver, Doyle, Merkle, and other headliners. Wahoo Sam was offered heavy sugar to go over to the independents."[16] It was something for Crawford to think about. He knew his future was limited in Detroit. Though he could still wallop the ball, he had lost a step in the outfield and with Cobb and Bobby Veach in the outfield, one more young and promising player could force him to the bench, and perhaps out of baseball. So Crawford had a lot to think about and had to make the right decision. He had plenty of time to mull it over while traveling around the world. The tour began in New York and played exhibition games as the group traveled west by train. The first game was October 19 in Cincinnati, the birthplace of professional baseball.

Once it got to the West Coast, the tour boarded a ship called the *Empress*. Players and their wives waved their farewells to the crowd and departed on their adventure that would see the players celebrate Christmas and a new year on board. For players like Crawford and Jim Thorpe, this trip was essentially a honeymoon for the newlyweds. The tour's first series of 1914 was in Australia, White Sox vs. Giants which were all-star teams made up mostly of those teams' stars. Crawford played for the White Sox and Red Faber was loaned to the Giants for the series. A storm struck the *Empress* that was so severe that the officers declared an emergency as the ship suffered damage and took on water in a November 29, 1913, typhoon on their way to Japan.[17]

Crawford remembered the series in Japan. "I still get a kick thinking of a home run I hit in Tokyo in 1913, that time John McGraw and Charlie Comiskey took all-star National and American League teams on a world tour. The Tokyo ball park was the biggest I ever saw and there was a tree out in right field, about 440 feet from the plate. Some Jap once hit the tree on the fly and they didn't think any American could match that. I got a hold of one and hit it clear over the tree—maybe 450 feet on the fly," Crawford told the *Chicago Daily News*.[18]

Unfortunately, [Faber's] snapshots apparently had not survived the subsequent nine decades. What scenes and events they would have captured! They would have shown a fantastic array of experiences, including rickshaw rides in Asia, a visit to the pyramids and Great Sphinx of Egypt, an audience with Pope Pius X and a luncheon hosted by Sir Thomas Lipton (then the richest man in the world) and a climactic final game before the king of England. Speaker and the other Protestants who went to the Vatican that day— Sam Crawford among them—came away impressed. Later, they told journalists that their visit to the Vatican was one of the most vivid memories they had of the tour. Most of the Americans with them were Catholic—including all three of the tour's leading lights, Comiskey, McGraw, and Billy Sullivan. The troupe could have heard a pin drop as Pius X assured them that he would bless their future endeavors and travels.[19]

King George appeared to enjoy the tight battle. He followed each pitch and each play intently. Sportswriters noted that even when a foul ball smashed a stadium window above him, the king barely noticed the falling glass. The game remained tied after the regulation nine innings. In the top of the 10th, the Giants notched two runs against Joe Benz. In the bottom of the 10th, holding a 4–2 lead and with no opponents on base, Faber stood just one out away from a royal victory. Whether it was due to nerves or fatigue or just bad luck, Faber walked Buck Weaver to keep the White Sox's hopes alive. That brought to the plate "Wahoo" Sam Crawford, then of the Detroit Tigers and a future Hall-of-Famer. A native of Wahoo, Nebraska, Crawford proceeded to slug a Faber offering for a home run. Suddenly, the game was tied 4–4.... (Tom) Daley launched a Faber pitch high over the left field fence for a game-ending home run.... Final score: White Sox 5, Giants 4.[20]

On March 6, 1914, the Cunard liner *Lusitania* at last steamed into New York harbor to conclude the final lap of Commy's (Comiskey) and Muggsy's (McGraw) global adventure. "You know I think that trip around the world did me a lot of good ... though ... I don't believe that any fellow was ever as sea sick as I was," Speaker said.[21]

Back in Detroit, Tigers owner Frank Navin knew he would have to come up with a good deal to sign Crawford so he wouldn't jump to the Federal League.

> Crawford, usually easy to sign, was tough this spring. He knew he was getting close to the end of his trail, and took advantage of his opportunity. However, both Cobb and Crawford were difficult to sign, with the Feds promising to double the salaries of outstanding stars. Both outfield aces skipped the Gulfport, Miss., training season, but eventually signed in New Orleans shortly before the Tigers moved north. Cobb got into big brackets, and for the first time went over $20,000. Navin offered him two contracts, one for one year at a higher sum, and another two-year contract for a somewhat lesser figure. Ty took the one-year document. Pitcher Ed Willett jumped to the new league. Navin eventually induced the former Nebraska barber to put a signature on a contract by virtually insuring his big-league future; Sam signed a four-year contract.[22]

Crawford had been around the world and now he returned to the Tigers in hopes of getting the team out of the second division and back into a pennant race. A pennant was not in their cards in 1914, but the Tigers showed definite signs of improvement and the possibility of being a contender once again.

1914: Back to the First Division

Tigers owner Frank Navin needed the Tigers to turn it around in 1914 with all the money he was dealing out thanks to the war with the Federal League. "Navin got back this additional salary outlay when the 1914 Tigers got off to a thrilling start."[23] The thrills began on Opening Day against St. Louis. The Tigers and Browns battled for nine innings only to remain in a scoreless deadlock. The Browns scored two runs in the top of the 13th inning off Jean Dubuc. The Tigers had their backs against the wall, but still had one of the best lineups in baseball. They had underachieved the past couple of seasons and wanted to start this season by achieving something. Ty Cobb tripled in two runs to tie the game, 2–2, bringing up Sam Crawford. Wahoo Sam hit a sharp grounder to pitcher Bill James, who held the ball to keep Cobb from scoring the winning run. Crawford took off and ran all the way to second, knowing if they tried to tag him Cobb would score the winning run. Left fielder Bobby Veach, who later led the league in runs batted in three times, was up next. He singled to score Cobb and give the Tigers the victory. It was the start the Tigers needed.

Crawford powered the Tigers for the rest of April. He homered to lead Detroit past Cleveland, 4–3, on April 18. On April 21, Crawford hit a single, double and triple and the

Tigers beat the Indians, 7–4. He had another three-hit game the following day and another two days later. Wahoo Sam slammed a home run, scoring Cobb ahead of him, in the first inning on April 25 to propel the Tigers to a 4–0 win over St. Louis while Harry Coveleski threw a shutout. Crawford started the season batting at a .529 clip (18-for-34) and had put all fears that he was slowing down to rest.

The Tigers topped the Chicago White Sox, 4–1, on April 28 and surged into first place. Meanwhile, Crawford continued his tear. He had three hits in a 9–7 win over Cleveland on May 4 and was 4-for-5 with an RBI triple in a 10–8 win in Chicago. Detroit was still in first place on May 19 but was playing without Cobb, who was suffering from a broken rib. A young outfielder named Harry Heilmann took his place in the lineup. He was 0-for-1 but had two hits the next day. Little did Tigers fans know that Heilmann would become a mainstay and eventually replace Crawford in Detroit's one-two punch. For the time being, Heilmann played just 15 games for the Tigers. "The Tigers showed the rest of the pack nothing but their striped heels as they tore through May. By May 21, Jennings' flying Felines had won 19 games and lost only 9, putting them three games ahead of the Athletic World's Champions. Detroit suffered as the Mackmen caught the Tigers around Memorial Day, but as late as July 22, the Tigers were in fourth place, seven and a half games behind Philadelphia."[24]

Without Cobb, Crawford picked up the slack in his absence, but the Philadelphia Athletics were breathing down the necks of the Tigers. On May 21, Crawford slapped three hits and the Tigers beat the A's, 6–4. Philadelphia won the next day, 9–6, and Joe Bush got the win in relief of Eddie Plank, beating Detroit, 8–5, on May 23, despite a pair of hits from Crawford. In the past, Plank had often shut down the Tigers after they faced Washington's Walter Johnson. This time, it was the other way around and The Big Train won, 10–1. The Senators won three of four games and the Tigers struggled to remain atop the American League standings. It was on to St. Louis next and the Tigers split a doubleheader to open the series on May 30. Crawford homered the following day, but it was the only run the Tigers scored. Adding insult to injury, the loss dropped the Tigers to third place at 23–17.

The Tigers returned home June 1 to face the White Sox. Red Faber and Detroit's Hooks Dauss locked up in a pitchers' duel, each pitching a shutout through nine innings. Both pitchers stayed in the game through the tenth, and each allowed a run in the 11th. Dauss held the White Sox scoreless in the top of the 13th inning. Faber could not say the same. "It was a case of Greek meeting Greek and both men were so effective that there was no scoring until the eleventh inning," E. A. Batchelor wrote. "Then the Sox got one run and thought that they had the game in their pockets. They reckoned without 'Wahoo' Sam Crawford, however. That mighty swatist was the first Tiger up in the Detroit half of the chapter and he proceeded to paste the ball over the wire screen in right field for four bases. The rival hurlers stalled off all attempts to score in the next inning, but in the thirteenth, a double by Moriarty, (Oscar) Stanage's sacrifice and Bush's clean drive to left ended it. It was the second straight game Crawford belted a home run."[25]

Detroit lost two of the next three and were still in third place. Cobb returned to the lineup on June 6 against the Athletics, just in time to keep the Tigers from extending their slide and to gain some ground on the American League leaders. It was another extra-innings pitchers' duel with Dauss and Carroll Brown each allowing two runs through ten innings. The Tigers couldn't overpower Brown and the Athletics, and outfielder Rube

Oldring made several fine defensive plays on the Tigers' smashes, so the sluggers came out bunting. Batchelor described the action in Cobb's memorable return:

> It was mainly to get the ball out of "Rube's" clutches that the Tigers began to bunt. Having seen the folly of trying to flog anything toward this destroyer, they wisely figured that he couldn't possibly get bunts so they commenced to lay them down. Baker and Brown, not being so gifted as "Rube" messed up the taps considerably and the result was a victory that sent 15,000 maniacs home to a cold supper flavored with pennant visions.... Moriarty opened this round [eleventh inning] with a bunt that Frank Baker knocked down with the hand calloused from pulling in world's series checks. The home run hitter couldn't make his play in time, however. Then Tyrus bunted and beat the throw. Crawford did likewise, both Baker and Brown going after the ball and the pitcher finding nobody on third when he wanted to try for a play there. This filled each and every sack. Veach caused momentary chagrin and disappointment by fouling to ... Baker. But the Tigers had their mad up by that time and wouldn't be denied. Marty Kavanagh bounced one over Brown's head for which Jack Barry dove and missed. Collins cut across and lunged for the ball too and then kept right on running for the clubhouse while Moriarty went home with the winning run. Cobb could have scored also, if the game hadn't ended when George passed the threshold. The return of Tyrus to the fray put a lot of pepper in the Tigers.[26]

The Tigers won again the next day, topping future Hall of Famer Herb Pennock and the Athletics, 4–1. Then Philadelphia stormed back to win the next two games, including a 7–3 win on June 9—the first game that Crawford, Cobb and Heilmann all played in. Crawford got one hit off Bob Shawkey while Cobb was 0-for-4 and Heilmann 0-for-1 as a pinch-hitter. Crawford was hitting at a .337 clip but the Tigers needed a healthy Cobb and some other hitters to step up. On June 18, Crawford pounded a single, double and triple off Walter Johnson, leading the Tigers to a 4–2 victory. Two days later, Harry Coveleski threw a shutout and Crawford had another single and triple and the Tigers secured second place. Johnson was on the mound the following day and Crawford again had his number, tallying another single and triple. But it was Johnson who had the last laugh as he hit a grand slam in the fifth inning to provide the Senators with a 9–7 victory. It was the first of six straight losses for the Tigers, who dropped to 36–30, back in third place.

Detroit returned to second place when Crawford's two hits knocked in two runs in an 8–1 win over the White Sox on June 30. He slammed a single, double and triple off Abe Bowman in a 4–0 win over Cleveland. Detroit improved to 40–31 while first-place Philadelphia was 39–25. Crawford had another two hits the following day and was hitting .333 on the Fourth of July. Heilmann was playing almost every game again since Cobb was out with another injury. This time it was a broken thumb, and it wasn't an injury he received on the field. Rookie pitcher Babe Ruth was next up against the Tigers. "Ruth was given his second chance against the Detroit Tigers, who were playing without Ty Cobb. Cobb had been in and out of the lineup all season because of an injury he received in a fight with a Detroit butcher with whom Mrs. Cobb had a disagreement; Ty always did enjoy a calm, reasonable discussion of the issues when he found himself at odds with someone."[27]

The Cobb-less Tigers continued to hang with the Athletics. At the halfway point of the season, Detroit was 44–35 after sweeping a doubleheader from Philadelphia on July 9. The Athletics were 44–31 and tied the Tigers, 8–8, after nine innings the next day. The Tigers got inconsistent after leaving Philadelphia. On July 13, Johnson threw a three-hit shutout, but Dubuc shut out the Senators the following day. The Tigers continued the win one, lose one trend for the rest of the road trip.

The most important series of the season loomed as the Tigers finally returned home on July 25. Detroit wasn't playing poorly, but they weren't playing well enough to make up ground against Philadelphia. That would have to change immediately as the Athletics arrived for a four-game series. Plank was on the hill in the first game and scattered eight hits to win, 10–4. The Athletics won the second game, 8–6, then Pennock beat the Tigers, 8–3. The Tigers had dropped to fourth place with the three consecutive losses and needed to salvage the final game. Crawford had been quiet the first three games, but put the Tigers on his shoulders in the finale on July 28. Crawford slammed a triple, added two singles and knocked in three of the Tigers' four runs as Detroit hung on for a 4–3 win. Detroit was still in fourth place at 48–45. The Athletics led at 56–33, followed by Boston (51–41) and Washington (49–41).

The next day (July 29), baseball took a back seat to bigger news. Austria had taken occupancy of Belgrade and the Russians were ready to fight. It was the lead story in newspapers across the world, including the *Detroit Free Press*. The conflict in Europe was escalating and eventually became what is now known as World War I.

While the United States continued to look east, the Tigers also looked east in the pennant race. They were still playing without Cobb, who was still recovering from a thumb injury. The rest of the players began picking up the slack. Crawford was batting. 329 and carrying the team. But for the first time all season, others carried the load. Bobby Veach doubled in three runs to beat the Yankees, 4–3, on August 2. The next day, young Heilmann, who was playing second base, singled, walked and scored two runs in a 4–1 victory.

On August 7, a historical event happened in Detroit, though no one knew it. Cobb returned to the lineup and he, Crawford and Heilmann all were in the starting lineup for the first time. Heilmann still was at second base and wouldn't move into the outfield until later. The Tigers beat Boston, 3–1. Heilmann went hitless while Crawford and Cobb each managed a hit. Cobb's was a triple and he was knocked in by Crawford. Kavanagh returned to second base on August 13, which forced Heilmann into mainly a pinch-hitting role. That same day, one million German soldiers began an attack on the Allies in attempts to invade France.

The Tigers lost any chance they had at a pennant when they were swept by the first-place Athletics August 18–20. The third loss left them at 55–56, under .500 for the first time since they opened the season 1–2. On August 31, Detroit bounced back to 61–60 and would not drop below .500 again.

Crawford still did his best to try to get the Tigers back into the race. On September 6, he tripled with the bases loaded to spark an eight-run fourth inning and a 13–4 win over Carl Weilman and St. Louis. But the Tigers hadn't performed in the clutch and they finished the season 80–73, in fourth place, 19 games behind pennant-winning Philadelphia. Detroit got a minor victory over the Athletics at the end of the season. Cobb beat Philadelphia's Eddie Collins for his eighth consecutive batting championship. Despite all his injuries, Cobb batted .368 in 97 games. Collins finished at .344 but played 152 games. Under present American League rules, requiring the batting champion to appear at bat 502 times, Ty would not have won since he hit just 414 times.

It was a season in which Crawford had put the team on his back and despite being 34 years old, he showed no signs of slowing down at the plate. He batted .314 and led the league with 26 triples—the ninth highest total in history. It wasn't enough for Crawford, however. He wanted to get the Tigers back to the World Series. Without a healthy Cobb, the Tigers lost their chance in 1914. But 1915 was a different story. Cobb would be healthy again and Crawford would have another monster season as Detroit chased another pennant.

9. RETURN TO THE RACE

The Tigers came into spring training with a lot of questions in 1915. Would Ty Cobb be healthy for the entire season? What would they do with the promising youngster, Harry Heilmann? Would a somewhat aging Sam Crawford slow down or continue to dominate against American League pitching? Would their pitching keep up with their hitting? And could they finally return to the World Series?

Cobb managed to avoid any major off-field scuffles and played every game. He brought his scuffles back to the base paths and would have one of the greatest base-running seasons in baseball history. With Cobb's return and Crawford's continued slugging, Heilmann was sent back to the minors at the beginning of the season. Harry Coveleski and Hooks Dauss anchored a pitching staff that finally reached its potential. But was that enough to win a pennant?

Detroit opened the season on a tear, reaching first place on April 19 with a 4–2 record. Crawford also opened the season on a tear of his own, batting .500 the first week of the season. On April 28, the Tigers' potent offense showed just how much of a force it could be. Facing the St. Louis Browns at Navin Field in Detroit, the Tigers scored ten runs in the eighth inning on their way to a 12–3 victory. Crawford singled and walked in the inning, scoring twice. He also had the first Wahoo special—a triple—of the season against the Browns' Bill James. Cobb also had a big game, slapping three singles and scoring four runs. Meanwhile, Hooks Dauss kept the Browns in check.

Four days later, Dauss was on the mound and again was benefitted by the hitters. Crawford had two hits, including another triple, and Cobb had another three-hit game as Dauss outlasted Eddie Cicotte in Chicago, 4–3. On May 7, it was Coveleski's turn to reap the benefits of the offense. Cobb had three hits and scored each time while Crawford knocked him in twice with a pair of singles and the Tigers beat the Browns, 11–2.

While the Tigers were pounding the ball, the Detroit pitchers were taking care of business on the mound. They had allowed more than five runs only twice as of May 8. The next day, Jean Dubuc pitched a masterful shutout of the Washington Senators. Dubuc allowed only one hit to center fielder Clyde Milan and walked one to beat the great Walter Johnson, 1–0. Even more impressive was the fact that Dubuc only had two strikeouts and both were of Johnson, the pitcher, who allowed six hits and an uncharacteristic five walks while striking out six. Crawford continued to hit Johnson well and rapped out three hits.

The Tigers were still in first place when the second-place Red Sox came to town on May 11. The series started well for the Tigers when Dauss threw a four-hitter and beat Babe Ruth, 5–1. The Boston pitchers tamed the Tigers hitters and allowed just five runs in the next three games and the Red Sox won all three to take over first place. The Yankees traveled to Detroit next and split the two games (two were postponed because of cold weather). The defending pennant winners, the Philadelphia Athletics, came to Detroit next. It was a very different team from the one that reached the World Series in 1914. The team had a lot of new faces, and a lot of the familiar faces of dominating players were no longer in the dugout. Manager Connie Mack's two best pitchers—Eddie Plank and Chief Bender—had both jumped to the upstart Federal League after seeing its success in its pilot year of 1914. Without the future Hall of Fame duo, the Athletics would not be contenders again until a new generation of stars would win them three straight pennants, 1929–1931.

"It was another season of Federal League confusion and unsettlement. After Plank and Bender jumped to the Feds, and other Athletic stars pointed Federal-League-loaded salary pistols at Mack's head, Connie broke up the great team which had dominated the American League ever since the Tigers had held sway."[1]

On May 21, Crawford had one of his finest games of the season, slamming four hits off Philadelphia's Bob Shawkey and Chick Davies, pushing his season average to .348, fourth in the American League. Cobb also had a pair of hits that day, moving him to an even .400, which led the league. But Cobb's old nemesis, Napoleon Lajoie, had three hits of his own off Bernie Boland and led the Athletics to an 11–8 victory. Dubuc and Dauss won the next two for Detroit, and Coveleski opened the series against Washington with a 4–0 shutout on May 24.

The Tigers were trying to claw their way back into first place and looked to their two sluggers. On June 4, Cobb had a single and a triple, coming around to score both times— once when he stole home. Crawford got into the act with a single that scored two runs, leading the Tigers and Dubuc to a 3–0 shutout in New York. In the second game in the Big Apple, Cobb homered and Crawford tripled—both scoring twice—and the Tigers rolled to an 11–2 victory over Ray Fisher. Crawford tripled again the next day as a part of a three-hit performance off his old teammate "Wild Bill" Donovan. Crawford's most important hit came the next day (June 7) when he singled in Cobb in the eighth inning to tie the game 2–2 with the Yankees. Detroit added another in the ninth and beat New York, 3–2, to return to first place for the first time since May 14. But the Tigers lost, 4–1, in the finale with New York and dropped back into second place behind the Chicago White Sox.

Things would get worse before they could get better for the Tigers. On June 19, Walter Johnson shut them out, 7–0. He allowed just two hits and matched with a double and triple of his own. The next day, Carl Weilman of St. Louis shut out Detroit, 1–0, and dropped the Tigers into third place (34–24), behind Chicago (37–20) and Boston (28–18). The Tigers needed to awaken their offense, and did so in the next game against St. Louis. Crawford pounded a single, double and triple and Cobb also rocked Bill James for three hits, helping the Tigers tie the score, 9–9, heading into extra innings. The Browns scored four runs in the top of the 15th inning to win the game, 13–9. It was a crushing blow for the Tigers, who actually managed to swing their bats, unlike the previous two games. Fortunately for Detroit, the hitting would continue. Crawford had two doubles and his second three-hit game in a row off of James and Detroit won, 4–2. Two more hits and three from Cobb led Detroit to a 9–3 victory and moved them back into second place (36–25) on June 24.

Crawford continued his timely hitting as Detroit swept three games from Cleveland. On June 30, Crawford had perhaps his best game of the season. "Sam managed to toddle up to the plate and get himself three safeties for a total of six sacks," E. A. Batchelor wrote. "His first was a triple, his second a single and his third a double, the latter by the way being the longest punch of the day. It struck the front of the bleacher on the fly but came back on a nice bound to [Billy] Southworth, who held the big gentleman at second."[2] Two days later (July 2), Wahoo Sam made his mark with his bat again. Facing Chicago future Hall of Fame spitballer Red Faber, Crawford slammed a home run in the second inning to put the Tigers up, 1–0. "The Crawford home run deserves a chapter by itself," Batchelor wrote. "It was undoubtedly the longest four-baser ever made at Navin Field, going into almost the exact center of the bleacher and clearing the screen by a comfortable margin. Numerous balls have been lifted into the southern end of the two-bit stand, but none other ever has wafted its way over the barrier so far down toward the flagpole."[3] The Tigers hung on to win, 2–1.

With Crawford swinging a hot stick, the rest of the Tigers finally joined in. On July 3, Cobb doubled to clear the bases in the sixth inning off Reb Russell and the Tigers beat Chicago, 9–4. Many Detroit hitters collaborated on the Fourth of July. Cobb had three hits, Crawford a single and a double, and Marty Kavanagh hit a home run, leading the Tigers to an 8–7 victory. Crawford had 22 hits in his last 12 games and didn't stop there. On July 11, he had a three-hit performance and led the Tigers to a 5–4 victory over Boston. "Sammy was a very important factor in the proceedings," Batchelor wrote. "He hit in the deciding [run] with a two-bagger, drove home the one that tied the score with a triple and scored one himself after getting on by means of a single.... If it hadn't been for the old boy's ability to come through in the pinches, Boston surely would have walked off with the game."[4] Crawford's triple tied the game, 4–4, in the seventh and his double won it in the ninth. The next day, he homered off Dutch Leonard and scored four runs in a 15–12 loss to the Red Sox. Three hits in each of the next two games gave him 37 hits in 21 games (82 at-bats) for an average of .451.

The Tigers were starting to come together but they needed something to push them over the top. On July 14, Jennings moved Crawford from fourth to fifth in the lineup. Wahoo Sam responded by going 3-for-3 in a 12–3 win over New York. It was only temporary, however, and Crawford was back in the cleanup spot the next game. He continued to move back and forth between those spots. Philadelphia came to town on July 18 and the Tigers promptly took the first four games in a five-game series. After the third game, the Tigers moved up to second place—but only by percentage points—and were back to third on July 21 after losing the final game against the Athletics.

An important road trip was in front of the Tigers. Detroit would be away from Navin Field for 21 games and had to perform if the Tigers had any thoughts about seriously contending for the pennant. After splitting the first two games in the Big Apple, the final game against New York on July 29 was more important than it looked on paper. The Tigers were headed to Fenway Park next to face the first-place Red Sox. Lose the final game to the Yankees and they would meet Boston on a downswing. Win and they would build some momentum going into what could be their most important four games of the year. Cobb tripled in two runs in the sixth and Crawford followed with a two-run homer in the eighth and the Tigers led, 7–2. It wasn't over, however, with Boland on the mound. He made it interesting, giving up four runs in the bottom of the eighth before Bill Steen relieved him and saved a 7–6 victory.

Now, it was on to Fenway Park on a high note. Boston's Dutch Leonard held Crawford and Cobb hitless in the opener, but the rest of the Tigers chipped in and Boland recorded a 7–6 victory in relief of Hooks Dauss. Harry Coveleski lost the second game, 4–1. After an off-day, Dauss was back on the mound and edged Collins, 5–3, on August 2. Coveleski was again the tough-luck pitcher the next day, falling 2–1 to Ernie Shore. The Tigers managed to split the series and keep the same distance behind the Red Sox. If the Tigers were aiming to catch Boston, they needed to pick up the pace. They did so by taking four of five from the Athletics to move back into second place at 62–38 (behind Boston's 61–34). Detroit finished the road trip by taking two of three from Washington, both games in Chicago and sweeping Cleveland in a four-game set, the last two a doubleheader sweep on August 17. Crawford and Cobb provided the one-two punch for the Tigers. "Ty, Sam and company greeted Oscar Harstad with a book of resounding whacks in the first inning of the opener and thereafter the roar was almost constantly in evidence," the *Detroit Free Press* reported. Cobb and Crawford singled in the first inning and came around to score on an error. In the sixth, Cobb singled and scored on a double by Wahoo Sam.

Detroit returned home with a 70–39 record. The Tigers were happy with the way the road trip went, but Crawford wasn't thrilled with his own play up until the Cleveland series. After starting the season on a tear, Crawford managed just six multi-hit games in the 21-game trip. He began to hit with more consistency at home, scoring twice in the first game against the Athletics, then rapping out a pair of two-hit games to lead the Tigers to a sweep of Philadelphia. The 11–1 rout on August 20 was the ninth consecutive victory for the Tigers. On August 22, the Tigers lost, 8–1, to Walter Johnson and the Senators, but won the second game of the doubleheader, 1–0. Detroit was comfortably in second place at 74–40 and had won ten of 11 games with its lone loss coming to perhaps the greatest pitcher in baseball history.

As far as the Tigers were concerned, it was a perfect time for the first-place Red Sox to come to town. Detroit needed to gain some more ground and Boston looked to put some more distance between themselves and the Tigers. The fate of the series, and subsequently the season, hinged on the first inning of the first game on August 24. The Tigers committed three errors in the first inning that led to three Boston runs, and the Red Sox went on to win, 3–1. Crawford had a multi-hit game off Shore but the Tigers were shell-shocked from that opening inning. It didn't get any better in the second game. The Tigers were down 1–0 in the ninth inning but fought back to tie in the bottom of the frame. Detroit sent the game to extra innings and had at least one runner as far as second base in the tenth, 11th and 12th but Dutch Leonard pitched out of every jam. Leonard led off the 13th with a single. Harry Hooper bunted him to second and Everett Scott singled Leonard in with the winning run. It was another crushing blow to the Tigers, who had lost once because of their own miscues, then lost the second game in heartbreaking fashion. The Tigers salvaged the last game, 7–6, in 12 innings. Cobb singled in the 12th and was sacrificed to second by Crawford. Veach doubled him home to give the Tigers the victory, but even with the win they were 75–42, falling further behind the 76–38 Red Sox.

The Tigers broke out of their funk after Boston left town, pounding New York, 8–1 and 11–3, in a doubleheader on August 27. Crawford went 6-for-7 on the day and scored three times. It was an important time for him to shine because Cobb went 0-for-18 in the series with the Yankees. Detroit leaned on Crawford and went on to win eight of nine games. He had six multi-hit games during the stretch, which lasted through September 2. With the surge, the Tigers actually were ahead of Boston in the win column, 82–81, but Detroit was still behind with 43 losses compared with Boston's 39.

Detroit would have one more shot at the Red Sox with the season on the line. The Tigers opened up a four-game series at Fenway Park on September 16. It started with a bang and of course involved Ty Cobb. "Both defeat and disgrace came to Boston today," E. A. Batchelor wrote.

> The defeat was administered to the Red Sox by the Tigers, who won a one-sided and featureless game by a score of 6 to 1. The disgrace attaches itself to the fans, who were guilty of the most atrocious exhibition of muckerism seen in a major league park in years. The ball club incidentally took its licking with very bad grace and when its doom was inevitable resorted to tactics that would be considered unethical in a bar-room brawl. For the last month, two of the Boston papers started a campaign to stir up the rooters to a hostile demonstration against the Detroit players. Almost every morning there have been articles designed to inflame the public temper. It was started over Ty Cobb's action in trying to inspire the Detroit fans to give some vocal aid to the Tigers the last time the Red Sox were at Navin Field. The Georgian's beckoning to the crowd to unlimber its vocal artillery and his waving three bats while awaiting his turn at the plate were represented as crimes of the blackest die and the Bostonian baseball fan was urged to avenge the fancied wrongs of Bill Carrigan's men at the earliest opportunity.[5]

The fireworks began in the eighth inning. Batchelor described the scene:

> Cobb was the first man to come up in the eighth and Carl Mays's first two pitches were so plainly designed to knock the Peach down that everybody in the park could see the evil.... "You yellow dog, you ought to be ashamed of yourself," said Tyrus to the hurler.... Mays came right back with another pitch that nicked the batter and sent him to first base, eventually to score a run. As soon as Cobb threw his bat, the fans forgot his extreme provocation and hissed and jeered him with renewed vigor. They kept it up in intervals of breathtaking until the end of the game and then came the crowning disgrace of the day. It so happened that the last Bostonian to go out flied to Cobb and no sooner had he caught the ball than the human insects who made up a portion of the bleacher crowd leaped out and made a rush for him. Prudence would have dictated that Ty take to his heels and make for the shelter of the dugout. He had the lead and the speed and could easily have distanced those who sought to mob him. But the greatest of ball players isn't made of that sort of stuff and he stood his ground until the foremost of his would-be assailants were upon him and then began to walk deliberately in. None of the mongrels in the crowd had the nerve to attack him, each waiting for somebody else to strike the first blow. With the usual lack of leadership that characterizes a mob, there wasn't a soul, though Ty was outnumbered 1,000 to 1, who wanted to be the man to precipitate the mauling of the game Tiger. Somebody tossed a pop bottle that hit Ty lightly, and he turned to single out the man who had done so. Before he could locate his coward a couple of big Irish policemen had arrived on the scene and the hoodlums were driven back. One ... made a rush for the Tiger and a copper caught him a beautiful punch in the jaw and knocked him sprawling 20 feet away. After that even the courage, if you could call it that, which impels members of a mob to curse and threaten a defenseless man ebbed away and the Peach continued his way to the clubhouse deliberately and unafraid. The whole Tiger squad, some of them clutching bats, went out to meet Cobb and formed a body guard ready to give the mob the busiest few minutes of its life if anybody had started a real fight. But nobody did and the last few yards of the march were in the nature of a triumphal procession.[6]

Ugly scenes were avoided the next day, but the Boston fans did cheer Cobb in jest the first time he came to the plate. He managed just one hit on the day while Crawford went hitless and Dutch Leonard beat the Tigers 7–2. The third game of the series, September 18, was both a thrilling and heartbreaking matchup. Harry Coveleski and Ernie Shore both pitched masterfully and allowed no runs through 11 innings. Pinch-hitter Bill Carrigan knocked in Duffy Lewis in the bottom of the 12th inning and the Red Sox won, 1–0. The next matchup had many similarities. It was another brilliant pitching duel between Dauss and Babe Ruth. The Tigers led, 2–1, after the first inning before both pitchers settled down. Dauss gave up a couple of untimely hits in the sixth inning, leading to two Boston runs, and Ruth held on to beat Detroit, 3–2, to close the series. The Red Sox took care of business after losing the first game with Detroit and ran off three straight victories to virtually clinch the pennant. Boston extended its record to 93–45 while the Tigers dropped to 91–51.

With only 12 games to go the Tigers needed to win every game and hope for a miracle. Crawford helped give the Tigers a chance when he singled in two runs during a ten-run seventh inning against Philadelphia on September 22. The Tigers swept the Athletics in three games, then won three of five from Washington. Detroit split two games with St. Louis and closed the season by beating Cleveland twice. The Tigers had won 100 games but it wasn't enough to claim the pennant. In fact, it was the first time an American League team won 100 games but did not reach the World Series. It had happened to the Cubs in the National League in 1909, preventing three straight Detroit-Chicago World Series matchups. Detroit finished 100–54 but the Red Sox hung on with a 101–50 mark.

Hughie Jennings in later years called his season of 1915 his "biggest disappointment in Detroit." The Tigers came home second with 100 victories, 54 defeats, and a percentage of .639, higher than any of Detroit's seven pennant-winning percentages with the exception of .656 in 1934. Carrigan's Red Sox won 101 games and lost 50 for a percentage of .669. Yet Jennings' 1915 club, as well as the Tiger fans, knew exactly where they blew the flag—in competition with their nearest rival, Boston. The swaggering Red Sox won the year's series from Detroit most emphatically, 14 games to 8. Cobb's seasons were so uniformly brilliant that it is difficult to point the finger at one, and say: "This was Cobb's greatest," but 1915 certainly was one of his very best. This time he didn't scuffle with any butcher boys, played the full season of 156 games (two were ties), led the batting race again with a .370 average—38 points ahead of second-man Eddie Collins—scored 144 runs, and established a modern record with 96 stolen bases. "I've always regretted I didn't make it a hundred steals that year," said Cobb, some years later. "With a little greater effort, I believe I could have gotten those four additional bases. It also was a great disappointment not to get into the World's Series that year. I was little more than a youngster in my three Series; by that time I had matured, and I think I could have shown those National Leaguers something." The Tiger 1915 outfield really was a punishing affair. Veach came fast that year, hit .313 in 152 games, and bombarded the fences with 40 doubles and 10 triples. And Crawford still had plenty of dynamite in his cudgel; he just missed .300—finishing with .299—but, like Cobb, he played out the full 156-game string and was second to Ty in number of hits.[7]

Sam was openly disappointed [about missing .300].

"One hit or, at most two, would have altered all that," he said. Few people are aware of the remarkable fact that for the past thirteen consecutive years Sam Crawford has averaged over 150 games per season. This is a record that stands unequaled. The only mark that could compare with Crawford's is that of [Honus] Hans Wagner. And the Flying Dutchman, during the past thirteen years of his labors, has averaged a shade less than 141 games per season. To add to the impressiveness of Crawford's total we might cite the fact that during the past three seasons, when he might confidently be expected to decline somewhat, he had averaged over 155 games per season.[8]

Crawford quietly led the American League with 19 triples and 112 runs batted in, keeping the Tigers in the race. But what Crawford and the Detroit fans didn't realize was that despite his lack of decline and his utter domination over American League pitching, they had seen Wahoo Sam as a full-time starter for the last time.

10. MR. ALMOST 3,000

Sam Crawford felt invigorated after the 1915 season. In the face of many saying he was too old and too slow, Crawford had proved them all wrong by leading the American League in triples and runs batted in to help the Detroit Tigers win 100 games and fight the Boston Red Sox tooth and nail for the pennant. Even on the decline, Wahoo Sam set the major league record for most consecutive games played at 472 from 1913 through the first six games of 1916. It wouldn't last long because he wasn't going to be an everyday player, despite his history of heroics at the plate.

The problem for Crawford was that the Tigers needed to find a spot for young Harry Heilmann, who had been up with the Tigers in 1914, but played most of 1915 with San Francisco of the Pacific Coast League. Detroit wanted Heilmann in the lineup and manager Hughie Jennings did everything he could to get him there. To start the season, Heilmann played first base with the usual outfield of Crawford in right, Cobb in center and Bobby Veach in left. Jennings wanted Heilmann to contribute but didn't want to disturb the superb outfield.

The 1916 season opened for the Tigers in newly enlarged Comiskey Park, where an estimated 32,000 White Sox rooters watched in astonishment as Harry Coveleski not only shut out their favorites 4–0 but collected two singles, a double, and a triple. Cobb, now hitting third in front of Veach and Crawford, contributed a single and a double. Two games later, severe colds felled Cobb and Crawford; both missed the home opener on April 21. After being out for two more games, Cobb returned to the lineup. Jennings announced that Crawford's slowness in right field hurt the team and the 36-year-old veteran of 17 major league seasons would no longer play regularly. Harry Heilmann took over for him, with Crawford now relegated to fill-in and pinch-hitting duties.[1]

"I am mighty sorry to have to admit that Crawford is through as a regular," Jennings told writer Fred Van Ness. "He has been a grand player and I hate to see him go to the bench, but he has slowed up. I have been playing Heilmann in his place. I intend to use him from now on as a pinch hitter. It seems to be the opinion that I benched Crawford because of his hitting. I want to say that is wrong…. If Sam had taken my advice, he would still be a regular. Two years ago I noticed Sam was slowing up and I wanted him to take up first base."[2]

Crawford got a hit in his first pinch-hitting role on April 29, helping the Tigers beat Cleveland, 5–3, in 11 innings. For his efforts, he returned to right field the following day and was 2-for-4 with three runs scored in an 11–6 loss to the Indians. He played the next four games in right and after being off two, played six consecutive games in the outfield and managed six hits. It was the longest consecutive stretch he would play until late July.

In fact, he was only allotted eight pinch-hit assignments in the next seven weeks. He went 3-for-7 and was not happy about his diminished role.

Jennings didn't have a problem with Crawford's hitting. It was his diminished speed in the outfield that bothered him. While in New York on May 21, Jennings unveiled a plan to have Crawford move to first base and Heilmann take over in right field. "Jennings is now trying to persuade Sam Crawford to put aside his prejudice against playing first base so that he can station the big fellow there and thus give the club the benefit of his batting ability without handicapping it through his slowness of foot and poor throwing in the outfield," E. A. Batchelor of the *Detroit Free Press* wrote.

> Sam doesn't take kindly to the idea of holding down the initial bag and it doesn't seem likely at present that he will consent to don the mitt. The Wahoo man has made several stabs at playing first since he has been a Tiger, but always has given it up in disgust. He feels that he isn't able to make a creditable showing there and as soon as he pulls a couple of bad plays, he wants to quit. He says now that before he attempted to become a regular initial bagman, he would want to put in a whole training trip practicing there. Jennings believes that his big slugger would be able to hold down the position in an acceptable manner without any long period of preparation.[3]

As Sam Crawford got older, younger players looked to supplant him in the outfield. Tigers manager Hughie Jennings put Crawford at first base several times during his later years when Harry Heilmann needed a spot in the lineup (National Baseball Hall of Fame Library, Cooperstown, New York).

Crawford took a lot of pride in every facet of his game. While he could not improve his speed, he still worked diligently to improve his hitting and fielding. After being one of the top players in all of baseball for 15 years, including the previous season, Wahoo Sam thought he deserved better treatment from the Tigers. Jennings abandoned the idea of Crawford at first, but always kept it in the back of his mind.

One thing is for sure: It wasn't helping the Tigers to keep Crawford on the bench. Without him, they continued at their .500 pace well into June. Crawford was riding the pine despite his .286 average on June 10. Cobb was hitting .321 while Heilmann was at .311 and Veach .256. Obviously, Jennings didn't consider Veach's defense a liability or Veach would have played less in favor of Crawford. Between May 21 and June 18, Crawford saw no action whatsoever. It is difficult for a hitter to keep his stroke while delegated to part-time duty, especially for the first time. Crawford was eager to prove he could still hit and would get that chance June 17 at home against Philadelphia.

"Taking the game by and large, it

wasn't what you could call inspiring, but there was one feature that everyone present will remember long after all the other details have been forgotten," Batchelor wrote.

> It happened in the seventh inning when Sam Crawford went to bat in place of Heilmann who retired because he wasn't feeling fit. The moment big Sam came out of the dugout brandishing a flock of bats, every man woman and child in the park except the occupants of the pressbox, who aren't supposed to be human, proceeded to make a noise. They yelled and howled and squealed and shrieked and stamped and clapped and did everything else that they thought would convey to the Wahoo slugger how much they love him. The Niagara of sound continued with no sign of abating all the while Sam was at the plate and it received added impetus when he showed his appreciation by hammering a three-bagger to the front of the bleacher, sending Veach home. They continued to cheer Sam until he was thrown out at the plate and disappeared in the dugout, and they started the whole thing all over again when he came out at the end of the inning to take his place in the field. As he approached the old familiar pasture in right, the bleacherites showed the grandstand patrons where the real lung power resides. They didn't confine themselves to vocalisms either but could be seen throwing away their new straw hats and trying to break up the benches in their enthusiasm. Never before has a ball player been given such an ovation in Detroit as a ... pure tribute to his personal popularity. Men who have made the deciding plays in Tiger victories have been more or less wildly hailed at the moment but this demonstration was different. It was Sam Crawford, the man, they cheered and not merely the athlete that could influence the result of this particular contest.[4]

Crawford's popularity and the display of the fans was something that shocked him. Fittingly, it was a triple—the Wahoo special—that Crawford delivered to such an ovation. "Sam Crawford may have gone back as a ball player, as manager Jennings asserts, but he is hitting just plain 1.000 in the popularity league," Batchelor wrote. "It must have warmed the Wahoo man's heart when the crowd handed him that ovation in the seventh inning. There can be no denying that baseball is worthwhile when such a handsome display of sentiment can be given so spontaneously."[5]

The Tigers won the game, 7–3, and moved up to third place (29–24). Detroit won the final game against Philadelphia without Crawford. First-place Cleveland came calling on June 20. Hooks Dauss pitched a gem in the first game and the Tigers won, 2–1. The following day, Harry Coveleski pitched a 3–0 shutout, allowing just three hits, and the Tigers climbed into a tie with the Indians atop the American League standings, with both teams sporting a 32–24 record. Cleveland won the next two games and retook the lead. The Tigers dropped from second to third with the two losses, then, showing how close the standings were in 1916, dropped to fourth with only two more defeats.

For the next few weeks, Crawford saw a lot of the bench. He pinch-hit just four times in June before starting at first base on June 29. He went 0-for-4 in an 8–2 loss to the White Sox. On July 3, Wahoo Sam was back in familiar territory—right field—because Cobb was suspended for throwing his bat the day before. Crawford responded with a single and a double, though the Tigers lost, 6–4, to the first-place Indians. With Cobb suspended one more day, Crawford started both games of a Fourth of July doubleheader. He went 3-for-4 with a double in a 6–2 Tigers victory in the first game but went hitless in the second game, which Cleveland won, 6–3. The games brought his season batting average up to .287, which in many ways was incredible considering Crawford never had time to get into a groove with his sporadic playing time. On July 11, Crawford slammed a pinch-hit double off Walter Johnson, but the Senators won, 3–1.

Crawford got another chance to play the outfield on July 22, when he was back in right field while Cobb was out with a laceration on his head. He got eight hits in the next six games, including a 3-for-3 performance with a triple in a 7–4 win over the Senators on July 27. He played so well, in fact, that he played all three games without the Georgia Peach, then played the next seven more after Cobb returned, as Jennings sat Heilmann for a few games. He had a pair of hits on July 30, though the Red Sox won, 9–1. "Both of Crawford's hits were scorchers," the *Detroit Free Press* said. On August 2, Crawford went back to a pinch-hitting role, tripled and scored in a 5–2 loss to Boston. He slapped a pinch-hit single the next day too.

Detroit lost four straight and Jennings decided that he needed Crawford's bat in the lineup more often. Heilmann moved to first base for a few games to make room for Crawford, who hit three triples and three singles in four games, moving his average up to a surging .316. He would remain in the outfield the rest of the season, while young Heilmann would be the top pinch-hitter off the bench. Crawford responded with three hits the next game and the Tigers moved back up to fourth place. The move worked. Beginning August 25, the Tigers won ten of their next 11 games and moved up to second place at 74–57 after sweeping Cleveland in four games at home. Six days later, the Tigers began a three-game sweep at Cleveland, as the once mighty Indians had fallen into the second division.

The Tigers were clinging to second place and trailed only Boston in the standings. Detroit had won four of five in a row thanks to Cobb, who had a single and a double and a triple in a 9–1 win over Cleveland. Cobb then slammed two home runs off future Hall of Famer Stan Coveleski in the finale, part of a four-hit game. Crawford also managed a single, double and triple off Coveleski and the Tigers won, 10–2. Heilmann had returned to first base and went 5-for-5, including a triple and a double.

Detroit took 1 of 3 from the Yankees and then hosted last-place Philadelphia. Tigers hurler Howard Ehmke hung on to beat the Athletics, 4–3, remarkably sending the Tigers into first place at 82–60. The Tigers won the next game as Harry Coveleski hung on to win, 6–5, in ten innings. At 83–60, the Tigers were ahead of Boston (80–59) by four percentage points. The Tigers dropped the finale to Philadelphia, 2–0, and with it dropped to second place.

The Tigers had a big chance to redeem themselves. Boston came to town for a three-game set, and the Tigers trailed the Red Sox by only three percentage points. Carl Mays was on the mound in the opener against Hooks Dauss on September 19. Mays was in several jams throughout the game, allowing Crawford, Cobb and Heilmann to each go 2-for-4. Crawford scored only once and the other sluggers were left stranded each time as the submarining Mays won, 3–1. Dutch Leonard got the best of Ehmke in the next game and hung on for a 4–3 victory. Any chance the Tigers had at the pennant would rest with the final game of the series. The Red Sox jumped on Coveleski for runs in each of the first four innings and cruised to a 10–2 victory, all but clinching the pennant. The *Detroit Free Press* chose this headline: "Boston massacres Tigers in final game of series—Jungleers' pitchers are duck soup for champions."[6] Babe Ruth pitched for Boston and scattered seven hits, including two by Crawford.

Jennings was again disappointed with another "almost" season. He could not blame Crawford, however. Wahoo Sam slammed seven hits when it counted—in the final Boston series—and continued to hit well the rest of the year. Would the Tigers have claimed the pennant if Crawford had played every day? Who knows, but it was certainly a question on the minds of a number of Detroit fans. Crawford finished the season at .286 and was still among the league leaders with 13 triples, despite playing in just 100 games, including 19 as a pinch-hitter. The Tigers closed out the season with a 6–3 loss to the Browns and their old adversary, Eddie Plank, who had returned from the Federal League. They finished the season 87–67, in third place behind Boston (91–63) and Chicago (89–65), who had sneaked into second when the Tigers were dominated by the Red Sox. After the Tigers split a four-game set with the Senators, the Red Sox clinched the pennant on September 27.

> The season of 1916 was another "might-have-been" year for Detroit. The Tigers were hot contenders in another stiff race, and with their 1915 percentage they would have won easily. Despite the loss of their greatest star, Tris Speaker—sold to Cleveland—the Red Sox repeated in the American League, but with 10 fewer victories than they posted in 1915. The Tigers, however, fell thirteen under their 1915 victory total, and wound up in third place, four games behind Boston, and two in back of the runner-up White Sox. Detroit's big thrill came on August 25, when, after running second to the Red Sox for weeks, the Tigers bolted into first place for the first time. "From here on watch our smoke," was the Tiger war cry, but the smoke quickly faded. The Felines held the lead only two days, when the pace became too severe; on the September home stretch, the Tigers fell back to second and then to third. The 1916 season also made history in that it saw Cobb finally dethroned as American League batting champion, after he had wielded the scepter nine successive years. Ty had his usual bright season, hitting .371—two points higher than in 1915—but Speaker, Cleveland's new expensive acquisition, shot by the Georgian and finished with .386. If Cobb had to lose the title, he probably rather would have lost it to "Spoke" than to any other man in the league. Ty was an out-and-out individualist, who made few close friends among players, and Speaker probably came closer to being an intimate of Cobb than any other player.[7]

Sam Crawford knew there wasn't much of a chance for him to return to a starting role in 1917, but he wasn't prepared for the even more limited role that the Tigers kept him in. Wahoo Sam was the top pinch-hitter for the Tigers and found his way into 61 games, but he only played in the field and batted more than once in a game 18 times all season.

A record crowd saw the Tigers open the season with a 6–4 loss to Cleveland on April 11. Crawford came up as a pinch-hitter, but didn't connect. Wahoo Sam pinch hit in each of the next five games and had one hit and a sacrifice fly in his five plate appearances. The Tigers started 1–5 with Crawford on the bench, so manager Hughie Jennings inserted him at first base on April 19. Crawford responded by slamming a home run and a double. In the first game that Crawford, Harry Heilmann and Ty Cobb started together in 1917, all three had two hits and scored at least one run, but the Tigers lost, 8–7, to the Indians.

Crawford started at first base the next three games, going 1-for-4 in each of the first two, which helped the Tigers win both games. Wahoo Sam unsuccessfully pinch-hit in a 7–2 loss to St. Louis on April 24, didn't play in the next game, then started the next two games at first base. He went 0-for-4 in each game, was benched the next game, then went 1-for-4 on May 7 at first base in a 4–3 win over Cleveland.

The Tigers were in a tailspin, falling into an unbelievable seventh place after starting the season 11–19. They didn't know what to do with their outfielders and it was affecting the entire team. Heilmann started the season playing center field while Cobb was in right field. Crawford was playing some first base, doing a lot of pinch-hitting and would be back in right field before the season was done. On May 26, Crawford had a pinch-hit single in the eighth inning and scored to spark the Tigers to an 11–8 victory over the Athletics.

It was back to the bench for a few games for Crawford before he played both games of a doubleheader on June 5. He had a pinch-hit single in the first game, which the Tigers lost, 5–2, to the Yankees. Playing at first base in the second game, Crawford went 1-for-4 and the Tigers won, 6–4. After a week with only one at-bat, Crawford was back in right field on June 15, taking over for Heilmann. He pinch-hit for Heilmann after two at-bats. Once again, he responded with two RBI singles in a 4–3 victory over Walter Johnson and the Washington Senators. Crawford started in right field the next day, and it was Heilmann who played first base. Both went hitless, though Howard Ehmke beat the Senators, 3–2, thanks to a triple and double by Cobb, who had started the longest hitting streaks of his career. Crawford drove in the winning run in a 1–0 win on June 18 but switched with Heilmann the next game and both went hitless again as Johnson shut out the Tigers, 3–0. It was the last time Crawford would play first base in his career.

Meanwhile, the Tigers were starting to pull out of the second division. Cobb homered to beat Eddie Plank and the Browns, 4–2, on June 24. Four days later Bobby Veach hit a home run in the ninth to force extra innings. Detroit beat Chicago, 6–5 in the tenth. The next day, the Tigers pounded St. Louis, 19–1. With Crawford on the bench, Cobb and Heilmann each had three hits and scored three runs. Both scored on Heilmann's home run. It was part of one of the biggest tears the Georgia Peach had ever been on, his first of six straight multi-hit games.

Crawford was doing his best at the plate despite his sporadic at-bats. He slammed a three-run, pinch-hit homer in the seventh inning against St. Louis, but the Tigers dropped the game, 15–9, to split a July 1 doubleheader. Cobb had five hits in the twin bill and slapped seven hits in the next five games. On July 6, Cobb went hitless against future Hall of Fame pitcher Red Faber, who mastered his famous spitball to beat the Tigers, 4–1. Cobb's hitting streak was snapped at 35 games and the Tigers fell back into fifth place at 36–35.

Crawford managed a pinch-hit double on July 8 and another on July 17 but had only two at-bats in between. He was starting to be used even more sparingly. He got another chance but failed to get a hit on July 18. After a walk on July 22, he went 20 games without seeing any action until August 13. Again, he failed to get a hit, and again the following day. He drew a pinch-hit walk on August 24, then got a surprise the next game.

On August 25, the Tigers celebrated "Sam Crawford Day" at Navin Field, and Wahoo Sam started in his old post—right field. It was his first start in two months and his first in right field since June 16. Manager Hughie Jennings and the Detroit ownership wanted Crawford to get the praise he deserved for his career, even if they felt he had slowed down. The Tigers honored Wahoo Sam with gifts and a 4–2 victory over Philadelphia.

"Sam had a nice party," E. A. Batchelor of the *Detroit Free Press* wrote.

> He was enriched by about $1,200 in cash, representing the Detroit club's net profit from the gate receipts, a valuable diamond ring presented by Detroit fans, and a fine gold watch from his admirers in Flint. The Wahoo man played the whole game and though he didn't get a hit, he would have had a home run with any sort of luck…. Sam slammed a long drive to right field. A brisk northwest wind carried the ball to the pavilion side of the bleachers when it seemed certain to land in the 20-cent section and (Charlie) Jamieson,

who apparently has no eye for the artistic and no sentiment in his make up, proceeded to pull a one-hand catch that was the feature play of the game.... The crowd showed its affection for Sam on every possible occasion, cheering wildly whenever he came to the plate and applauding his two fielding achievements in a most enthusiastic way.[8]

It was the last time the Detroit fans would see Crawford start. In fact, it wasn't until almost a month later that they saw him at all. On September 15, he pinch-hit in the second game of a doubleheader and made an out. The following day, Crawford had the final at-bat of his big league career, though neither he nor the fans knew it for sure. Again he failed to make a hit off of Cleveland's Jim Bagby and the Indians won, 8–4.

The Tigers had 12 more games to go in the season, which Crawford was forced to watch from the bench. It was a tough season for Crawford, who was at the crossroads of his career, and the Tigers, who finished fourth at 78–75.

Crawford had a lot of thinking to do that off-season. He knew if he stayed in Detroit, he would play even less than he did in 1917, which was only 61 games. He hit .173 with two home runs and no triples. "Don't talk to me about batting averages," Crawford told *Baseball Magazine*.

> No man on earth can sit on the bench a week then go in and play two or three games, then sit on the bench another week and go in as a pinch hitter and hit up to his regular standard. My batting average for the season may be poor just now but how on earth could it be anything else? It is true that I am not the fastest man in the world. It is also true that I am probably not as fast as I was at twenty-five. But after all, right field is one place where speed does not count for as much as it should elsewhere on the diamond and there are other slow men playing right field. I think, without exaggeration, I can cover a fair amount of ground and stop most of the balls that come my way in right field. And I am confident I can hit nearly as well as I ever could. They told me I had slowed up, that I would have to begin to take my turn on the bench, that I must relinquish right field at least part of the time to a younger man. Now I have always known that I would grow old sometime. I have always been prepared to meet the day when it arrived and I flatter myself with as good grace as the next man. But I wasn't ready to say good-bye in 1916.[9]

Crawford had to decide whether to hang up his uniform for good or try to hang on and get his 3,000th hit. "If only I could have played another 50 games that year, I could have made it," he told Fred Lieb. "But I ran out of gas. I had a fine career; I enjoyed every minute of it."[10]

Crawford, with becoming modesty, saw nothing particularly unusual in his long years of service. "Why," he said, "when I was in Cincinnati we had a player on that club named Bid McPhee who had played in one position, second base, for nineteen years. I will have to job along two or three seasons more to equal that."[11] He did all he could to help the team reach another World Series. But Cobb didn't get along well with Crawford, and the Tigers finally made a choice.

"After the Great War, the elastic in Sam Crawford's throwing arm showed wear, and in 1918 the veteran of 19 major-league years was released by Detroit and joined Los Angeles of the Class AA Pacific Coast League. Wahoo Sam left behind an important record, one that ... still stands—309 career triples. No hitter since Crawford has surpassed him in cumulative three-basers—not even Cobb (295), Ruth (136) or Willie Mays (140). Crawford's durable feud with Cobb continued after he left the Tigers. When I asked Cobb why the breach never healed, he said, 'Crawford was a hell of a good player. Hall of Famer. But he was only second best on our club—a bad second. He hated to be an also-ran.'"[12] It wasn't the first time Cobb had gotten his way.

A vaudeville-like name was given Detroit in the years when the club ran out of the money: "Cobb and others." "Tigers" was spelled "Tygers" by some writers. Cobb himself seldom praised his teammates. His snubbing of Sam Crawford, who retired with bitter feelings in 1917, of Jones, of Matty McIntyre, was a way of getting even for the past. Steady-hitting Bobby Veach came to Detroit in 1912 and lasted in the outfield until 1923. Deferential to Cobb, the genial Kentuckian came around in time to saying, "If T.C. didn't like you he could run you off the club. He had that king of drag with the front office from about 1914 on. He was a sorehead. I hit .355 one year to his .384 and I swear he was jealous of me. What an odd bird." Veach could not forget that in 1914, with postseason exhibition games left on the schedule, their leader dropped out to attend the World Series between the Boston Braves and the Athletics. He was paid a high fee to write a commentary, "Cobb Says." "You can guess what that did for our morale," said Veach. Sam Crawford had said it before and said it again. He felt rather sorry for the one who walked mostly alone, not sharing in team camaraderie. Crawford noted, "That's no way for anyone to live. But I know one thing—he was never sorry for what he did." For as long as he lived Cobb retained a copy of a letter he sent to J. G. Taylor Spink of *The Sporting News*, reading:
   Dear Taylor:
   Crawford never helped in the outfield by calling to me "plenty of room" or "you take it" on a chance. Not only that, when I was on base and tried to steal second to get into scoring position, with Crawford at bat, he would deliberately foul balls off so I'd have to go back to base, so that the first baseman would have to hold me on ... giving Crawford a bigger hole to hit through. I ran hundreds of miles having to return to first.
   Crawford, upon learning of the letter in 1946, shook his head. "Cobb dreamed that up," he told several reporters. "He could come in on a ball with the best. He wasn't so good going back for a big lofter in the wind. So he blamed me. As to my fouling them off, it was always a way to pick at pitches until I got one to my strength. Cobb was just the same way."[13]

Whether it was because of his feud with Cobb, or because management thought he had slowed down too much, Crawford's days with the Tigers, and subsequently in the majors, were over. He finished his career just 39 hits shy of the magical 3,000, which would have helped his name be remembered outside Detroit. His record of 309 triples has never even been approached since Cobb, and he knocked in 1,525 runs while finishing with a .309 career average. He led the league in triples six times, runs batted in three times, home runs twice, doubles once and runs scored once. He also batted .300 for 11 seasons and led the league in fielding percentage in 1905, 1914 and 1915.
   Crawford played in the Pacific Coast League with Los Angeles for the next four years and, in his true ironman form, played 175 games in 1921 at the age of 41, batting .318. In 1920, he had one of his more memorable games, but not for the reason one would imagine.

Sam Crawford was in his twenty-second year of professional baseball when he stepped up to the plate in the eighth inning of a game between Sacramento and Los Angeles on June 30, 1920. Long and eventful had been his career as a big leaguer, and now he was tapering off in the minors.... Even so, Crawford could still put the wood to the ball in fine style. At the age of thirty-nine, he batted .360 in the fast Pacific Coast League. And he was barging along at a clip well above the .300 mark when he came to bat that day in the Los Angeles ball park. Crawford stepped into the batter's box with the bases loaded. Sam made them sit up and take notice by hitting a "phantom home run," the likes of which might never again be seen in a lifetime of watching ball games. The big outfielder took a toe hold and slammed the ball into deep center field. The way his bat met the ball, good and solid, he was sure he had an extra-base hit going. But the three baserunners weren't so sure. They saw what Sam, tearing along toward first with his head down, didn't see. Bobby Schang, the Sacramento center fielder, was making a dart of a run for the ball and the chances were that he might catch it. But he didn't. Rollie Zeider, the runner on first, had edged off a little and was waiting to see if Schang would make the catch for the second out of the inning. He was startled when something went whizzing past him. It was Sam, going down to second as though a dozen devils were chasing him. Sam rounded second and headed for third, still unaware that he had passed a base runner, when he heard a bull-voiced wag shout, "Hit the dirt." Thinking the ball had been recovered and was being thrown into get him out, Sam heaved himself into a magnificent slide, knocking the third baseman at least a rod into foul territory. After making the slide, Sam saw the ball wasn't anywhere around. So he got to his feet and started on the last quarter of his trip around the bases. He topped it off with a dazzler of a slide across the plate. Under the illusion that he had belted a base-clearing homer, Sam was amazed when the umpire told him he was out for having passed a runner at first base. But the show wasn't over. Marty McGaffigan, Sacramento's second baseman, also was in the grip of an illusion. Having taken the throw from the outfield, he raced to third and touched the bag. Then he held the ball aloft and yelled, "He's out—he never touched third." By that time, there wasn't a dab of ennui (boredom) left in the ball park. Laughter was making ribs ache all over the place. Sam himself, after looking sheepish for a spell, came to the conclusion that he had done something funny and laughed along with everyone else.[14]

Batting .338 in four seasons, he tallied 781 hits in the PCL, leading the league in 1919, which many believed was basically another major league at the time. There was no big league ball on the West Coast and just 16 major league teams, unlike the 30 today. That total gave him 3,742 hits, and while they weren't all in the majors, it is easy to see that he could have had the chance to reach 3,000 and would have easily reached it had the Tigers kept him. Also, his time in the Western League could have counted since the league joined the American League in 1900, one year after Crawford played in Grand Rapids. The National Commission originally ruled that all players would be credited with their 1899 statistics, which would have given Crawford 3,051 hits.

Crawford himself wrote Hall of Fame president Paul Kerr on the matter on November 6, 1964. It read:

Dear Paul,
    I have your letter of October 29. You are quite right concerning the National Commission and the year it was organized, 1903. It was at this time we were given the hits one made in the Western League in 1899. American League was just getting into full swing at this time. However as long as you and the Directors would not believe (H. G.) Salsinger and his *Detroit News* story concerning my 3,000 hit claim I really thought the National Commission story would show the Directors that a really bad mistake had been made and that you and the Directors would rectify it and give me what I rightfully earned. I appreciate your cooperation with all good wishes.
    Sincerely,
    Wahoo Sam Crawford

But somehow the matter was later disputed and dropped. "The Western League was not a major in 1899 and it was not a major when it changed its name to the American League in 1900," Hall of Fame historian Lee Allen wrote in a column for *The Sporting News* in 1968. "And the National Commission ... did not concern itself with the playing records at all, but concentrated on the endless contractual disputes between players and their clubs."

So Crawford still remains on the outside of the 3,000 hit club. He finished his major league career with 2,961 hits, a record 309 triples, 1,525 runs batted in, 458 doubles, 97 home runs, 1,391 runs and a .309 average in 2,517 games during his 19-year career.

Crawford continued in baseball as an umpire in the Pacific Coast League and joined the Association of Professional Baseball Players in 1927 to provide services to retired ballplayers in need. As a player who had very few run-ins with umpires during his playing career, being behind the plate was eye-opening for Wahoo Sam. "It was hard to imagine that this was the same great Sam Crawford whose reputation as a player during the early years of baseball was that of a tough, battling competitor," Babe Herman told the *Lincoln Star*. "As an umpire, Sam was a pussy cat. He may not have been the most talented umpire, but he was certainly the most gentle, the kindest person ever to wear an umpire's uniform. Confrontations saddened him. I could never criticize a decision of Sam's without subsequent feelings of remorse and guilt."[15] Crawford described umpiring as a thankless job and a lonesome life. The only friend an umpire had was his partner. Everyone else was just waiting for the umpire to make a mistake.

Following his wife's death, Crawford married Mary Blazer in 1943. Following his stint as an umpire (1935–1938), he worked in a defense plant during World War II. After his career was over, he moved around in the Northwest, ending up in Hollywood of all places. He actually appeared in a silent film called *College*, one of a handful of former players to appear in the baseball portion of the film in 1927. Not somewhere you would expect to find a quiet person like Crawford. But that is where writer Lawrence Ritter found him while interviewing players from the Dead Ball Era for his book *The Glory of Their Times*. Here is an excerpt from the interview:

> No, I don't have a telephone. If I had a lot of money I wouldn't have one. I never was for telephones. Just don't like them, that's all. Anybody wants to talk to you, they can come to see you. I have a television over there—it was a gift—but I never turn it on. I'd rather read a book. Don't even watch the ball games. Oh, maybe the World Series, but that's about it. I like to do what I like to do, that's all. I don't see why I should watch television just because everybody else does. I'd rather read a book, or fix up the garden, or just take a walk with my wife, Mary, and see what's going on, you know.
>
> Heck, I don't even buy a newspaper. Nothing but trouble in it. Just spoils your day. You get up in the morning, fell pretty good, get a hold of a paper, and what do you see? Nothing but trouble. Big headlines about bombs and war and misery. It ruins the day. That's the way I look at it, anyway. Maybe I'm wrong, I don't know....
>
> Did you ever hear of Tim Hurst? He was a very famous umpire back then. A real tough character. He was wise to this deal, of course, where the runner doesn't come anywhere close to touching third base. Well, Jake Beckley was playing first for us—with the Cincinnati club in 1899 or 1900 or so—and he came sliding into home one day. A real big slide, plenty of dust and all, even though no one was even trying to tag him out. Tim had been watching a play at second all the while. "You're out," yells Tim.
>
> Jake screamed to high heaven. "What do you mean, I'm out?" he roared. "They didn't even make a play on me."
>
> "You big. S.O.B.," Tim said, "you got here too quick."
>
> Yeah, old Tim knew what was going on. I was an umpire too, for awhile, you know—in the Pacific Coast League from 1935 to 1938—long after I finished playing. Umpiring is a lonesome life. Thankless job. Thankless. You haven't got a friend in the place. Only your

partner, that's all. He's the only man in the whole place that is for you. Everybody else is just waiting for you to make a mistake. There's a bench over here, and a bench over there, and thousands of people in the stands, and every eye in the whole damn place is watching like a hawk trying to get something on you.

I had a good partner, too. I booked in with a fellow named Jack Powell, a wonderful umpire and a wonderful person as well. He'd tell me not to fraternize with the players. I felt that I could kid around with them a little, you know. What the heck, I'd been a ballplayer myself. But he said, "Don't do it, don't fool with the players, don't have anything to do with them. If you do, sooner or later they'll put you on the spot."

And that's the way it turned out. He was right. It's a thankless and lonely way to live, so I quit.[16]

Crawford was finally elected to the Hall of Fame in 1957—well after his playing career was over—and when he was 77 years old. In fact, Cobb was the one who pushed for his old teammate after he was overlooked for so many years. They feuded, yes, but Cobb and Crawford always appreciated each other's ability. Long gone are the days of their fighting and aggression. They will forever be remembered as one of the best one-two punches in baseball history and as Hall of Fame teammates. Cobb himself played a big role in helping his teammate reach Cooperstown, and he did it in secret. Writer Jack McDonald kept Cobb's secret safe all his life, but once Cobb died in 1961, he told all in an *Associated Press* story:

McDonald recalled a morning in February 1957. He had answered the phone and heard the excited voice of Cobb. "Did you hear what happened? He made it. He made it," Ty blurted. "Who made what?" "Crawford. Old Wahoo Sam. He just made the Hall of Fame." Nobody, including Crawford himself, McDonald recalled, could have been more elated about it than Ty. McDonald had access to correspondence in Cobb's home, answers to letters Cobb had written to hundreds of influential baseball people in Crawford's behalf. "I am going to write the story of how you have been working tirelessly for years to get Crawford into Cooperstown," McDonald had told Cobb. "If you do I'll never tell you another thing in confidence as long as I live," he said. "All right Ty, then I'll write it the day you die," he said. McDonald said he used to ask: "Why are you working so hard for a guy you hated and didn't speak to for years?" "Look at the man's record," Cobb had replied. "He made the majors his first year in organized ball. With the rabbit ball they're playing with today he'd have been one of the greatest home run hitters of all time." McDonald also said that Cobb would never discuss his feud with Crawford, even off the record.

Crawford entered the Hall of Fame in 1957 with Yankees manager Joe McCarthy, who was pleased to go in with a player like Crawford. "Sam was the first player I ever saw who used the widespread stance, like DiMaggio's. I don't remember anyone using it before. He was a mighty good player. I'm glad Sam made it when I did." Crawford's wife was just as thrilled. "I'm all excited about it and I know he will be thrilled by it, too," Mrs. Crawford said. "You know Sam always has gotten a kick out of learning that old friends from his baseball days were being named to the Hall of Fame. But he never dreamed that he would be selected himself." The telegrams began coming in. One of the first was from Ty Cobb. Wahoo Sam was thrilled to be a part of the ceremonies in Cooperstown. He wrote a friend of his trip. It read in part: "Mrs. Crawford and I are getting back to normal after our wonderful trip back east. We talk of Cooperstown a great deal and the opportunity it gave us to make so many new friends and to visit with our old friends once more."[17]

Crawford also wrote a letter that H. G. Salsinger published in the *Detroit News* after his election:

In all the publicity and excitement which has come to me on being elected to the Hall of Fame, my kindest thoughts are for Detroit where I spent most of my baseball career, and those who have helped me toward the great climax of my life. I must be thinking in retrospect for surely there cannot be many people now living in Detroit who remember those rip-roaring days of 1907, 1908 and 1909 and who would remember me as taking part in them. If there are people there who remember me I am very grateful to them.... I am just starting to get back to earth and am thrilled to know that my plaque will be among all the diamond brilliance from so many stars.... I will humbly enter this great Shrine at Cooperstown, knowing that the great Harry Heilmann and the peerless Ty Cobb will be waiting and welcoming me. The Tiger outfield will be together again and rarin' to go.[18]

Crawford was formally inducted into the Hall of Fame in Cooperstown, New York, on July 22, 1957. Upon his return to Wahoo on August 2, 1957, 700 people greeted him with a ceremony to honor Crawford by naming the city ballpark Wahoo Sam Crawford Field.

"This is the nicest tribute that I could have," he told the Wahoo newspaper. Crawford threw the first pitch out at the ceremonial game between Wahoo and Fremont. Crawford was elected to the Michigan Sports Hall of Fame in 1958.

Crawford and his wife, Mary Blazer, moved to Hudson Avenue in Hollywood and also bought a small house near Pearblossom in the desert, "where we often go and rest and relax and get away from the noise and traffic," Mary Crawford said.

Mrs. Crawford said that she and her first husband and Sam and his first wife, the former Ada Lattin of Wahoo, had been very close friends for many years. They were married 15 years earlier after losing their mates several years before. Wahoo Sam had a son, Samuel E. Jr., who was a disabled veteran and lived in San Francisco. His daughter Virginia lived in South America and he had two grandchildren.

Crawford continued his honorable reputation after his career was over. In 1965, he stood up against the pension plan Major League Baseball had put into effect at that time. He wrote a letter that was printed in newspapers across the country, including the *Christian Science Monitor*. Writing from his Oroville, CA, home, Crawford claimed, perhaps with merit, that since the player of his day played a major role in making baseball the big attraction it has become in recent years, they should be taken care of in a pension plan that seems to have more than enough money to take care of everybody. Here, in part, is Crawford's letter:

> I am writing to you in regard to an article you wrote on Judge Robert Cannon.... He probably merits your laudatory remarks, but I do not agree with him when he says that the baseball players have the greatest pension plan in the world when the old-timers are excluded.
>
> Pensions generally go to the older people who have earned the right to share in them. In the baseball pension plan it is the younger players who are in.... Mediocre players who have bounced back and forth in the two big leagues for a number of years rate a pension, while us old fossils who took the bumps in the early days and helped to make the game what it is today don't get a dime.
>
> I contend that we are the players who put these so-called stars in the drivers' seat with their big salaries. I would like to hear what the Judge has to say about this.
>
> It seems that some committee has decided that any player who played prior to 1946 is not eligible to share in the pension plan.... There are plenty of past stars who could use a past pension.

He didn't return to the ball park often, but he did when it was important. Crawford threw out the first pitch in a May 1968, game at Anaheim Stadium. He was there to congratulate Al Kaline, who was on his way to pass Crawford's Detroit mark in games played and hits.

Crawford died Saturday, June 15, 1968, in Fullerton, California, after complications from a stroke. He is buried in the Inglewood Park Cemetery in Inglewood, California. Just as he was the longest tenured American League player at the time of his retirement, he was the oldest living member of the Hall of Fame.

Crawford's All-Time Team He Selected After His Retirement[19]

1B–Hal Chase
2B–Napoleon (Larry) Lajoie
3B–Bill Bradley
SS–Honus Wagner
OF–Tris Speaker
OF–Ty Cobb
OF–Joe Jackson
C–Ray Schalk
LP–Eddie Plank
RP–Walter Johnson

11. Forgotten Legacy: Sam Crawford

Three thousand hits has become a standard for longevity of elite hitters for decades. Every generation has a handful of stars that were able to play long enough and well enough to reach the milestone. But only 29 players in the history of the game have reached 3,000 hits. Sam Crawford is one of seven Hall of Famers to finish his career within 100 hits of the milestone. Just about all of them (except Frank Robinson) played before there were enough people in the 3,000 hit club to make it a club. When Crawford retired in 1917, only Cap Anson, Honus Wagner, and Napoleon Lajoie had reached the mark. Anson reached it in the 1800s before Crawford's career began, while Wagner and Lajoie both made it an actual club in 1914. So it is hard to fault Crawford, as well as Sam Rice, Al Simmons, Rogers Hornsby, Willie Keeler and Jake Beckley, for retiring prior to reaching the mark. Had they known what a big deal 3,000 hits would be, they surely would have reached the milestone, as Sam Rice, who was just 13 hits short, often said. So Sam Crawford finished his career with 2,961 hits, and though he went on to amass hundreds more in the Pacific Coast League, will forever remain 39 hits short. But unlike Rice, Crawford knew he was closing in on the mark. He shared his thoughts in *Baseball Magazine* in an article titled: "My Three Thousandth Hit: An Early Ambition and How I Have Come Very Near To Its Realization":

> One July afternoon many years ago some player on the bench happened to mention "Pop" Anson and his remarkable record. The fact was brought out that the famous old slugger was the only player who had ever made three thousand hits. It seemed a staggering total. I was fairly swamped by it. But then and there the idea crystallized in my mind that some day in the far off future, I, too, would like to register my three thousandth hit. I will not say that I deliberately set about to accomplish that seemingly impossible feat. It would have been foolish to make any such mental reservation in a game so uncertain as baseball. But I will admit that it has been my chief ambition for a good many years to make three thousand hits. And as the passing of each season has brought me nearer the goal I have thought more and more upon that particular afternoon to come when I would meet the ball fairly and rap out a good clean drive for a complete score of thirty hundred safeties. Since that visionary idea came to me so far back that I can hardly remember it clearly, two players have passed Anson's great mark. One of them, Hans Wagner, is tottering on the verge of his final season in the big show. The other, Nap Lajoie, one of the greatest batters who ever lived, has hung up a record which few can ever possibly equal.... And with this going I find myself the oldest player in point of service in the American League, the oldest player, with the exception of Hans Wagner, in the major leagues....
>
> It is an unpleasant experience to think about that ambition now as I stand on the very

verge and cannot see the certainty of its realization. It is all the more unpleasant because I have come so near it and because I feel it within myself, the ability to realize it....

When I completed my seventeenth season in the big leagues I counted up and found that according to the records I had made 2,869 hits. I needed 131 more to realize my ambition. And I won't deny that as I looked at those figures I counted that record as good as won.

I was in excellent condition, had just played a full score of 156 games and was confident that several more good seasons lay before me.... Bear in mind that I needed but 131 hits. And for fifteen straight seasons I had not failed to make more than that number of hits a season. The season before I had registered 183 and for more than ten years I had averaged at least 183....

Instead of annexing my 131 hits last season I took part in but an even 100 games, much of the time as a pinch hitter and rapped out 92 hits.

I began this season with exactly 39 hits to go. Now there was a time when I could have made 39 hits in a single month of healthy swatting. The only thing that troubles me now is whether or not I shall make these 39 hits in an entire season. At my present rate I should say it was doubtful but perhaps things will break a little better before the year is over.

On most accounts, I have no cause to complain. Baseball has been good to me and I appreciate the fact. Neither have I any criticism of the management of our club. The management is after results and if those results can be better obtained by having someone in my shoes, why the management would be foolish not to follow that plan. I am not criticizing anybody nor anything accept the unusual succession of events which have brought me so near the realization of my dreams and then threatened to leave me just short of its attainment. For I am not through, I will not admit that I am through. I can still hit that old baseball. I can still play the game up to major league standard. I can still get those three thousand hits if only I have the chance.[1]

It is amazing how 39 measly hits can affect how someone is remembered. Had Crawford played one more season in Detroit, he would have become the fourth member of the 3,000-hit club, reaching the mark three years before teammate Ty Cobb achieved the feat in 1921.

Instead, because of his quiet nature, and the fact that he finished 39 short, Crawford fell into obscurity for decades, living so quietly in California that many neighbors and friends had no idea that he ever played baseball, let alone that he was one of the best players in the history of the game. He is still the all-time triples leader and was the first player to lead both leagues in home runs. "I am the only fellow who ever led both leagues in home runs. I hit sixteen for Cincy in 1901 and then led the American with seven in 1908 after I had joined the Tigers. Imagine leading a league with seven homers! But, one spring ... the manufacturers were monkeying with the ball and made it right lively," Crawford told the *Chicago Daily News*. "No one knew anything about it and I hit .378 in spring training. I'd like to have had a chance against the ball they used back in the '20s."[2]

When the first class of the National Baseball Hall of Fame was announced, Crawford was nowhere near the top of the list. His teammate, Ty Cobb, received the most votes by the baseball writers in 1936 with 222 (98.2 percent), while Babe Ruth and Honus Wagner each received 215 votes (95.1 percent). With 75 percent needed for election (still the standard), New York Giants pitcher Christy Mathewson garnered 205 votes (90.7 percent) and Washington pitcher Walter Johnson got 189 (83.6 percent) to round out the inaugural class of Hall of Famers.

Crawford, meanwhile, received one vote. One. Two players who never came close to making the Hall of Fame, catchers Johnny Kling and Lou Criger, received seven and six votes, respectively. While each was a fine catcher in the big leagues, Criger had an abysmal career batting average of .221. The next year, Tris Speaker and Napoleon Lajoie—both members of the 3,000-hit club—made it along with all-time wins leader Cy Young. Crawford's vote total jumped to a whopping five. Crawford's other outfield teammate, Harry Heilmann, received ten votes that year. But the most insulting part of the vote was that nine non-Hall of Famers finished ahead of Crawford on the ballot.

As Crawford fell into obscurity, the number of baseball writers who actually saw him in his prime dwindled. Eventually Crawford dropped off the writers' ballot. Fortunately for Crawford, and for baseball, the Hall of Fame had established a Veterans' Committee to vote on older players. It took until 1957, but Crawford finally was elected to the Hall of Fame. Would Crawford have had to wait 21 years if he had reached 3,000 hits? There is no way of knowing, but all of the players to reach 3,000 hits at that time—Anson, Wagner, Lajoie, Cobb, Speaker, Eddie Collins and Paul Waner—were elected within three years of their first appearance on the ballot.

If Crawford got those extra 39 hits, would he have been at the first induction ceremony in 1939 with the first four classes? Maybe not, but it likely wouldn't have taken 21 years, either. But of all people, Cobb was the one who lobbied hardest for Crawford's election.

> Maybe out of a deep need to maintain as much of a living connection with that time as he still could, Cobb started going back for the Hall of Fame inductions and reunions of old ballplayers. Beginning in 1951, he made the long trip to Cooperstown every two years or so. Sid Keener remembered seeing Cobb, Cy Young, Ed Walsh, and Connie Mack walk arm in arm from the stately Otesaga Hotel to the 1953 ceremonies. Getting Sam Crawford into the Hall of Fame became something of a cause for Cobb. Although Cobb and Crawford had never cared for each other personally, Cobb had always admired his old outfield mate's ability and achievements. He talked up Crawford's qualifications when he was at Cooperstown and regularly wrote letters to the ... veterans committee urging his admission. In 1957 Crawford was finally voted into the Hall of Fame. He arrived from rural California in the company of Davy Jones. When Crawford, Jones, and Cobb sat together and swapped reminiscences at the annual banquet, the rancor that had marked their years as teammates seemed forgotten.[3]

Flashing forward to today's impact of not reaching 3,000 hits, what is affected is the number of times Crawford's name is mentioned to current fans. When Derek Jeter became the 28th member of the 3,000 hit club in 2011, the names of the other 27 were mentioned, as they were when Craig Biggio achieved the feat in 2007. So current fans learned a little bit about players like Paul Waner, Cap Anson and Eddie Collins, who might not be household names like some of the other members of the group (Aaron, Mays, Wagner, Cobb, Clemente, etc.). Even for Detroit fans, Cobb and Al Kaline are the only members of the club.

So the only time Crawford's name is mentioned is when players reach a milestone in triples, which is much rarer. He was mentioned when Carl Crawford (no relation) reached 100 triples in 2010 and when he got 19 triples during the 2004 season—still seven away from Sam Crawford's 26 in 1914. But the best triples hitter during the past decade (Carl Crawford) still has nearly 200 fewer career triples than Sam Crawford, which is astounding. And since triples are so much rarer than home runs, Wahoo Sam's name hardly ever comes up.

Playing in the Dead Ball Era also hurt the chances of Crawford's name being passed on. Statistician Bill James calculated that Crawford would have hit 494 home runs had he played in a different era. Had he hit 494, he surely would have stuck around to reach 500.

That would have made Crawford the first hitter in the history of baseball to reach 500, even before Babe Ruth.

So if his career had begun a little later, he could have been the first player to reach 3,000 hits and 500 home runs, something that only Hank Aaron, Willie Mays, Eddie Murray, Alex Rodriguez and Rafael Palmeiro have done. That would have kept him in people's memory.

But that wasn't the fate of Crawford, who, despite not reaching the major milestones in baseball, was still the premier slugger in the game during his career and one of the best hitters in the history of baseball.

For all the what-ifs that surround his career, Crawford probably would have preferred it to happen the way it did. He never liked the limelight, and taking the slow, quiet road to Cooperstown is the way he would have wanted to go. It's just a shame that there have been generations of baseball fans—even Detroit Tigers fans—with no idea just how great a player Crawford was. Or how good a person he was, especially to children. Here is a story Arthur Daley wrote for the *New York Times*:

> Wahoo Sam made it a habit of taking into the ball park with him all boys he found waiting outside the players' gate. Then one day the gate attendant barred the way.
>
> "I'm sorry, Sam," he said. "I've just had orders from the management that I can only admit you and no one else."
>
> Sam looked around and saw almost two dozen disconsolate youngsters, staring pleadingly at him. He whispered to them and they brightened. Sam went inside to dress and the boys hurried beyond the right field fence as Crawford had instructed them to do.
>
> Once in uniform, Crawford stepped into the batting cage and took dead aim. He hit one over the fence and the boy who recovered the ball beyond the barrier traded it to the gateman for free admission. Sam hit twenty-two baseballs over the fence and twenty-two happy young friends came in for free.[4]

That was Sam Crawford. Great player. Great man. Quiet player. Quiet man. But not too quiet to be remembered as one of the game's greats.

APPENDIX: CRAWFORD'S RECORD 26 TRIPLES IN 1914

Date	Opponents	Pitcher	Date	Opponents	Pitcher
April 17	St. Louis	Hamilton	July 2	Cleveland	Bowman
April 19	Cleveland	Kahler	July 9	Philadelphia	Bressler
April 21	Cleveland	Hagerman	July 23	New York	Keating
April 24	St. Louis	James	July 28	Philadelphia	Bush
May 6	Chicago	Scott	July 30	Washington	Harper
May 8	Chicago	Benz	August 5	New York	Caldwell
May 20	Boston	Collins	August 31	New York	Brown
May 28	Washington	Shaw	September 4	St. Louis	Hamilton
June 10	Boston	Collins	September 6	St. Louis	Weilman
June 12	Boston	Johnson	September 7	Chicago	Faber
June 18	Washington	Johnson	September 22	Boston	Collins
June 20	Washington	Ayers	September 25	New York	Warhop
June 21	Washington	Johnson	September 26	New York	Fisher

❖ *Part II: Harry Heilmann* ❖

12. BOY FROM THE BAY

The San Francisco Bay Area is known for producing baseball superstars, many of whom went on to make the Baseball Hall of Fame. Joe DiMaggio, Joe Cronin, Tony Lazzeri, and the list goes on. But the first superstar to come from the Bay Area was Harry Heilmann.

Harry Edwin Heilmann was born August 3, 1894, in San Francisco. The Heilmann family lived in the South-of-Market district. It was "during the stormy years of union strikes and protests which pervaded the area from 1900–1906. Harry and his older brother, Walter, were members of the Saint Rose parish, attending the parish school and playing on the Saint Rose baseball team. It was during this time, prior to the 1906 earthquake, Harry began to develop the skills that would eventually carry him to stardom. Soon, Harry would be labeled 'the best juvenile catcher that San Francisco's sand lots ever knew.'"[1]

A former Golden Gate Park player, he attended Sacred Heart High School in his native city and then St. Mary's. His mother was of Irish extraction, his father of German origin, and the Heilmanns were much concerned in the early days of Harry's ball playing. When he brought home some of his early baseball pay, they feared Harry was doing something which wasn't honest. "Nobody pays such kind of money to a boy for just playing a game," Heilmann's father said.[2]

Heilmann was with Portland, Oregon, of the old Northwestern League, in 1913, when Fielder Jones, manager of the 1906 "Hitless Wonders" White Sox, was president of the circuit. He recommended the young slugger to Detroit owner Frank Navin, and the price tag supposedly was only $1,500.

Referring to the youngster as the best ever known implies that organized youth baseball in San Francisco had some history to it.

In fact, the games Heilmann played as a child during the first decade of the twentieth century had been institutionalized, in some form, for over fifty years, dating back to the gold rush days, when dreamers and fortune seekers from Eastern and Midwestern cities came West, bringing with them the embodiment of baseball in a game called townball as early as 1852. By the end of the 1850s, both cricket and baseball had become popular recreational hobbies in the San Francisco Bay Area. The first organized baseball team in San Francisco, the Eagle Base Ball Club, was established in 1859.[3]

Even though Heilmann excelled at baseball and loved the game, he hadn't planned on it being his career. He finished school, graduating from Sacred Heart High School in 1911, and eventually became an accountant.

So how does a bookkeeper named Slug get into the Hall of Fame? It happened because of a lost topcoat and a lot of tinkering by manager Ty Cobb. Harry Heilmann was a 19-year-

125

old accountant with a biscuit company in San Francisco, who was more interested in crunching numbers than a baseball career. One day he walked from his office and a few blocks from the store and realized he'd forgotten his coat. On his way back to the office Heilmann ran into a man whose friend—the manager of a baseball team—needed a fill-in for a sick third baseman. Heilmann was offered $10 to play in a game in Bakersfield. He accepted. He doubled in the winning run in the eleventh, and ecstatic fans showered the field with money. Heilmann collected $150, which was more than one month's salary for him. He was hooked on baseball.[4]

His minor league career began with Portland of the Northwestern League in 1913. In the Class B league, Heilmann batted .305 in 122 games before getting promoted to Portland's team in the Pacific Coast League—Class AA at the time. Then Heilmann spent a brief time in the majors in 1914. The Tigers realized he was slow and did not field well. That is where the nickname "Slug" came in. He hit just .225 in 1914 and was sent back to the minors.

Heilmann returned home in 1915, playing for the San Francisco Seals of the Pacific Coast League, one of the most storied franchises in the history of minor league baseball. Heilmann did not disappoint the hometown fans, surging to a .364 average with 23 doubles that season. After a disappointing start to his major league career, Heilmann, who married Mae Maynes of San Francisco, was looking for a second chance. He would not need a third. His life in the minors was done after 222 games and a .330 average. He was headed back to Detroit, and would not look back.

13. The Big Leagues

It was an inauspicious beginning in the major leagues for Harry Heilmann. The outfielder from San Francisco made his debut for the Detroit Tigers on May 16, 1914. Hardly anything to write home about, but Heilmann cranked two hits the next day playing for Ty Cobb, out with a broken rib, and was on his way to becoming one of the greatest right-handed hitters of all time.

He was a good hitter from the beginning, but wouldn't dominate the game right away. The youngster played just 68 games for the Tigers in 1914, filling in for Cobb. On June 9, Heilmann, Cobb and Sam Crawford all played in the same game for the first time. Crawford got one hit off Bob Shawkey while Cobb was 0-for-4 and Heilmann played only in the field.

On August 7, a historical event happened in Detroit, though no one knew it. Cobb returned to the lineup and he, Crawford and Heilmann all started a game for the first time. Heilmann was at second base and wouldn't move into the outfield until later. The Tigers beat Boston, 3–1. Heilmann went hitless while Crawford and Cobb each managed a hit. Cobb's was a triple, and he was knocked in by Crawford. Marty Kavanagh returned to second base on August 13, which forced Heilmann into mainly a pinch-hitting role.

That same day, one million German soldiers began an attack on the Allies in attempts to invade France. It was the beginning of a war that would change the course of the world and would affect America and baseball, though it would be a while before the United States dove in. Meanwhile, the Tigers finished the season 80–73, a disappointing fourth place.

The Tigers returned to contention in 1915, nearly winning the pennant in a race that went down to the wire. Detroit finished the season 100–54, but lost the American League flag to the Boston Red Sox, who finished 101–50. Detroit saw legend Sam Crawford return to glory with 19 triples and 112 runs batted in, leaving Heilmann out of the picture. He was sent down to San Francisco of the Pacific Coast League for the season in order to have the chance to play every day and get ready for his future in Detroit. He batted .364 in 98 games with the Seals.

Surprisingly to everyone, after Crawford's dominating season in 1915, the Tigers delegated him to a mostly pinch-hitting role in 1916, which gave the young Harry Heilmann a chance to make the big league club again, but this time remain in Detroit.

Detroit wanted Heilmann in the lineup, and manager Hughie Jennings did everything he could to get him there. To start the 1916 season, Heilmann played first base while the usual outfield remained Crawford in right, Cobb in center and Bobby Veach in left. Jennings wanted Heilmann to contribute but didn't want to disturb the superb outfield. His most famous act during that time, however, was on July 25, 1916, when he dove into the Detroit

River to save a woman from drowning. He received a thunderous ovation at the ballpark the following day.[1]

On August 2, Detroit had lost four straight and Jennings decided that he needed Crawford's bat in the lineup more often. Heilmann was at first base for a few games to make room for Wahoo Sam, who hit three triples and three singles in four games, moving his average up to a surging .318. He would remain in the outfield the rest of the season, while the young Heilmann would be the top pinch-hitter off the bench. Crawford responded with three hits the next game and the Tigers moved back up to fourth place. The move worked. Beginning August 23, the Tigers won 11 of their next 13 games and moved up to second place at 74–57 after sweeping Cleveland in four games at home.

The Tigers were clinging to second place and trailed Boston in the standings. Detroit had won five in a row thanks to Cobb, who had a double and a triple in a 9–1 Detroit win over Cleveland, then slammed two home runs off future Hall of Famer Stan Coveleski in the finale—part of a four-hit game. Crawford also managed a single, double and triple off Coveleski and the Tigers won, 10–2. Heilmann, at first base, went 5-for-5.

Detroit took two of three games from the Yankees, then hosted last-place Philadelphia. At 83–60, the Tigers were ahead of Boston by percentage points (80–59). The Tigers dropped the finale to Philadelphia, 2–0, and with it dropped to second place.

The Tigers had a big chance to redeem themselves. Boston was next in town for a three-game set and the Tigers only trailed the Red Sox by a little more than a game in the standings. Carl Mays was on the mound in the opener against Hooks Dauss on September 19. Mays was in several jams throughout the game, allowing Crawford, Cobb and Heilmann to each go 3-for-4 in the game. Crawford scored only once and the other sluggers were left stranded each time as the submarining Mays won 3–1. Dutch Leonard got the best of Howard Ehmke in the next game and hung on for a 4–3 victory. Any chance the Tigers had at the pennant would rest with the final game of the series. The Red Sox jumped on Detroit's Harry Coveleski for runs in each of the first four innings and cruised to a 10–2 victory, all but clinching the pennant. The Tigers closed out the season with a 6–3 loss to the Browns and their old adversary Eddie Plank, to finish the season 87–67 in third place behind Boston (91–63) and Chicago (89–65), who had sneaked into second after the Tigers were dominated by the Red Sox. After the Tigers split a four-game set with the Senators, the Red Sox clinched the pennant on September 27.

Heilmann got into 136 Detroit games in 1916, as Hughie Jennings tried to see where he fit best, playing him at first base, second, and in the outfield. The young Californian hit .282.

A record crowd saw the Tigers open the 1917 season with a 6–4 loss to Cleveland on April 11. Crawford came up as a pinch hitter, but didn't connect. The Tigers started 1–5 with Crawford on the bench, so manager Hughie Jennings inserted Wahoo Sam at first base on April 19. Crawford responded by slapping a single and slamming a home run. In the first game that Crawford, Harry Heilmann and Ty Cobb started together, all three players had two hits and scored at least one run but the Tigers lost 8–7 to the Indians.

Heilmann started the season playing center field while Cobb was in right field. Crawford was playing some first base, doing a lot of pinch-hitting and would be back in right field before the season was done. Crawford was back in right field on June 15, taking over for Heilmann. He pinch hit for Heilmann after two at-bats. Wahoo Sam responded with a pair of RBI singles in a 4–3 victory over Walter Johnson and the Washington Senators. Crawford started in right field the next day and it was Heilmann who played first base. Both went hitless, though Howard Ehmke beat the Senators, 3–2 thanks to a triple and double by Cobb, who had started the longest hitting streaks of his career. Crawford switched with Heilmann the next game and both went hitless again as Johnson shut out the Tigers, 3–0. It was the last time Crawford would play first base in his career. And 1917 would be the last time Wahoo Sam played for the Tigers, who finished fourth (78–75).

The season was strange enough for Heilmann, going from the bench to the field and back so many times,

Harry Heilmann won his first of four batting titles in 1921 when he hit .394. He was close to the legendary .400 mark, but would get more chances at that throughout the decade (National Baseball Hall of Fame Library, Cooperstown, New York).

but there were some strange things that happened on the field that season, too. Heilmann was in the middle of one of the strangest, and it came in a game where he was facing his future friend, Babe Ruth.

Those were the days when Ruth was gradually switching over from pitching to outfielding because of his power as a batter.

Well, on this particular day, Howard Ehmke was having his share of qualms as Ruth stepped to the batter's box. Harry Heilmann, playing first base in the game, saw he was jittery and decided some encouragement was needed. "You can get him, Howard; he's your meat," Harry shouted. Ehmke looked over at him as much to say, "What makes you think so?" Ruth brought his bat around viciously on the first pitch. And the ball went back down toward Howard about ten times faster than he had thrown it. The Tiger pitcher put on a spectacular display of reflex action. Importantly, he got his glove up in front of his Adam's apple. The ball struck the glove and Howard was knocked flat by the impact. After upsetting Ehmke, the ball hit the ground a few feet in front of second base. Seemed as if it might have drilled right through the pitcher. Donie Bush, the Detroit shortstop, had moved to his left when Ruth came to the plate, as was the custom. That enabled him to get to the ball and make the catch. But he didn't throw to first for the put-out on Ruth because he saw nobody was covering the bag. Heilmann had left his position. The moment Ehmke was knocked down, Harry sprinted to him. By the time Ruth had crossed the base, Harry was bending over his fallen teammate. "You hurt, Howard?" he asked. Howard pulled himself to a sitting position, took stock to be sure his head was where it should be, and assured Harry he wasn't injured. After Howard got rid of the shakes, play was resumed. But an aftermath of the incident was coming up for Harry. Hughie Jennings, the Detroit manager, was out in front of the bench waiting for the big fellow when he came off the field at the end of the inning. Then and there, Hughie plastered a fifty-dollar fine on him for having left first base unguarded. Hughie called off the fine that evening. But the experience had left its imprint on Harry. "From here on," he announced, "I'm going to count up to a hundred and fifty before I go to anybody's help."[2]

For the first time in 15 years, the 1918 Tigers opened a season without Sam Crawford on the club. Crawford had been at odds with Ty Cobb and manager Hughie Jennings for a few years. Cobb didn't like Crawford and Crawford didn't like that he was being pushed to play first base. So Crawford "retired" from Major League Baseball following the 1917 season, but he continued his career for four more seasons in the Pacific Coast League. It left a big hole to fill in the outfield, but a hole the Tigers were sure Harry Heilmann could fill. Heilmann had shown some flashes of brilliance—especially at bat—and was up to the challenge of starting full-time.

The 1918 season opened up cold and damp, with storm clouds looming over much of the East Coast and Midwest. It was a fitting start to America's game since a storm cloud had been looming over the country for a couple of years. That storm was World War I, and the United States had finally gotten involved in 1917 by officially declaring war on Germany. It had been a long time coming. Germany had sunk two U.S. submarines without warning in international waters and President Woodrow Wilson asked Congress to declare war, which it did on April 6, 1917.

The declaration of war meant the military draft was soon to be initiated, leaving many baseball owners and fans wondering what would happen to the national game. Ultimately, the game struggled, but continued, and players did their best on the field knowing any day could be their last before they changed from a baseball uniform to a military uniform.

Many of the game's best stars would be called for duty. Two of the best pitchers in the game's history—Christy Mathewson and Grover Cleveland Alexander—would go, as well as two of the best hitters of all time, who happened to be Detroit Tigers—Ty Cobb and Harry Heilmann. The Detroit duo began the 1918 season with the Tigers, but both would be in a different uniform by the season's end.

The season opener on April 16 was rained out in Detroit, as was the game the following day. The Tigers finally began the season with a 6–2 loss to Cleveland and future Hall of Fame pitcher Stan Coveleski. Neither Cobb nor Heilmann played in the game. Detroit fielded Bobby Veach in left, Frank Walker in center and Babe Ellison in right. The Tigers moved to Chicago for the next series and had three straight games rained out before finally facing the White Sox on April 22, beating Ed Cicotte, 7–3. Two more rainouts occurred in the next four days.

Heilmann finally made his season debut in right field, batting fifth in the lineup with two hits in a 3–2 loss in 12 innings to Coveleski on April 27. Cobb went hitless against the future Hall of Famer. Rain called off the next game. Heilmann doubled and scored the following day but the Tigers lost, 12–3, to the Browns in St. Louis. The Tigers and Browns were rained out the next day, giving Detroit ten rainouts in the first 15 days of the season. The dreariness of the weather was about to change, but the entire season would keep that feel for the Tigers.

Improved weather actually allowed the Tigers to play 11 consecutive days beginning May 1. The Tigers went 5–6 during the stretch, dropping to 7–10 overall and into seventh place. The second division was not something the Tigers were accustomed to. Since Cobb joined the Tigers in 1906, the Tigers had finished in the second division only three times, claiming sixth place in 1906, 1912 and 1913. Every other season had been one of contention, but sadly, 1918 was to be one of the few poor seasons in Tigers history. Heilmann faced his future friend Babe Ruth for the first time on May 15 and went 0-for-4 in a 5–4 loss. The Tigers lost the next two to the Red Sox and with a 3–1 loss to Boston in the series finale on May 18, the Tigers fell into last place for the first time (7–15).

On May 23, General Enoch Crowder issued the "work or fight" edict, which was to go into effect on July 1 and threatened the future of baseball. Owners were hoping baseball would be exempt because of its popularity and its place as entertainment. The edict read: "Persons, including ushers and other attendants, engaged in an occupation in and in connection with games, sports and amusements, excepting actual performers in legitimate concerts, operas or theatrical performances." It shocked the baseball world that actors would be exempt, but not ballplayers. But league officials did what was best for their country and tried to take it in stride. American League president Ban Johnson said he "will never object to a ball player shouldering a rifle and will do everything to encourage such a practice, but we do not think it is fair to take out players and put them in industrial plants where they are wanted mainly to play ball on the side."[3]

The Tigers were rained out in the nation's capital that day, but enjoyed a rare treat the following day as President Wilson watched the game from the stands at Griffith Stadium. The Tigers and Senators battled to a 2–2 tie when the game was called because of darkness after 16 innings. Hooks Dauss, who would go on to become the all-time wins leader for the Tigers, threw a 1–0 shutout the next day—the first shutout by the Tigers all season. Walter Johnson turned around and shut the Tigers out, 4–0, the following day. Cobb was sidelined with a shoulder injury on May 26, and Heilmann picked up the slack with a double and home run, but the Tigers lost, 7–4. He had three hits with Cobb out the next game and the Tigers won the series finale, 4–2, over the Senators.

Despite success in the previous two games, Heilmann's average was .260, while Cobb was at .294. Not quite what Detroit had hoped for or expected. Cobb played the next game but went 0-for-2. His shoulder injury was worse than he originally let on. He sat out on May 30, then was used as a pinch-hitter for a few games. Since he had trouble throwing, Jennings moved Cobb to first base for nine games. It got the best hitter back in the lineup, but did little to turn around the fortunes of the Tigers. Detroit did beat the first-place Red Sox two straight games to move out of the cellar on June 2. The first was a 13-inning nail-biter as Harry Heilmann became a hero for the first time in Detroit with a game-winning hit. *Detroit Free Press* writer Harry Bullion described the scene:

> Harry Heilmann, who right fields for the Tigers in the summer time and tears up all the landscape in San Francisco with his automobile in the off-season, made himself dear to the hearts of Detroit fans Saturday afternoon, when, in the thirteenth inning of the most hectic contest staged at Navin Field this season, he flogged one of Carl Mays's choicest shoots far over Amos Strunk's head. Under certain conditions a blow of the sort would create mere passing comment, but since "Pep" Young happened to be perched on second base crying for just that kind of help and in possession of the winning run, Harry's thump sent the crowd, close to 8,000, home in a hysterical mood.[4]

Unfortunately for the Tigers, the success was short-lived. The next day, Detroit was shut out by Dutch Leonard, 5–0, then lost a 7–6 thriller to Carl Mays, thanks to the third home run of the series by Babe Ruth. Detroit fell back into the cellar and remained there after being one-hit by Walter Johnson on June 9. The next day, Heilmann homered off Elmer Myers and Cobb slapped a double and a triple to lead the Tigers past Philadelphia, 6–4.

Cobb's shoulder had slowly began to heal and he returned to center field on June 15, leaving the Tigers with one too many outfielders, Jennings wanted to keep everyone's bat in the lineup, so Heilmann moved to first base, where he went 1-for-4 in an 11–6 loss to New York. On June 18, Heilmann hit a game-winning home run off Allan Sothoron with Cobb on base to beat the Browns, 3–1.

Heilmann remained at first base for the next 23 games, then played two games at second base before returning to first. Cobb actually played one game at second base on July 8. He went 4-for-5 with three runs scored in a 16–9 loss to the Athletics. Heilmann didn't start the game but singled and scored as a pinch-hitter. On July 13, Heilmann singled in the winning run against Washington in the first inning. Donie Bush walked, Cobb singled and Heilmann followed with a single to knock in Bush. Bill James went on to shut out the Senators, 1–0.

On July 18, baseball was declared non-essential labor by Secretary of War Newton D. Baker. Ball players would be exempt from the "work or fight" edict until September 4, when the season would be over. The leagues agreed to finish the season early in order to have a championship. Players who were on pennant-winning teams were exempt until September 15, when the World Series was over. Baker was in favor of keeping the World Series.

Heilmann wasn't waiting until the season ended. He had left the night before to go to San Diego and volunteer for the Navy. Heilmann rarely spoke of his active duty and even his immediate family didn't know much except that he served at least part of the time on a submarine.[5]

Cobb joined the U.S. Army as a captain in the gas and flame corps on August 27. Four days later, Boston clinched the American League pennant. They would go on to beat the Cubs in the World Series and would not win another championship until 2004.

14. Return from the War

There were a lot of questions heading into the 1919 season, and it wasn't just the Tigers who had them. Each team was dealing with the return of players from World War I. When would they return? Would they be as productive as in their pre-war careers?

The Tigers were perhaps the team most affected 1918–1919. Two of their top players didn't finish the 1918 season because they left for stints in the war. Ty Cobb, the best player in the game, volunteered to join the Army late in 1918, and Harry Heilmann, whom the Tigers were expecting big things from, had joined the Navy.

Both returned in 1919. Cobb picked up right where he left off, leading the league in hits and winning his 12th, and final batting title. Heilmann, on the other hand, had been a platoon and utility player, filling in the gaps where the Tigers needed, and had yet to emerge as the star manager Hughie Jennings hoped he'd be. Jennings wasn't sure what to expect from a young player who was away from the field for so long while in the Navy. It turned out that everyone was in for a shock. For the first time in 1919, Heilmann would play the entire season at one position (first base) and would reward the club by batting over .300 for the first time in his career. His emergence as a dominant hitter started a second wave of Detroit's 1–2 punch which began with Cobb and Crawford and moved to Cobb and Heilmann heading into the 1920s.

It began with a turn-around during the 1919 season. The Tigers opened the season on April 25 with Heilmann playing first base and batting fifth in the lineup behind Cobb and Bobby Veach. Unlike past years, Jennings stuck with the lineup and kept Heilmann at first base for the entire season. It worked, as the Tigers offense came alive. It just didn't work right away. The Tigers started the season with a 4–2 win over Cleveland and future Hall of Famer Stan Coveleski. It quickly went downhill for Detroit, who lost four in a row, before oddly enough, beating Coveleski again, 8–1, on May 1. Heilmann was 5-for-8 against the Cleveland hurler in the two games with a double and runs scored. The Tigers won again the next day, 14–6, as Heilmann and Cobb each packed a punch with two hits. Another four-game losing streak, however, put the Tigers' record at 3–8 and sank them to last place in the American League. Another six-game skid dropped them to 5–14.

The Tigers were sinking fast and needed something to turn the tide. With Cobb, Heilmann and Veach hitting well, the tide would need to be turned by the pitching staff. George "Hooks" Dauss responded by stopping the skid with a 6–0 shutout of the Washington Senators, one day after future Hall of Famer Walter Johnson had dominated the Tigers, 8–2. It sparked the Tigers to win five in a row and eight of their next nine games and move up to fifth place at 13–15. One of those wins was the Detroit debut of Hubert "Dutch" Leonard, who had pitched the previous six seasons for the Boston Red Sox. His 0.96 ERA in 1914 remains the lowest in American League history (Luis Tiant holds the "modern" record—post–1920—at 1.60 in 1968). Leonard had compiled a 90–64 record with Boston before coming to Detroit and would be a key figure in the Tigers' turnaround with a 2.77 ERA.

Detroit took three of four from the St. Louis Browns, beginning May 30, then swept the first-place White Sox in three games to give the Tigers their first winning record of the season at 17–16, moving up to the first division at fourth place. The Tigers headed to Fenway Park next and Leonard pitched against his former teammates for the first time. He pitched well but was outdueled by Babe Ruth, who won, 2–1. Another pitching battle squared off the following day with Red Sox lefty Herb Pennock, a future Hall of Famer, getting the best of Detroit's Howard Ehmke 3–1. The Tigers returned to .500 when Dauss beat the Red Sox, 10–5, thanks in large part to two hits and two runs scored by both Heilmann and Cobb.

Unfortunately for the Tigers, another downslide began in the next series when the team traveled to New York, lost three of four to the Yankees and dropped back into the second division in sixth place at 19–21. Detroit split a four-game set in Washington, then traveled to Philadelphia. If the Tigers were going to turn it around, Philadelphia was a good place to start. The Athletics had been one of the best teams in the American League during the first 15 years of the league's existence, but after winning three World Series and two more pennants between 1904 and 1914, the Athletics dropped to last place for seven years, going from first to worst in 1915. Owner and manager Connie Mack sold off many of his stars like second baseman Eddie Collins, who was on his way to 3,000 hits and a Hall of Fame career. Collins went to the White Sox, where he helped their resurgence as a force in the American League. Other future Hall of Famers had come and gone like Frank "Home Run" Baker and pitchers Eddie Plank, Rube Waddell and Charles "Chief" Bender.

The Athletics were on their way to another poor season in 1919—one in which their two best starting pitchers would go 9–15. One of those was Walt Kinney, who stunned Detroit by beating Hooks Dauss, 6–5, in the series opener on June 18. Heilmann managed only one single off Kinney, and Cobb was nursing a leg injury which would keep him in the dugout the next 15 games. The Tigers needed a better showing against Philadelphia, and without Cobb, other hitters would have to pick up the slack. Harry Heilmann almost single-handedly beat the Athletics the next two games. He homered in a 2–1 loss on June 19, then doubled and homered again the following day, driving in four runs and sparking an 11–9 victory.

Detroit left Philadelphia with a disappointing loss of three of the four games in Philadelphia, but was heading back home after 15 games on the road. First up was a makeup game against first-place Chicago on June 22. Heilmann was 3-for-3 with two runs scored as Dauss hung on to win, 5–4. The Tigers swept a two-game set with the Browns, then opened a four-game series with Cleveland. Heilmann was again the hero. With the game a scoreless duel between Detroit's Bernie Boland and Henry "Hi" Jasper after 11 innings, Heilmann tripled in the bottom of the 12th and scored the winning run on a single by Ira Flagstead. The extra-inning victory jump-started the Tigers, who went on to sweep Cleveland in four games. Dauss beat Jim Bagby, 6–1, then Leonard topped Coveleski, who had lost three of his four starts against the Tigers so far in 1919, 3–1. Ehmke capped the series with a 4–0 shutout.

The Tigers won all seven games on the brief homestand and were above .500, back in the first division with a 29–26 record, good for fourth place. It was back on the road, where the Tigers had struggled all season and the struggles would continue. Playing well at home made up for not having Cobb in the lineup, but on this road trip, his absence would be evident.

Detroit's offense was nowhere near as potent without Cobb in the lineup. The Tigers opened their road trip with four games in St. Louis. The teams split the series but the Tigers scored just 15 runs in the four games combined. Heilmann, who had done so well picking up Cobb's slack, had just four hits. If there was any team the Tigers didn't want to face next, it was the first-place White Sox, but as fate would have it, the struggling Tigers were headed to Chicago for a crucial five-game series. Win the series and the Tigers would bounce back and gain some ground on the White Sox. Unfortunately for Detroit, the opposite happened. The White Sox dominated the Tigers and won four of the five games, holding the Tigers to 12 total runs. Heilmann had one hit in every game but drove in just one run. Cobb returned but was just 4-for-18 in the series. His leg was clearly not back to 100 percent, but he wanted to do everything he could to stop the Tigers' slide. The Tigers left Chicago 32–32, in fifth place.

It was back home again for Detroit, where they had played significantly better all season. It would happen again as the Tigers took three of four from the Senators, four of five from the Yankees and capped the win streak with a four-game sweep of the Athletics. Heilmann put the exclamation point on the series with a home run in the finale. But he wasn't the only one hitting. Heilmann's average jumped to .313, while Cobb was hitting .348 and Bobby Veach right on his heels at .343. Detroit scored a whopping 64 runs in the 13 games, winning 11 of them and surging back into fourth place at 43–34.

Boston was next to visit Detroit and stopped the streak when Herb Pennock pitched an 8–0 shutout on July 20. The Tigers faced Babe Ruth the next day. He batted cleanup, in addition to pitching, and belted a home run off Ehmke. It wasn't the last homer Ruth would hit against the Tigers. He was on his way to the single-season record. Heilmann packed some punch that day too, doubling off Ruth and scoring to lead the Tigers to a 6–2 victory. The Tigers split the last two games with the Red Sox to end the homestand with a 45–36 record.

The Tigers were finally playing well in all facets of the game, but a 17-game road trip loomed for a team that struggled on the road. If the season continued like it had gone, the Tigers would have erased their winning record. But something different happened on this road trip. The Tigers began to win.

Detroit's first foe was a familiar one: Stan Coveleski. For some reason, the Tigers had the future Hall of Famer's number that year and beat him for the fourth time in five games, winning 4–2 on July 24. Heilmann and Cobb both singled and scored runs. The Tigers offense roared through the next game as Heilmann laced three hits and Cobb two. Heilmann had two singles, a double, scored twice and knocked in three runs as Hooks Dauss pitched well enough for an 11–5 victory. Ehmke struggled the next game, losing 9–1, but Boland came back strong to squeak out a 2–1 victory in the finale. Coveleski was once again the losing pitcher, having come on in relief.

It was on to Boston, where the Tigers were part of another slugfest on July 29, led by the greatest slugger in the history of the game: Babe Ruth. Ruth, playing left field, torched his former teammate Dutch Leonard for two doubles and a home run, tying the American League record with his 16th home run of the season—and it was only July. He had the game-winning hit in the 12th. The Tigers did their share of slugging too as Cobb and Heilmann each singled and scored runs, and the Tigers hung on to beat the Red Sox, 10–8. Detroit and Boston split the next day's doubleheader before future Hall of Famer Waite Hoyt beat Doc Ayers, 2–1, in 12 innings on July 31.

The Big Apple was next on the road trip, and the Tigers were rudely awakened by a 5–4 loss on August 1. The next game was about as close as you could get for a six-run victory. Going into the tenth inning, the game was tied, 8–8. Heilmann had homered earlier in the game and came up in the top of the tenth inning with the bases loaded. "Slug" powered a grand slam to spark a six-run tenth inning and lead the Tigers to a 14–8 victory. Harry Bullion of the *Detroit Free Press* thought it the biggest game of Heilmann's young career:

> Though Harry Heilmann still is a young man, and, therefore, barring injuries, doubtless certain to enjoy many years of life in the majors, it is questionable whether he will ever duplicate his achievement in the tenth inning of this afternoon's game, which ended 14 to 8, Detroit's way.
>
> To the giant from the Pacific coast, too, goes the honor of snatching from the outstretched hands of the Yankees as hectic a ball game as 30,000 fans, grouped in a single stadium, as they were in the Polo Grounds today, ever thanked the good fortune that guided their steps to a ball yard.
>
> The Tigers had just fought off a determined rally on behalf of the Yankees ... and went into the tenth round of a game in which they were behind twice, only to fight back to the level of a tie.
>
> (After "Pep" Young walked and Cobb doubled, New York hurler Jack Quinn walked the dangerous Bobby Veach to get to Heilmann.)
>
> Anger written on his countenance, because of what he termed a slight on the part of Quinn, Heilmann fouled off the first ball, let the next sail over wide and met the third pitch squarely.
>
> Like a rifle-shot it headed for the center field fence, with Bodie and Chick Fewster in hot pursuit. On it sped to the wall, caromed off and long ere the relay could get it back to the field of play the maker of this robust wallop scored behind the three mates who, a second before, were in possession of the bases.
>
> Once before in this game Heilmann made the circuit of the bases ... behind a blow of similar dimensions. Still, with those samples of the hitsmiths art, and five runs previously, the Tigers were obliged to enter an extended period to give Heilmann the chance to add fame to his name and luster to the Tiger's career.[1]

The Tigers remained in fourth place, but had closed the gap on the rest of the first division. After a 10–2 loss closed the series in New York, the Tigers headed to the nation's capital with a 51–41 record. The greatest pitcher in the history of the game awaited them in Washington on August 5, but Bernie Boland edged Walter Johnson, 2–1, to open the series, with Heilmann slapping two hits off The Big Train. It was a good sign for the Tigers, who, like most teams, rarely got the best of Johnson. Astonishingly, the Tigers jumped from fourth to a tie for second place with the victory. The next day, Heilmann tripled and scored in the second inning, and the Tigers won, 4–1. When Dauss pitched two shutout innings in relief to win, 4–3, in ten innings, the Tigers had completed a rare road sweep.

Only one series remained on the fateful road trip, and it was in Philadelphia. The Tigers were still miffed that the last-place Athletics had won three of four in their last trip to the City of Brotherly Love. The Tigers wanted payback and got it with a three-game sweep. The Tigers finally put together a solid road trip, going 12–5 and winning the final six games to push their record to 57–41. Only the Chicago White Sox were ahead of the Tigers at 62–38.

The Yankees were the first opponent to visit the triumphant Tigers at Navin Field following the road trip. Heilmann, who tore up Yankees pitching in New York, continued to do so in Detroit. In the opener on August 14, he went 4-for-7 with two doubles and two runs scored, but the Yankees won, 5–4, in 15 innings. The next day, Heilmann had a double and triple and drove in two runs in a 7–0 victory. In the series finale, Heilmann homered to lead the Tigers to a 3–2 victory. "Apparently the giant Californian doesn't require anything more than the sight of the Yankees to inspire him to action and as long as Harry stays in the league there will be misgivings in the ranks of that team, unless the Gotham club owners obtain a restraining injunction against further exhibitions similar to the big fellow's conquering wallop over the left field wall in the aforementioned period with Bobby Veach prancing around second base,"[2] Harry Bullion of the *Detroit Free Press* wrote.

The Senators were next in town and Johnson got his revenge with a 4–2 victory in 11 innings. But the Tigers won the next two, then swept Philadelphia in three games, improving to 64–43 and remaining in second place. Boston arrived next and the series opener was one of the first heroic matchups of Ty Cobb's brain versus Babe Ruth's brawn. Not to say that Cobb was without brawn or Ruth was without a brain, but Ruth was beginning to make his mark by hitting the ball as far as he could. Cobb was the best player in the game but rarely hit a home run. He beat teams in every other way. Both showed their special skills on August 23. Ruth homered for the 19th time in the third inning, a grand slam, but it wasn't as captivating as something Cobb pulled off in the bottom half of the same inning. Not to be outdone by Ruth, Cobb stole home as part of a triple steal with the bases loaded and sparked the Tigers to an 8–4 win over future Hall of Famer Waite Hoyt.

Detroit lost the next two games and faced an important series in Cleveland, who after being supplanted as the second-place team, had hung right behind the Tigers and were waiting to strike. In the first game, despite a double by Heilmann and triple from Cobb, Cleveland won, 7–2, behind the pitching of Jim Bagby. The result brought Cleveland up to a tie for second place with Detroit at 65–46.

Stan Coveleski was next on the hill for Cleveland, and after losing four of his five starts to the Tigers, he was ready for a little payback. The future Hall of Famer gave up four hits each to Cobb and Veach but outpitched Hooks Dauss to beat the Tigers, 7–5, and move his team past Detroit into second place.

The Tigers headed to St. Louis on August 29, and Dauss bounced back to beat Browns ace Urban Shocker, 5–2, to put the Tigers back into second place. It was short-lived, however, as the Tigers split a doubleheader the next day and dropped to third as Cleveland won a pair. Doc Ayers closed the series with a 4–1 victory in relief.

After two months of up-and-down performances, the Tigers' season was basically on the line at the beginning of September when they faced first-place Chicago at home. Sweep the three games and the Tigers were still in the hunt. Lose and it would be extremely difficult to catch both Chicago and Cleveland. Unfortunately for the Tigers, it was the latter. Lefty Williams and Eddie Cicotte swept the Tigers in a doubleheader on September 1. The Tigers, led by Heilmann, stormed back to take the finale, 4–3, in 16 innings. Heilmann had a single and two doubles and scored a run off Dickie Kerr to help the Tigers, but the chance of a pennant hang by a thread. Detroit hung in the race after splitting a four-game set with the Browns and looked to get back in the thick of things when they traveled to Philadelphia and Washington, the two worst teams in the league.

Detroit opened in Philadelphia on September 9 and lost a closely-fought 4–3 game in which Cobb drove in all three Tiger runs. The Tigers looked in control behind Hooks Dauss in the second game, leading 5–0 in the ninth inning. But the lowly 33–90 Athletics rallied for six runs in the bottom of the ninth to beat the stunned Tigers, 6–5. It marked the beginning of the end for the Tigers. After winning the finale, 3–2, the Tigers lost two of three to the Senators (none against Walter Johnson).

The Tigers finished their road trip with stops in Boston and New York. Detroit beat the Red Sox two of three but was swept by the Yankees, sending the tail-spinning Tigers into fourth place. Heilmann continued to swing a hot bat and had four hits, including a homer, against New York, and was hitting .323.

In the final two home games of the season, the Tigers beat Cleveland, 4–1, on September 24—the same day Ruth slammed his 28th home run to set the major league record. That same day, the White Sox clinched the pennant with their 88th victory. The Tigers closed the season with a win over Cleveland, then moved to Chicago for a sweep over the White Sox, who rested most of their starters.

The Tigers, who were in second place for most of the stretch run of the season, finished at 80–60 in a disappointing fourth place, eight games behind the 88–52 White Sox. Cleveland finished second at 84–55 and New York moved into third, finishing just a half-game ahead of the Tigers at 80–59.

The White Sox would go on to face the Cincinnati Reds in the World Series, which would be marred by the infamous "Black Sox Scandal" in which eight members of the team—including Shoeless Joe Jackson and pitchers Eddie Cicotte and Lefty Williams—conspired with gamblers to throw the Series. The eight were later acquitted in court but a year later newly appointed baseball Commissioner Kenesaw Mountain Landis would ban the eight players for life. Landis even barred third baseman Buck Weaver, who didn't take any money or play poorly in the Series, because he knew about the fix and didn't "promptly inform his club"—or basically rat out his teammates.

It was a disappointing season for the Tigers and all of baseball. But they couldn't be disappointed in the emergence of Harry Heilmann as one of the premier hitters in the game. Heilmann batted .320, which put him tenth in the American League. Cobb won his 12th and final batting title at .384, well above runner-up, teammate Bobby Veach, at .355. Heilmann also finished sixth with 172 hits and tied Cobb for fifth with 256 total bases, thanks to his 15 triples (second) and eight home runs (sixth). His 53 extra-base hits were fourth and led him to a .477 slugging percentage, which was seventh in the league, as was his .843 OPS (on-base plus slugging percentage). In the field, Heilmann made a league-leading 31 errors at first base in 1,511 chances, which was not bad for someone who was brought up as a second baseman and outfielder.

Now that Heilmann had shown his potential, the only question was whether his outstanding performance was a fluke or shades of what was to come in the 1920s.

15. BATTING CHAMPION

The 1920s ushered in a new era for the Detroit Tigers. The greatest player in franchise history—and in baseball history up until that point—began a new role with the Tigers in 1921 as a player/manager. Even though previous manager Hughie Jennings was not an active player, it was pretty commonplace during that time. Other baseball legends like Tris Speaker and Napoleon Lajoie had worn both hats and had some success.

But there was some apprehension about Ty Cobb taking the reins. Just because he was a great player didn't mean he would be a great manager. Though the Tigers—or Tygers as they were often called under Cobb—had dropped off the previous four seasons under Jennings, Hughie had an enormous amount of success with the Tigers between 1907 and 1920. He won American League pennants his first three seasons at the helm, and finished second twice and third twice, keeping the Tigers in the first division all but four years.

Another question mark was Cobb's temper. Would he be able to control it as manager? Or would he be even more out of control in his spats with the umpires and his players? Only time would tell. No one expected a pennant immediately because the Tigers were no longer the dominant force they were when Cobb began his playing career. They could still hit the ball, but the days of the dominating pitching of Wild Bill Donovan, Ed Killian and George Mullin were long gone. Cobb had to take some baby steps with the team to build a winner. One of the telltale signs of Cobb's job as manager of the Tigers was how Harry Heilmann responded in 1921, after batting a solid .309 with 89 RBI in 1920 for the seventh-place Tigers. Heilmann had turned himself into a .300 hitter the past two years as a regular, after failing to reach .300 in each of his first four seasons—mostly as a part-time player. Now established as the right field starter after playing first base the previous two seasons, he would bat fifth in the lineup most of the season.

Whether it was directly because of Cobb or not, Heilmann's performance at the plate soared to new heights, as "Slug" began his transformation from a good hitter to the best right-handed hitter in the American League in 1921, when he would claim his first batting title.

Opening Day was scheduled for April 13 in Detroit, however a heavy rain pushed it back a day. Heilmann found his stroke the following day, lacing three hits—including a single that knocked in the game-winning run—to help the Tigers beat the Chicago White Sox, 6–5. The conditions were still wet, as Heilmann found out in the sixth inning. "Harry Heilmann gave the crowd a laugh in the sixth when he hit the mud at second base and slid 10 feet before he could stop himself,"[1] the *Detroit Free Press* reported. The next day, future Hall of Famer Red Faber held Heilmann to a single and beat Howard Ehmke, 3–2. The

139

finale was rained out and the Tigers traveled to Cleveland, where snow postponed the first two games of the four-game series. Future Hall of Famer Stan Coveleski pitched well and the Cleveland bats came alive to beat the Tigers, 12–3. Heilmann helped even Detroit's record with a 4-for-4 performance and three runs scored in a 9–6 victory.

The Tigers traveled to Chicago and lost the first two games of the series, including an 11-inning pitchers' duel between spitballers Dutch Leonard and Faber. Heilmann went 0-for-5 against Faber and reliever Shovel Hodge, one of only four times he would fail in five at-bats in 1921. He made up for it the next day, however, as he singled, doubled and homered to lead the Tigers to a win in the series finale. Cobb also slapped three hits for Detroit.

It was on to Cleveland where Jim Bagby held the Tigers at bay in the opener on April 25. Cobb went 0-for-5, though Heilmann managed two hits, and Detroit lost, 5–3. The next day, Cleveland raised its 1920 World Series Championship flag and looked as good as they did the previous season with a 9–8 win over the Tigers despite three hits by Heilmann, who had two more the next day as the Tigers beat Coveleski in ten innings. But the success was very short-lived as Cleveland pounded 18 runs off Leonard in the finale to win, 18–5, and send the Tigers into seventh place.

If that wasn't enough, Heilmann sustained a spike wound on his ankle and would miss some time. He sat out the first game of the homestand against the St. Louis Browns on April 29, a 5–3 victory, then tried to play the following day. It didn't affect his hitting as he went 3-for-4 to help the Tigers knock off Browns ace Urban Shocker, 7–5. Heilmann had one of the best Mays in baseball history up to that point. He became the first Detroit Tiger to amass 45 hits and 35 RBI in April. Only Ty Cobb (1925) has matched that feat. But he came back from the injury too soon and didn't start the next few games. On May 1, he slapped a pinch-hit single in a 2–1 win over the Browns, which evened Detroit's record at 7–7 as they leap-frogged into a tie for third place. Heilmann pinch-hit again the following day but didn't get a hit. He then sat out three games altogether, but the Tigers made up for his absence by scoring 33 runs (24 in two games against the White Sox). In the third game, Red Oldham blanked Urban Shocker and the Browns, 9–0, for Detroit's first shutout victory of the season.

Heilmann returned to the starting lineup in St. Louis on May 6 and picked up right where he left off, pounding a single, double and home run in an 11–7 victory. Two games later, Heilmann was 4-for-5 with a triple and four runs batted in, but was upstaged by Cobb, who also went 4-for-5 but had two doubles, a triple, a home run and four runs scored. Despite all that offense from Detroit's one-two punch, Dutch Leonard got shelled by the Browns and St. Louis won, 16–8.

The bats of Heilmann and Cobb weren't the only things flashing thunder in St. Louis. In the eighth inning on May 9, lightning struck the St. Louis stadium and knocked several people to the ground. "The finish was anything but peaceful," Harry Bullion of the *Detroit Free Press* wrote.

> The eighth for the Tigers had closed when [Marty] McManus approached the plate, and was set to face "Red" Oldham's shoots as he had in earlier innings. Umpire George Hildebrand adjusted his mask, and had called for Oldham's delivery to the plate and with that setting there was a mighty crash. Sparks flew out from the sky and the concrete grandstand rocked and swerved for several seconds. For about five seconds everything was dark. When the

clouds disappeared the fans were startled by seeing Hildebrand, McManus, Lee Fohl and Bush on the ground. Hildebrand's mask had popped off and rolled 4 feet away. Fohl, who was in the coaching station at third base, had been knocked fully 20 feet by the shock, while McManus was sprawled out around the plate."

Fortunately, no one was seriously injured. Hildebrand recovered and called the game, and the Tigers, who were leading at the time, won 11–5.

The Tigers had to catch a train back to Detroit and were rattled by what had happened. With no day off, the New York Yankees came to town on May 10. It was Babe Ruth's first trip to Detroit since leaving the Boston Red Sox. He greeted the Detroit crowd with a towering two-run home run in the first inning and Carl Mays hung on to beat the Tigers, 2–1. The next day, future Hall of Famer Waite Hoyt was edged in a pitchers' duel by Detroit's Harvey "Suds" Sutherland, 2–1. It was the fifth career win for Sutherland, who would go on to a 6–2 record, but never played in the majors after 1921.

The Yankees and Tigers were known for their hitting, and after two pitching duels, both teams brought the lumber on May 12. Heilmann hit a single and a triple and scored three times while Cobb was 1-for-3 with two runs scored. But it was Ruth who had the last laugh as he homered to help the Yankees win the slugfest, 11–10. The Yankees took the series with a 6–4 win the following day, which dropped the Tigers into fifth place and down to .500 with a 13–13 record.

Despite losing the final two games against New York, the Tigers bats had returned. Detroit took three of the next four games against the visiting Washington Senators, knocking out the great Walter Johnson in a 13–10 victory. Detroit scored 34 runs in the four-game series, with Cobb scoring five and Heilmann three, to improve to 16–14. The Tigers likewise took three of four from the Red Sox, including a 6–5 win over future Hall of Famer Herb Pennock on May 21 to return to third place at 19–15. It was one of just three times the Tigers would be four games over .500 all season, however.

Even though the Tigers were struggling, Heilmann was not. He was hitting at a .455 pace to lead the American League on May 21, while Cobb was fifth at .394. Heilmann was showing his skills day-in and day-out. On May 19, he singled against Hank Thormahlen. The next day, he slapped two hits. Though nobody knew it, Heilmann had begun the longest hitting streak of the season. Here is a look at the streak.

Game	Date	Opp.	Hits	Pitcher	Outcome
1	May 19	Red Sox	1	Thormahlen	3–2 Tigers
2	May 20	Red Sox	2	Myers	12–2 Tigers
3	May 21	Red Sox	2	Pennock*	6–5 Tigers
4	May 22	Athletics	1	Rommel	9–6 Athletics
5	May 23	Athletics	1	Harriss	5–2 Tigers
6	May 24	Athletics	1	Keefe	7–6 Athletics
7	May 25	Athletics	1	Perry	5–3 Athletics
8	May 26 (G1)	White Sox	1	Faber*	11–1 Tigers
9	May 26 (G2)	White Sox	3	Kerr	6–5 White Sox
10	May 27	White Sox	1	Faber*	3–1 White Sox
11	May 28	White Sox	4	Mulrenan	11–3 Tigers
12	May 29	White Sox	1	Wilkinson	8–2 Tigers
13	May 30 (G1)	Indians	2	Coveleski*	6–5 Indians
14	May 30 (G2)	Indians	3	Bagby	9–5 Tigers
15	May 31	Indians	2	Mails	7–4 Indians

Game	Date	Opp.	Hits	Pitcher	Outcome
16	June 2	Athletics	1	Keefe	5–4 Tigers
17	June 3	Athletics	2	Naylor	15–9 Athletics
18	June 4	Athletics	3	Hasty	7–5 Tigers
19	June 6	Athletics	3	Keefe	12–8 Tigers
20	June 7	Senators	2	Zachary	3–2 Senators
21	June 8	Senators	2	Mogridge	6–2 Senators
22	June 9	Senators	1	Johnson*	10–6 Tigers
23	June 10	Senators	2	Courtney	6–3 Tigers

denotes future Hall of Famer

Heilmann had racked up 42 hits during a 23-game hitting streak, batting .420. He had seven doubles, three triples and three home runs. He also scored 24 runs, helping the Tigers go 13–10 during the stretch. Future Hall of Famer Waite Hoyt finally held Heilmann hitless on June 11 at the Polo Grounds in the first game of a four-game set with the Yankees. The Tigers were still four games over .500 at 29–25, and the series against the Yankees would turn out to be the most crucial of the season. It was the first time the Tigers would face Babe Ruth in the Polo Grounds, where the Yankees played until Yankee Stadium opened in 1923. The New York fans were also eager to see Ty Cobb and the surprising batting leader, Harry Heilmann, for the first time all season.

The New York fans were not disappointed. They got to see everything they wanted to see. Heilmann slugged seven hits in the series, including three triples. Cobb also had seven hits, including a home run. Yankees fans, however, wanted to see their star outperform the league's two top hitters. Ruth did not disappoint, clubbing a home run in every game, and two in the final two games for a total of six clouts and a dozen RBI in the four-game series. Detroit pitching could not stop the slugging Yankees, who, sparked by Ruth, swept the series and score 41 runs. Perhaps the most impressive feat Ruth accomplished wasn't even at the plate. The Babe pitched five innings of relief in the third game to earn the win, also propelling the Yankees offensively with two homers.

The Tigers had dropped all the way back to .500 at 29–29, and it wasn't going to get any better. Fenway Park proved to be just as unfriendly as the Polo Grounds. The Red Sox

Harry Heilmann joined the Detroit Tigers in 1914. The young slugger played second base, first base and all three outfield positions. He became a mainstay on the team in 1916 and formed what turned out to be an all–Hall of Fame outfield with Ty Cobb and Sam Crawford (National Baseball Hall of Fame Library, Cooperstown, New York).

swept the Tigers in four games in which Heilmann was just 2-for-17. In the finale, the Tigers made eight errors to give away a game in which Hooks Dauss actually pitched well, but couldn't overcome the defensive miscues in an 11–7 defeat. A makeup game with Cleveland awaited the following day and the Indians handed Detroit its ninth consecutive loss, 8–7.

The season was headed downhill and not even Heilmann's .423 average on June 25 could help. The Tigers hovered around .500 and were 34–36 when Cobb took himself out of the lineup at the end of June to concentrate on managing. It was an interesting move for someone who loved to compete, but his competitive juices needed to be used as a manager, too.

It didn't help. Cobb went the next 26 games without starting, though he made a few pinch-hitting appearances. The Tigers came out of the stretch no better than before at 47–49. Their biggest tormenter again was Babe Ruth, who hit the longest home run at Navin Field up until that point and sparked the Yankees, who were on their way to the pennant, to another four-game sweep. Heilmann had 36 hits in the 26 Cobb-less games and was still atop the batting leaders. Cobb left the team for two more games on August 1 after his wife gave birth to a son, Ty Jr.

The press was beginning to sour on the Tigers. On an off-day, the August 11 headline in the *Detroit Free Press* read, "To get anywhere, Bengals must undergo rebuilding."[2] The struggles were starting to take their toll on everyone. Heilmann went hitless in three games at St. Louis (0-for-11), the only time he went hitless in consecutive games all season. The Tigers' slump affected others even worse. On an August 17 off-day, Detroit waived shortstop Donie Bush, who had been with the Tigers since 1908 and helped the team win two pennants. He batted just .250 in his career but had a .356 on-base percentage after leading the league in walks five times and runs once. The loss of Bush didn't end the tailspin. It got to the point where the Tigers were so bad that when they actually won six in a row beginning August 19 (Heilmann went 10-for-25 with three doubles, two home runs and 12 RBI), the Tigers improved only to 58–64. The pattern continued the rest of the season. Heilmann would hit well, but it wouldn't be enough for the Tigers to win. Heilmann went 5-for-5 on September 7, the only time he accomplished the feat all season, but the Tigers lost, 5–4, to Jim Bagby and the Indians.

The Tigers were not completely lacking drama in September, though, despite holding down sixth place. Cobb's long absence had held his batting average frozen for a month and he was gaining on Heilmann, who was playing every day. On September 17, Heilmann homered and singled to keep his average at .400. Cobb was on his heels, but Heilmann managed to go 1-for-9 and finished at .394 to win his first batting title. His hit on the final day of the season also gave him a league-leading 237 hits. He hit 19 home runs and 43 doubles, scored 114 runs and drove in 139 runs.

The Tigers had a lot to prove going into the 1922 season. After Heilmann's breakout season, he wanted to prove it wasn't a fluke, the aging Cobb wanted to prove he could keep up with his teammate and the Tygers wanted to prove they could become contenders under Cobb. All would be vindicated as winning came back to Detroit.

Ty Cobb was so intent on becoming a good manager that he didn't start the opening game of the 1922 season. In fact, he skipped the first five before starting in center field on April 20. He went 0-for-3 and went seven more games with only two at-bats as a pinch hitter. While he was focused on being a manager, the Tigers were without their best hitter as he tried to figure things out. The result was easy to predict. The Tigers started off 4–12. Adding insult to injury, Chicago White Sox pitcher Charlie Robertson threw a perfect game against the Tigers on April 30. He joined only future Hall of Famers Cy Young and Addie Joss in accomplishing the feat in the 20th century up to that point. It had been done twice in 1880 (five days apart with Lee Richmond on June 12 and future Hall of Famer Monte Ward on June 17) and would not be repeated again until 1956, when Don Larsen threw one in Game 5 of the World Series against the Brooklyn Dodgers.

Without Cobb in the lineup, Harry Heilmann, who was reveling in the birth of his son Harry Jr., on March 28, 1922, was carrying the bulk of the load, hitting .346 up until Robertson's perfect game. Four days after the gem, Heilmann had his biggest moment of the season. With the Tigers trailing 5–3 in the bottom of the ninth inning and two on, Heilmann launched a pitch from St. Louis Browns starter Elam Vangilder to lead the Tigers to victory in walk-off fashion, though the term "walk-off homer" wasn't around yet. The *Detroit Free Press* used its own phrase about the blast, saying it "altered the whole complexion of the verdict."[3] Heilmann slammed another home run five days later at Fenway Park.

Even with Heilmann hitting and Cobb back in the lineup, the Tigers were working out the kinks. On May 10, future Hall of Famer Herb Pennock started but left after one inning, with Quinn getting the 10–9 loss, but Detroit was still in seventh place (10–14). It was far from where the Tigers thought they would be, especially with their first trip to the Polo Grounds and the defending champion Yankees looming. Babe Ruth had belted the Tigers the previous season and always seemed to hit well at Navin Field, as well as his home park. But the Tigers were in luck as the series opened on May 12. Ruth had been suspended by American League President Ban Johnson and would miss the whole series. The Tigers dropped the first game, as future Hall of Famer Waite Hoyt held on for a 10–8 victory. Heilmann powered the Tigers to an 8–5 victory with two hits off Bob Shawkey, then an 8–2 win the following day with a single, double, triple and three runs batted in off Carl Mays. With the pair of victories, the Tigers had leaped from seventh to fourth place. The Tigers clinched the series with a 6–1 win on May 15 and were suddenly tied with Cleveland for third place at 14–15.

Heilmann, whose average had dipped to .308 on May 19, found his power stroke and helped the Tigers reach the .500 mark. He homered on May 20 in Philadelphia off of Slim Harriss. Four days later, he slammed two more, one against Harriss, who was on his way to leading the league with 20 losses. Heilmann proved he could hit against the best pitchers, too, as he slugged a home run the next day against Cleveland ace Stan Coveleski. The Tigers topped the future Hall of Famer, 7–3, and reached a winning record for the first time all season at 18–17. Heilmann had upped his average to .336 while Cobb was at .402 following three multi-hit games in a row.

Cobb and Heilmann were finally hitting at the same time until May 29, when an incident on the field in St. Louis stopped them both in their tracks. Heilmann, who had played right field all season, started the game in right before finishing at first base. The mild-mannered slugger argued a close call at first base and was tossed out of the game. Cobb, like any good manager, rushed out to defend his player and of course was thrown out as well. When American League President Ban Johnson got wind of the situation, he suspended both stars indefinitely. The slugging duo missed the next five games and the Tigers lost four of them to drop to 20–24. The final two losses came in Cleveland. The Indians didn't stop hitting once Cobb and Heilmann returned on June 3 and beat the Tigers, 5–4, then 14–6 the next day, sending the flailing Tigers all the way back to seventh place.

The Tigers needed a win desperately and it just so happened they were on their way to Navin Field for a 23-game homestand. It turned out to be just what the doctor ordered. Detroit pummeled Philadelphia 14–1 in the first game behind its two sluggers. In the sixth inning, Cobb tripled with the bases loaded and Heilmann followed with a homer. Detroit took three of four from the Athletics. Washington was next into town and Walter Johnson, perhaps the greatest pitcher of all time, was on the hill for the Senators. But The Big Train was chased from the game and the Tigers went on to win 5–4 in ten innings on June 10 thanks to a Heilmann home run off of reliever Ray Francis. Heilmann homered again the next day—his tenth of the season and Detroit won 8–0. The Tigers won three of four from Washington.

The Tigers faced their most important series of the season with the first-place Yankees. This time, Ruth was not suspended and would be eager to make good on missing two games the last series. But it was Heilmann who starred in this series. In the opener on June 14, Heilmann slugged a three-run homer and a double to lead the Tigers to a 6–2 victory. The next day, he helped with the game-winning rally as Cobb singled and scored on Heilmann's single. Shortstop Topper Rigney followed with a single to score Heilmann and the Tigers won 2–1 over Carl Mays. The Tigers had launched themselves back into third place by taking the first two games from the Yankees. But two games remained and the Tigers would face New York's strong starting pitchers in Waite Hoyt and Bob Shawkey. Heilmann singled, doubled and scored two runs off Hoyt as Detroit pitchers Bert Cole and Hooks Dauss combined for the 9–4 victory. The win kept the Tigers in third place, but stunningly knocked the Yankees out of first place. The St. Louis Browns had quietly taken over the American League lead. Heilmann could do no wrong against the Yankees and clubbed four hits off Shawkey in the series finale, pushing his season average back up to .348 and leading the Tigers to a 9–8 victory and a four-game sweep of the mighty Yankees. It was the turning point of the season as the Tigers would remain in the first division the rest of the way. After all, if they could sweep the Yankees, who couldn't they beat?

Detroit continued the roll when Boston came to town next on June 18. The Tigers hitters, who all finally seemed to be clicking at the same time, jumped all over the fourth outstanding pitcher in a row. Heilmann had his second four-hit game in a row and Cobb added two hits and scored three runs as the Tigers routed future Hall of Famer Herb Pennock, 8–1, and went on to take three of four from the Red Sox. Heilmann continued his slugging when St. Louis came to town. He hit two singles and a homer in a 10–6 win on June 23 and upped his average to .380 with two hits the next day. Detroit split the four-game set with the Browns, losing the last two. The Tigers finished their homestand with two losses to the White Sox as Heilmann was forced to watch from the bench with a sore back and shoulder.

The Tigers were 20–26 in seventh place when the homestand began and finished the St. Louis series 35–31—a 15–5 record before losing the last two games to make it a still impressive 15–7. Heilmann led the way, going 36-for-75 on the homestand, hitting at a stunning .480 clip.

It was back to the road for the Tigers, and it wasn't just any road trip. This trip was the toughest the Tigers had all season—one of the toughest in Heilmann's career. The Tigers faced 21 games in 19 days, including five doubleheaders. Four of the twinbills came in a span of six days. The Tigers split the first with the White Sox on July 3, then faced two more games the following day back home against Cleveland and were swept. The Tigers hung on to beat the Indians 6–5 in 11 innings the next day to end their quick homestand in the middle of the grueling road trip. After an off-day, the Tigers had two more double-headers in a row and took three of four from the Senators in Washington. The Tigers lost both games of the final doubleheader to the last-place Athletics on July 11.

The Tigers were exhausted and it was beginning to show. Heilmann homered the next day to lead Detroit to a 7–3 win over Philadelphia. He did even better the following day with two homers—solo home runs in the sixth and eighth. Bobby Veach added a solo homer in the sixth but the Tigers lost, 9–4, as Howard Ehmke struggled. The struggles became contagious—even to Heilmann. He was the hero against the Yankees in Detroit, but would be held in check by Yankees pitchers in the Polo Grounds. He went 0-for-4 against Carl Mays and Bob Shawkey but managed two hits off Waite Hoyt and Sad Sam Jones. The Tigers split the series with the Yankees. Heilmann rapped out three hits against St. Louis on July 23 but went into a slump. He went 1 for his next 14 as the Tigers split four games with Washington. His average was still a robust .342 after July 28, but that was 38 points lower than it was a month earlier. A four-game set against the last-place Athletics was just what he needed. Heilmann went 10-for-13 as the Tigers swept the series to improve to 54–47.

When teams like Boston and New York visited Detroit, Heilmann again struggled. In the eight games (four against each), he went an abysmal 5-for-27, though one of his hits was a home run. Detroit rallied to beat Boston in three of the four games, then lost three of four to the Yankees. Ruth hit his 20th home run of the season in the opener, then did it again in the final game. But Cobb stole the show by leaping over the center field fence to catch what would have been Ruth's 22nd. Heilmann's average continued to plummet as he went 4 for his next 19 in Cleveland and New York and dropping his average to .339.

It was a streaky season for Heilmann. He would be on a tear for ten games, then not be able to hit water if he was in a boat the next ten. So, fittingly, after his horrid hitting against the Indians and Yankees, he was due for another hot streak as the team headed to Fenway Park. Heilmann hit a three-run homer in the first game of a doubleheader on August 19, then singled in the only run in the second game. He pounded three more hits the following game, including two singles (and runs scored) in Detroit's ten-run sixth inning. The Tigers took three of four from the Red Sox. It turns out Heilmann was just getting started. At Philadelphia, Heilmann slugged homers all three days, going 10-for-17 against the Athletics as the Tigers again took three of four. It was on to the nation's capital, where Heilmann doubled and scored in a 3–2 win over the Senators on August 25.

But Heilmann's streak was about to come to a shrieking halt. He managed two hits the next day, but was on course for trouble in the sixth inning when he collided with Washington first baseman Frank Brower and fractured his right collarbone. Just when he was catching fire, his season was done. He finished the season with a .356 average, 162 hits, 92 runs, 21 home runs and 92 RBI. It was a great season, but one can only imagine how Heilmann would have done if he hadn't missed those 32 games.

Unfortunately for the Tigers, without Heilmann, they were never able to make a September run at the pennant and finished where they were for most of the season, in third place at 79–75. After watching Heilmann win it the previous year, Cobb made a strong run at the batting title, flirted with the .400 mark for much of the season and finished with a stunning .401 average. What was even more stunning was that St. Louis first baseman George Sisler did even better, finishing with a .420 average.

Heilmann didn't like watching from the bench as Cobb and Sisler fought for what he had won the previous year. Even worse, Heilmann felt like the Tigers could have made a run at the pennant if not for his injury. But he would have a chance to make amends the following year when he and the Tigers would have a stellar season.

16. .400

In 1923, the Detroit Tigers had a lot of questions to be answered. Can the Tigers contend for another pennant after finishing third in 1922? Will Ty Cobb still be one of the best hitters in the game after batting .400 the previous season? Will Harry Heilmann bounce back from a 38-point drop in his batting average (.394 to .356)? Tigers fans knew if the latter two happened, the American League pennant was a strong possibility.

Detroit got what it was looking for. Heilmann elevated his game to a new level. Cobb continued to hit like he always had and was getting better as a manager. There was also a young, raw outfielder who joined the Tigers that year. His name was Henry "Heinie" Manush, and before the season finished, he would give Detroit a glimpse at their future and create a crowded outfield with stars like Heilmann, Cobb and Bobby Veach, the three-time RBI champion. More questions would arise after the season.

First the Tigers would give the Motor City another exciting year. Opening Day was on April 18 in St. Louis. Heilmann, batting fifth and playing right field, went 4-for-5, including a double and a home run off reliever Dave Danforth. He scored twice, and coupled with Cobb's 3-for-4 performance with three runs, the Tigers beat the Browns, 9–6. Heilmann had three more hits the next day and singled in Cobb to give the Tigers an 8–3 victory. The Browns won the third game, 5–3, the game in which Manush made his debut, singling in a pinch-hitting role. Heilmann managed just one hit in the game, but took his frustrations out the next day, going 3-for-3 with two RBI and three runs scored as the Tigers routed the Browns, 16–1, with Hooks Dauss pitching masterfully for Detroit.

The Tigers opened at home on April 26 with a new look to Navin Field. The stadium was remodeled with a steel upper deck that stretched from first base around home plate to third base. A crowd of 35,000 was in attendance but went home disappointed after Browns pitcher Urban Shocker beat the Tigers, 4–3.

Heilmann slammed 24 hits in the first games to push his average to .545 on April 28. Two days later, the Tigers played with a historic lineup, though no one knew it at the time. It was the first game in which Heilmann, Cobb and Manush started in the outfield together. All three would eventually make the Hall of Fame, and it was the first time the Tigers had such a corps since Heilmann began his career with Cobb and Sam Crawford. No team—not even the Yankees—had fielded two separate combinations of three future Hall of Fame outfielders at this point. In fact, it would be rare for a team to accomplish the feat once. Cobb would be a part of another when he joined the Philadelphia Athletics and patrolled the outfield with Al Simmons and Zack Wheat in 1927 and Simmons and Tris Speaker in 1928. But those were players supplanted from their original teams (except for Simmons) and joined together for one season only. The Tigers had three Detroit-seasoned future Hall of Famers in the outfield for the second time and would for the next four seasons. But Manush wasn't yet a regular. The next day, May 1, he didn't play. Bob Fothergill was in left field and hit a game-winning single. Fothergill singled in the winning run again the following day and earned some more playing time over Bobby Veach.

All of the outfielders would get plenty of chances the following week thanks to Heilmann, who was suspended by American League President Ban Johnson after an argument with an umpire on May 2. Heilmann didn't like a call by Red Ormsby and presented him with a derby hat at home plate in the eighth inning. It came after a decision Heilmann felt comical, and he gave the umpire a hat a comedian like Charlie Chaplin would wear. Was it a joke? Either way, Ormsby took it as a personal insult. Harry Bullion of the *Detroit Free Press* sided with Heilmann, for he wrote: "The only offense Harry committed was against the fan whose hat he tried to make Ormsby a present of. The owner of the bowler was out there again Thursday, willing, under the same circumstances, to risk again the loss of the cover for his dome."[1]

Heilmann clearly showed up the umpire, which is something you don't get away with in baseball. It usually only merits being thrown out of the game and maybe suspended one game, depending on the umpire and the league official involved. Ban Johnson suspended Heilmann for five games, much to the chagrin of the Tigers and their fiery manager, Cobb. Bullion wrote: "Giving derbies to umpires has become, therefore, a costly practice. In itself the incident was trivial, but the consequences don't set well with the Tigers, who feel that the penalty paid by the suspension of their leading factor on the attack was far more severe than the offense against Ormsby merited.... Now the question arises, what would the penalty be were the bonnet of the felt straw or cap variety?... Red cried to Johnson, who cannot appreciate a joke either, it appears, and Heilmann got five days."[2]

Heilmann, who was hitting an even .500 at the time of the suspension, returned to the lineup on May 8 and was 1-for-2 in an 8–2 loss to Washington. The Tigers desperately needed him back in the lineup after dropping three of the first four games during his suspension, before salvaging the last game behind three hits from Manush and a home run by Cobb.

After two days of a record May snowstorm in Detroit, Heilmann finally got hot again. He went 2-for-3 on May 11, including a home run in the second inning to beat the Senators, 4–1. He rapped two more hits the next day in the series opener against New York, but Babe Ruth smashed a home run at Navin Field to help the Yankees to a 3–2 victory. Detroit came into the series tied with Cleveland for second place (12–10) behind New York (13–7). Detroit would be in fourth place after losing three of four to the Yankees and dropping to 13–13. The losses were no fault of Heilmann, who smashed eight hits in the four games, scoring four runs.

On May 17, Detroit opened the next series against Boston and something happened to Heilmann that hadn't all season. He went hitless. Heilmann was 0-for-3 though he scored a run and the Tigers beat the Red Sox, 6–2. It snapped a 21-game hitting streak for Heilmann. He would have only 20 hitless games all season, but two more of the games came during the next week. He had to cool off at some point and his average *dropped* to .419 at the end of May. He rebounded with two doubles and a home run in a 9–1 win over Cleveland and future Hall of Famer Stan Coveleski on June 2.

Heilmann wasn't just leading with his bat. On June 14, he made two spectacular catches in right field to preserve a 4–1 win at Fenway Park for pitcher Kenneth Holloway. He went 3 for 4 with a home run in the game, too, upping his average to .436. Harry Bullion wrote:

> Taking nothing away from Holloway it must be admitted, though, that he owes his success in turning the Red Sox back largely to the brilliance of Harry Heilmann's execution of Norm McMillan in the eighth, and of Joe Harris in the ninth, where it appeared that Holloway was not so strong as when he started. Heilmann's catches off drives that McMillan and Harris turned in the direction of the right field bleachers made the handful of patrons gasp in astonishment and forget to razz Cobb, to whom the fans were just beginning to warm up, when Harry stabbed the first one. And they were still thinking about it when the big fellow, whose reduced weight has made him a great outfielder, killed the other. ... Had Heilmann merely devoted himself to these stunts he could have called it a day. But Harry hit home the first run with a single ... and hit a home run.[3]

Heilmann, Cobb and Manush all started for the second time on June 16 in Fenway Park. All three managed a hit for the first time starting together, but the Tigers lost, 9–1. Nevertheless, Manush started in left field much of the rest of the season, with Veach and Fothergill getting less playing time. The problem was pitching, and Cobb was sticking with this lineup as long as he was able. The Tigers were 25–28 and buried in sixth place. They were starting to come around, but it was a slow process.

The outfield, however, was not the problem, and the future Hall of Fame trio continued to bring the big sticks. Heilmann was 3-for-4 with a home run, Manush homered and Cobb added three hits off future Hall of Famer Herb Pennock on June 20 to beat the Yankees, 9–7.

Back home, the Tigers hosted Chicago. The White Sox used five pitchers and beat the Tigers, 9–8, in the second game. Strangely, the Tigers scored eight runs without much help from the outfield. Heilmann and Cobb went hitless while Manush managed one hit and scored a run.

Heilmann proved that the game was a fluke as he slammed home runs in the next three games. In the first game, unfortunately, Heilmann's solo shot was the only run scored off future Hall of Famer Red Faber in a 7–1 loss. He and Manush belted homers the next day in a 7–6 win. But again Heilmann's third homer came off Browns ace Urban Shocker, who beat the Tigers, 6–2.

Cobb took himself out of the lineup for a couple of games to focus on his managing and give himself a break, inserting Veach back into the lineup. The Tigers won the next two games to move into fifth place. On July 7, the Tigers swept the Athletics in a double-header, 9–6 and 5–3, to move into a third-place tie at 35–36. Heilmann homered in the second game.

Bobby Veach was hitting well for the Tigers and Cobb wanted to keep him in the lineup. So he moved Heilmann to first base, playing Veach, Cobb and Manush in the outfield. The first game was disastrous. For the first time, Heilmann, Manush and Cobb all went hitless and the Tigers lost to Philadelphia, 7–5. All three managed hits the next game and Heilmann homered, but the Tigers lost again, 6–5. Heilmann homered again the next day and the Tigers finally won, 7–3, against the Red Sox, then took the second game of the doubleheader, 5–1.

It only took the next two games before Cobb had enough of that lineup. He took himself out of the lineup, moved Heilmann back to right field and kept Veach in center. Heilmann had struggled while at first base and his average dropped to .392. The Tigers crawled back to .500 (44–44) on July 25 for the first time since June 5 (22–22).

The Tigers traveled to the nation's capital and promptly lost, 11–1, to the Senators. Walter Johnson was on the mound in the second game of the series and won a 1–0 pitching masterpiece over Hooks Dauss. It was the 100th career shutout for Johnson, who would end his career with a record 110 shutouts. Heilmann went hitless and had back-to-back hitless games for the first time in a 12–5 victory in the finale on July 31. Detroit was in Philadelphia on August 3 when they got word of the death of President Warren G. Harding. Games that day were postponed, as were the games one week later on the day of the funeral.

Detroit returned to the field, but two days later was without Heilmann. He strained a shoulder ligament in the second game of a doubleheader in New York on August 11 (the Yankees swept) and missed three games. Veach filled in and homered on August 15 to lead the Tigers to their third straight victory. Heilmann returned and went 1-for-3 with a run scored in a 3–0 victory. Dauss, who had the hard luck of facing Walter Johnson in his 100th shutout earlier, pitched a masterful shutout of his own on August 16.

Heilmann was still near the American League lead in hitting at .394, but after Heilmann's recent struggles, Babe Ruth was up to .401 on August 18. Four days later, Ruth and the Yankees traveled to Detroit for a three-game series. The Motor City was buzzing as their star would go head-to-head with Ruth for control of the batting race. Heilmann batted .300 for the series, going 5 for 15, dropping to .388. Ruth was 3-for-9 and dropped to .400. Now, the pressure was on Heilmann. He responded with a 5-for-6 game on August 26, winning the game with a bases-loaded single in the 13th inning.

Heilmann had only two multi-hit games in the next eight. It would have been a great week for anyone else, but in a heated batting race, Ruth kept the lead, .393 to .390. Heilmann kept pace with multiple hits in six of the next seven games, including three triples, to move to .395. The next week, Ruth would have a tremendous advantage. Heilmann would be playing six consecutive doubleheaders. Detroit went 5–6 in the games (one tie) and Heilmann collected 19 hits to take a .394-.386 lead over Ruth in the batting race. Fittingly, the Tigers were at Yankee Stadium following the week of 12 games. Heilmann batted .444 in the series and the Tigers won two of three. Could he hold off Ruth and even approach .400 for the year? Heilmann homered in the first game against Cleveland in a 1-for-4 performance. The Tigers won three of four from the Indians, whom they were chasing for second place. Heilmann finished the series going 7-for-11 to reach .400. He finally reached the magic mark, but could he keep it?

He had one week remaining in the season. The batting race was clearly on Heilmann's mind, but in Detroit, Tigers fans were wondering if the team could reach second place. The Yankees had already clinched the pennant, but Detroit was in a fight for second with Cleveland. Heilmann went 3-for-5, then sat out the next three games after being "shaken up" on October 2 in Chicago. It created a minor scuttlebutt, since missing games preserved a .400 average for the season and the batting title. Heilmann had a pinch-hit single on October 6, scoring a run in a 12–4 win over St. Louis. Meanwhile, Cleveland lost both games of a doubleheader and the Tigers were in second place with one game to go. Heilmann pinch-hit again the next day—the last day of the season—and walked to help the Tigers win, 7–6, and hang on to second place. They edged Cleveland by a half-game, 83–

71 to 82–71. It was Manush who won the game for Detroit, slamming a double and a homer and scoring twice.

Heilmann won the batting crown with a .403 average, ten points ahead of Ruth, who led the AL with 41 home runs, 131 RBI, 151 runs, 170 walks, a .545 on-base percentage and .764 slugging percentage on his way to winning the American League MVP Award. Heilmann had 44 doubles, 211 hits, 121 runs, and 115 RBI, beginning a seven-year stretch in which he would drive in 100-plus runs. Ruth also had Heilmann where it counted, his team winning the pennant by 16 games. Somehow, Heilmann finished third in the MVP voting, behind Chicago second baseman Eddie Collins, who batted .360 with 48 steals and 89 runs scored. For the only year of his career, Ty Cobb was overshadowed by Heilmann. Cobb slapped 189 hits and batted .340.

Heilmann's season made him the last Tiger to hit .400 and the only one in franchise history, other than Cobb, to reach the mark. But could he keep it up consistently? So far, Heilmann had shown he could have a brilliant season every other year for the Tigers. He, and the rest of Detroit, wondered if he could repeat his heroics in 1924. Maybe, just maybe, the Tigers could knock off Ruth and the Yankees, too.

Coming off the best season of his career, Harry Heilmann had high hopes again for the 1924 season. He proved once again that he belonged at the top of the hitting world. The Tigers also proved they could hang with the New York Yankees. The Yankees would be overtaken in 1924, but not by the Tigers.

Once again, the Tigers had a young outfielder ready to crack the starting lineup. With Heilmann's and Cobb's positions set in stone, the Tigers were looking to make room for Heinie Manush in the starting lineup. They liked him so much that they traded mainstay Bobby Veach to Boston after he had led the league in RBI three times and batted .321 in 1923.

The Tigers opened the season on April 15 against Cleveland. Heilmann picked up right where he left off and went 2-for-3 with a walk and a run scored as Hooks Dauss pitched Detroit to a 4–3 victory. The Tigers beat future Hall of Famer Stan Coveleski, 5–1, the next day behind a home run and three

In 1923, Harry Heilmann enjoyed the finest season of his career as he became just the second Detroit Tiger to hit .400 in a season, joining teammate Ty Cobb. Heilmann batted .403 in 1923, had 211 hits, 121 runs scored and 115 runs batted in. He still finished behind Babe Ruth and Eddie Collins in the voting for Most Valuable Player (National Baseball Hall of Fame Library, Cooperstown, New York).

RBI by Heilmann. After losing the finale, 5–3 (Heilmann went hitless), Detroit welcomed the St. Louis Browns to town. Heilmann feasted on their pitching. He rocked ace Urban Shocker for a home run in the opener and finished the series 5-for-9 with five runs scored and six RBI, leading the Tigers to a sweep (7–4, 9–2, 8–4).

Detroit moved to Cleveland, where they lost two of three but remained in first place at 6–3. The Tigers returned home after the short road trip and took three of four from the White Sox, then set off for a long and critical road trip. It began in St. Louis, and the Tigers were confident after sweeping the Browns at home the week before. But home-field advantage played a huge part as the Browns stunningly swept the Tigers in four games (8–7, 4–1, 6–5, 6–5) in St. Louis. Heilmann was held hitless in the finale, but pounded two home runs the day before. It was a problem that had hung around the Tigers for a few years and would continue to plague the team throughout the 1920s: Heilmann was the only one hitting, with a .512 average late in April. Meanwhile, Manush was batting .194 and no one else was steadily driving runs in for Detroit. Obviously, Heilmann couldn't get the big hit every day, and when he didn't (or even sometimes when he did), the Tigers were beatable.

The Tigers won two games in Chicago, lost the next two to Washington and the first game in Philadelphia before taking three from the Athletics. Detroit dropped three out of four in Boston and was buried in fourth place at 15–14 as they traveled to Yankee Stadium on May 23 to face New York for the first time in 1924. The two best hitters in the American League—Heilmann and Ruth—would face each other for the first time since their epic batting race the season before. Ruth got the better of Heilmann in the first game, pounding a home run to lead the Yankees to a 7–6 win. Heilmann singled and doubled. In game two, Heilmann had two singles, a double, a triple, scored a run and knocked in a run as the Tigers roared back for a 7–3 victory. Detroit made it back-to-back wins with a 6–5 victory the following day thanks to two more hits from Heilmann. In the finale, the spotlight was shifted back to Ruth, who doubled and homered as the Yankees won, 8–2, to split the series.

Detroit returned home to face the Browns, and the Tigers were anxious for some payback after getting swept in St. Louis. Despite just four hits from Heilmann, the Tigers won three of four games to move up to third place. The Tigers remained in third until the middle of June, just mere percentage points out of second place on June 1 and June 9. Winning enough to hang in the race, Detroit was back in third place after a loss to Philadelphia on June 10. The Yankees traveled to Navin Field for the first time that season and Earl Whitehill outdueled Joe Bush, 7–2, and the Tigers jumped from third to first with one victory (28–22). Detroit lost the next three to the Yankees to plummet back to third place, but swept Boston in four games and was back within percentage points of first place on June 18.

The roller coaster continued in July as the Tigers fell from second to third. Detroit reached its turning point of the season on July 10 in Washington. The Tigers had split the first two games against the first-place Senators and had battled even for 12 innings before earning a 12–10 victory in the 13th inning. The great Walter Johnson started the game against Detroit's Ken Holloway. Johnson allowed three runs before coming out of the game in the fifth inning. Holloway departed after three innings. Neither bullpen fared much better, as the game was tied 10–10 after nine innings. Heilmann had two singles and a triple and knocked in a run for the Tigers. It was a game Detroit hoped to feed off of.

The Tigers surged to win 11 of their next 13 games, including a five-game sweep in Boston and three of four at Yankee Stadium. Unfortunately, Detroit lost three of four to

Washington to fall into third, then split with the Yankees in Detroit, reaching first place again on August 3 with a 5–2 win over the Yankees. After dropping back to second place the following week, the Tigers beat Boston, 13–7, and were ahead of New York by percentage points. Heilmann did his part with two doubles and three RBI.

Detroit was hanging on in the race, but the next day would embark upon a 25-game road trip. After reaching first place twice in the past week, this epic road trip came at the worst possible time for the Tigers. They split with Philadelphia, then lost four of five to the first-place Senators, dropping to third place—where the Tigers would remain the rest of the season.

The Tigers finished 86–68, six games behind the pennant-winning Senators. Detroit had the hard luck of facing either the Yankees or Senators every time they reached first place or got on a roll in 1924. Instead of rising to the occasion, the Tigers watched as Washington rose to the occasion to knock off the mighty Yankees and win the pennant and the World Series—the only championship the nation's capital has ever seen.

To add insult to injury for Heilmann, Ruth earned a little payback in the batting race, winning the crown with a .378 average. Heilmann had another strong year but finished with a .346 mark. He had 197 hits, a league-leading 45 doubles, 107 runs, ten home runs and 114 RBI. Heilmann finished ninth in the MVP voting as Walter Johnson ran away with the award after posting a 23–7 record with a 2.72 ERA, leading the Senators to the championship. Johnson was on the mound in relief in Game 7 as the Senators topped the New York Giants to hang on for the title.

The Senators weren't going anywhere and, unfortunately for the Tigers, this meant there were now two teams to beat in the American League.

17. RETURN TO THE CROWN

After underachieving but still hanging in the race in 1924, the Tigers were looking to put everything together and make another run at a pennant in 1925. Detroit had watched the lowly Washington Senators shock the nation by overtaking the powerful New York Yankees to claim the pennant and was looking to be the next team to make a shockwave.

It started out well for the Tigers as they knocked off the Chicago White Sox in the season opener on April 14. Though no one knew it at the time, it would be the only day the Tigers could say they were in first place all season. Detroit lost four of its next five and dropped to sixth place. After a 4–3 win over Cleveland on April 21, the Tigers dropped 11 of 12 games to fall into last place at 4–14.

Pitching was definitely a major problem for the Tigers. Detroit was 8–16 on May 10. In five of those wins, the offense provided at least nine runs of support. The pitchers were not winning the close battles. The Tigers' staff was a far cry from the days of Wild Bill Donovan, George Mullin, Ed Siever and Ed Killian, who led the Tigers to three straight pennants. Hooks Dauss went from a 20-game winner two years before to 16–11, and Earl Whitehill dropped from 17–19 to 11–11 in 1925. With their two best pitchers struggling, the rest of the staff didn't pick up any slack as the team earned run average was 4.61, sixth in the American League.

The Tigers could still hit and proved that even when their pitching struggled, batting an astounding .302 as a team in 1925. First baseman Lu Blue batted .306, and Al Wingo batted .370 while getting most of the playing time in left field. Like Cobb, Wingo was from Georgia. He was a rookie with the 1919 Athletics and was signed the year before from Toronto for $50,000 to fill Veach's shoes in left after he was traded to Boston. Heinie Manush batted .302 off the bench and Bob Fothergill added a .353 mark. Joining Ty Cobb and Harry Heilmann, the Tigers had by far the best hitting outfield in the game. Cobb would bat .378 for the season, but for the second and final time took a back seat to Heilmann.

"Slug" proved to be just that as he passed the .400 mark on May 7 after tallying five multi-hit performances in his last six games. He knocked in ten runs in six games and hovered close to .400 the rest of the month, finishing May at .401. On June 4, Heilmann clubbed four hits and drove in four runs to reach .406 but the Tigers lost, 12–7, to the White Sox. It was the theme of the season. The offense had strung enough big hits together to climb into the first division—barely—by June 20. Fourth place was where they stayed for most of the season.

On July 12, after being held hitless by the Athletics, Heilmann dropped below .400 to .399. He would not reach the .400 mark the rest of the season—but there was still a title to be won.

Heilmann was hitting as well as he had at any time in his career, but Cobb and Cleveland's Tris Speaker were right on his heels. It was an interesting situation with Cobb being Detroit's manager—the race was between the master (Cobb), the rival (Speaker) and the apprentice (Heilmann).

Detroit owner Frank Navin was still hoping for more managerial success from the greatest player in the game. "It was a heartbreaking experience for Navin, who thought the club was ready for new pennants," Fred Lieb wrote in *The Detroit Tigers*. "In the privacy of his office, he would let his hair down to Wish Egan, his confidant among the scouts. Standing wistfully before the pictures of Donovan, Mullin, Schaefer, Crawford, and the old game, he would ask sadly: 'Are those days never to return? Is Detroit never to have another winner?'"[1]

Heilmann's successful batting race of 1925 saw one of the epic finishes of major league history. Tris Speaker apparently had an unbeatable lead as the clubs reached the last month of the season. The great Spoke's legs bothered him in September; he sat out most of the month, playing only a few innings or appearing as a pinch-hitter. His average stayed around .390. On Labor Day, Heilmann was some 20 points behind, but he put on a whirlwind September batting campaign. Still, Speaker kept in front up to the very last day of the season, October 4. "While Tris sat on the bench in the final Cleveland-White Sox game, Harry the Horse galloped to the batting championship in St. Louis with six hits in nine times at bat. He had three singles in six times up in the first game, and 3 for 3 in the second, one of them being a homer. The final figures gave him .393 for 150 games; Speaker .389 for 117 games."[2]

After Heilmann made three hits in the first game, several of his teammates figured he had passed Speaker by the width of the hair. They suggested: "Why don't you lay off in the second game? You've got the title won."

"Not me," said Heilmann, who led the league with 134 RBI. "I'll win it fairly, or not at all. I'll be in there swinging."[3]

He swung his way to his third American League batting title, though the Tigers could swing no higher than fourth place, 16½ games back. The Washington Senators won their second consecutive pennant, but this time fell to the Pittsburgh Pirates in the World Series. The Pirates returned to glory for the first time since Honus Wagner led the team past a young Ty Cobb and the Tigers in 1909. Detroit was hoping for that kind of resurgence in 1926.

Unfortunately for the Tigers, the team was going in the other direction. Under Cobb, the Tigers fell to sixth place in 1926, 12 games out of first. Surprisingly, only two spots from last place, Detroit still finished with a winning record at 79–75. But no one was catching the Yankees, who rebounded after missing two straight World Series and finishing seventh in 1925. New York had a first baseman named Lou Gehrig who, with Ruth, would become part of the greatest one-two punch in baseball history. Gehrig cemented the Yankees' dynasty for more than a decade and spelled doom for the rest of the American League.

Although they were sixth in the league standing, 1926 was another great year for the Tigers in the batting race with three of the top four spots. Heinie Manush, who hit .378 (more on this in the Manush section), won the batting championship. Ruth followed at .372. Heilmann and Fothergill were tied at .367. Cobb took part in only 79 games because of injuries and ailments and hit .339. In his first year as regular second baseman for Detroit, future Hall of Famer Charlie Gehringer hit .277.

"The red-letter day of the year was Harry Heilmann Day, August 9. A crowd of 40,000 Heilmann fans crammed into Navin Field to pay homage to "Harry the Horse." Larry Fisher, the automobile king, came across with a new car, the Knights of Columbus with a diamond stickpin, and Paddy Pexton with a hunting dog with a huge green ribbon around his neck. And they put the usual jinx on their hero. Heilmann went hitless in a free-hitting game which Detroit lost to the old Yankees foe, 9–8. But Slug whacked out plenty on days when he was not the special guest of honor."[4]

It was a torn situation for manager Cobb, who had guided Heilmann into a dominant hitter, but could do little to help the pitching staff keep the Tigers a contender. "Maybe I was not a managerial success, but just as surely I was not a managerial failure," Cobb said.

I took over a seventh-place club in 1921, and with the exception of that year, all of my clubs won more games than they lost. Four years in the first division. We played interesting, exciting ball, drew well at home, and next to the Yankees were the best attraction on the road. I was continually handicapped by inadequate pitching, but Whitehill and several other good prospects were developed. Heilmann developed into a full-fledged star under my management; he was a natural hitter, and I taught him everything I had learned in my long career. We always had hitting clubs, so I must have imparted some of my own hitting knowledge to my players.[5]

18. Slug's Surge

The 1927 season was one of the most memorable in baseball history. The Yankees had "Murderer's Row," which rolled over every team in the American League to win 110 games and leave the rest of baseball in the dust, including the National League champion Pittsburgh Pirates, who were routed in a World Series sweep. But 1927 was memorable for Detroit Tigers fans for many other reasons. For starters, it would be the first season since 1904 without Ty Cobb. Baseball's greatest player had struggled as a manager and left the Tigers after 22 seasons to join the Philadelphia Athletics. Cobb would bat .357 for the Athletics after being replaced as Detroit manager by George Moriarty—a former teammate who helped the Tigers win the 1909 pennant. Moriarty would help the Tigers return to the first division after finishing sixth in 1926. It would also be the last season for Heinie Manush in a Tigers uniform. His average dropped to .298 and he was traded to the St. Louis Browns that winter.

The biggest reason the season was memorable in Detroit, however, was because Harry Heilmann—whose year would be memorable no matter what thanks to the birth of his daughter Mary Ellen—would be locked into another heated batting race with the hopes of winning his fourth title in seven years. Unlike seasons past, Cobb was neither his manager nor teammate, and as Tris Speaker's career was winding down like Cobb's, a new rival surfaced in the form of Philadelphia's Al Simmons. It was so captivating that Navin Field saw 773,716 fans come through the turnstiles in 1927, second to only the Yankees' 1.1 million.

Heilmann went hitless on Opening Day, but slashed out multi-hit games the next four days, raising his average to .500 on April 20. He came back down to earth with an 0-for-4 performance, dropping him to .409 the next day. On May 9, Heilmann had his best game of the spring, clouting two home runs against Boston going 4-for-5 with three runs scored and four RBI. Prior to that performance, Heilmann had gone three straight games without a hit.

Meanwhile, Simmons upped his average to .424 on May 16 while Heilmann was at .337. No one would have guessed the two would battle till the season's final day for the batting crown. Heilmann dropped all the way down to .326 on May 23 before slowly picking up some steam.

When the hits came, they came in bunches for Slug. Heilmann slammed five hits in nine at-bats in a doubleheader split against Cleveland on May 30, surging to .349. Simmons was still above .400 at that point, however, sitting at .401. On July 13, Heilmann slugged seven hits in a twin bill, including a 5-for-5 performance in the second game. He scored four runs and had three doubles and two singles. The Tigers won the first game, 7–3, and the second, 13–9, against the defending champion Senators, and Heilmann improved to .351.

Simmons, however, was hanging tough at .401. He dropped to .393 on July 24 before missing six weeks with an injury. The longer he was out with his average holding steady, the more difficult it would be for Heilmann to catch him. If he struggled in August, he would be sunk. But Heilmann was a veteran and a star. He had been through this kind of a situation before and knew what it took to become a batting champion. After all, he had won three already and had batted .400 once.

With the pennant race all but over, thanks to the dominating "Murderer's Row" Yankees, the American League turned its attention to the batting race. A four-hit game surged Heilmann to .373 on August 4. He hovered around .370 for two weeks before being faced with seven games in four days. Meanwhile, Simmons remained at .392. The Tigers had three doubleheaders scheduled at Navin Field beginning on August 19. Heilmann could have become tired and given up, especially after going hitless in the first game against Boston, but he turned it around in the second and went on a tear. He was 2-for-4 in the second game, then 2-for-3 in the first game against Washington. His signature game came in the second half of the August 20 twinbill as he went 5-for-7 with a triple, home run and two runs scored, though the game was ruled a 6–6 tie after 15 innings since night had fallen. In the one single game of the stretch, Heilmann went 3-for-4, then went 4-for-6 in the second doubleheader with the Senators on August 22. The league-leading Yankees were in town next and Heilmann pounded them for four hits, raising his average 27 points in nine days to reach .398. He had 27 hits in an 11-game span to regain the top spot in the race. Heilmann remained above .390 through August and was at .397 on September 6 when Simmons returned to the Philadelphia lineup. Two days later, Heilmann and the Tigers came to Philadelphia but Simmons was back on the shelf, missing another six games. He returned on September 14 and after a hitless game, picked up where he had left off before the injury with five multi-hit games in a row. The Tigers were in the middle of a 20-game road trip and would only have a doubleheader at home against Cleveland to end the season. Without a friendly crowd, Heilmann briefly dropped behind Simmons before the second game of a twin bill at Fenway Park on September 17, when he cranked out four hits and leapt to .391—one point ahead of Simmons.

It was neck-and-neck until the final day. Simmons closed the season with a single game in Washington, while Heilmann had a chance to win or lose in two games with the Indians. Simmons bagged two hits in five at-bats, giving him a closing average of .392. Due to the difference of time, Heilmann knew almost before he started what he had to beat. Jack McCallister of Cleveland used George Grant in the opener and big Garland Buckeye in the second game. Heilmann was looking to cement his place in history. Win the title, and he would join the great Cleveland second baseman, Napoleon Lajoie, for the most American League batting championships by a right-handed hitter with four.

"In his first two times up, Heilmann smacked doubles. In his third time at bat, he rolled to third base and was out. The next time up, he pulled a Lajoie—he bunted, caught the third baseman flat-footed, and beat it out. It gave him three out of four. Some of the fans implored him to retire. "You've got Simmons beat; call it a day, Harry," they yelled. But not Slug; he knocked the next one out of the lot for a home run. Would he come back for the second game and risk the championship which now was his? Every man, woman, and child in the park cheered him as he went out to right field at the start of the second game. His bat churned out a homer, a double, and a single this time in four at-bats. What an exhibition of guts when the chips were down! He beat Simmons by six points at .398 and was every inch a champion. Heilmann also amassed 201 hits, a career-high 50 doubles and 120 RBI to help the Tigers finish fourth at 82–71."[1]

Heilmann had answered every call and returned to being the top hitter in the game. But just as in previous years, he could not put together two dominating seasons in a row. His average fell to .328 in 1928 and the Tigers returned to sixth place—this time with a losing record of 68–86. It was another season of abysmal pitching with the Tigers collectively posting a 4.32 ERA. Unlike previous seasons, the hitting did not bail out the pitching, due to a major off-season trade. Detroit sent Manush and Lu Blue to the St. Louis Browns for outfielder Harry Rice and pitcher Elam Vangilder. Unprotected in the middle of the lineup, Heilmann batted a solid .328, though it was a 70-point drop from the previous season. Without Cobb, Veach and Manush, Heilmann didn't have much help in the lineup, something he experienced for the first time. The outfield was still solid with Bob Fothergill batting .317 and the newcomer, Rice, batting .302. It was a lot different from having Heilmann, Cobb and Manush all over .370, however. The only infielder to bat .300 was Charlie Gehringer, who in his second season as the full-time second baseman hit .320. The Tigers were beginning a youth movement and Gehringer would be the cornerstone, though no one knew it at the time. Heilmann was looking for some major improvements the following year after seeing such a sharp drop in his average. The 1929 season would be a little better—but not by much.

Harry Heilmann won his third batting title, nearly hitting .400 again with a .393 average in 1925. He slapped 225 hits and drove in 134 runs for the Tigers that season (National Baseball Hall of Fame Library, Cooperstown, New York).

19. The Beginning of the End

The Detroit Tigers franchise was in a bit of a freefall as the 1920s came to a close. For the first time in team history, the Tigers were in a rebuilding stage. After three consecutive pennants, 1907–1909, Detroit kept most of its core for the next decade, losing a couple of key pitchers. The team gained stars like Harry Heilmann, Heinie Manush and Hooks Dauss to balance the loss. Now that Ty Cobb was two years removed after leaving the Tigers for Philadelphia, there were fewer big bats in the lineup. Manush and Lu Blue were doing well in St. Louis after being traded by the Tigers, and Manush would go on to have another decade in his Hall of Fame career. Detroit got virtually nothing out of the deal, at least long-term, as it turned out. Harry Rice batted .300 for two seasons, then was traded, while Elam Vangilder was 11–11 for Detroit in two years. Meanwhile, the Tigers had switched managers again in 1929, welcoming Bucky Harris into the dugout. Harris had led the Washington Senators to back-to-back pennants in 1924–1925, but inherited a team in transition.

The only other bright spot in addition to Heilmann was young and talented Charlie Gehringer, who would go on to be the best second baseman in Detroit history and arguably one of the top five second basemen ever to play the game. But the Tigers would need more than Heilmann and Gehringer to compete in 1929, and it turns out, they found it—at least at the plate. Rookie first baseman Dale Alexander batted .343 with 215 hits and 137 RBI while Harry Rice hit .304 and outfielder Roy Johnson added a .314 average with 201 hits. Meanwhile, Gehringer slapped 215 hits and batted .339 while Heilmann led the team with a .344 mark and added 120 RBI in just 125 games. For the first time, Heilmann was not able to win an odd-year batting title like he had in 1921, 1923, 1925 and 1927. He was still no slouch at .344, finishing eighth in the league.

It was again the pitching that was the problem. Detroit's ERA was 4.96, the worst in the American League. Only the team's hitting brought it out of the basement to a sixth-place finish at 70–84, a whopping 36 games behind pennant-winning Philadelphia.

The 1929 season began with a 5–4 loss to Cleveland in 11 innings, leading to four losses in Detroit's first five games. Six wins in a row from May 3–8 propelled the Tigers to a winning record at 12–9 and moved them into fourth place (reaching third for a couple of days), where they would remain until late July, when a 10–7, extra-inning loss to George Earnshaw and the Athletics sent them to fifth place at 45–45.

The Tigers stayed in fifth place until the last two weeks of the season, when seven straight losses sent them to a sixth-place finish at 70–84. It was demoralizing for Heilmann, who was hoping to play on another team in contention. He did his part, but the pitching was the worst it had been in franchise history. Detroit finished the season with an 8–7 loss to the Chicago White Sox on October 6, with former manager George Moriarty serving as the home plate umpire. Heilmann came up as a pinch hitter and failed to get a hit. Little did anyone know it would be the last time he would appear in a Tigers uniform. Eight days later, his contract was bought by the Cincinnati Reds. To add insult to injury, Heilmann lost much of his fortune in the stock market crash and was headed to a new city while the country was headed into the Great Depression.

The Cincinnati Reds were coming off another awful season. At 66–88, they finished in seventh place in the National League in 1929. The team's top stars were first baseman George "High Pockets" Kelly, the former New York Giants star, who batted .293, and aging pitcher Eppa Rixey. Both would eventually end up in the Hall of Fame, but both were in the final two years of their careers and showing their age. The Reds needed a new draw, a fresh face for the fans. With Heilmann proving he was still in the prime of his career with a .344 average in 1929, Cincinnati was able to purchase the contract of the four-time batting champion from the Detroit Tigers.

Tigers fans had watched the team get rid of batting champions Ty Cobb, Heinie Manush and now Heilmann. The team was obviously looking for a youth movement as the 1930s began and would have a pennant in 1934, led by Charlie Gehringer and Hank Greenberg. Of course the fans couldn't predict that. They just saw a 75–79, fifth-place ball club in 1930 with Gehringer and Dale Alexander providing the only punch in the lineup. In 1931, Detroit would drop to seventh before finishing fifth twice, then winning the pennant in 1934 and the World Series in 1935.

Heilmann had hoped to stay in Detroit long enough to see that turnaround, but he was in the National League and trying to help his new team complete a turnaround. Heilmann showed the NL what the AL already had seen in his first game in Cincinnati on April 15. He slugged a single and double and scored the first run of his National League career in a 7–6 loss to Pittsburgh. Cincinnati was hoping Heilmann and Kelly could provide a one-two

In 1927, Harry Heilmann continued his trend of winning batting titles every other year. He surged to a .398 average to win his fourth and final batting title. With 201 hits and 120 RBI, Heilmann finished second in the MVP voting to Lou Gehrig (National Baseball Hall of Fame Library, Cooperstown, New York).

punch similar to what Heilmann and Manush brought to the table in Detroit. It didn't happen. Kelly's average stayed below .300 and he was released by the Reds on July 10. He signed with Minneapolis of the American Association on July 17 and was traded to the Cubs on August 18. He would retire following the 1932 season with a .297 career average. As with the Tigers, pitching was an issue. In fact, it was even worse in Cincinnati. No Reds starter posted a winning record, the team ERA was 5.08, and they finished seventh again.

Heilmann did his part, however, completing his first National League season with a .333 average. What was most impressive about his final mark was that he was doing this against pitchers he had never faced in his career. But age was taking its toll on Heilmann, who after one year away from Detroit decided to retire after the 1930 season.

After a year away, however, he was lured back by the Reds to be a player/coach and appeared in 15 games in 1932, batting just .258. His final hit came in his final game. He singled against Pittsburgh on May 31 in a 4–1 loss. Heilmann finished his career with a .342 batting average. He knew his playing days were over, but he could not stay away from the game for long.

20. To the Booth

In 1933, Harry Heilmann launched the second half of his career in baseball. He became the radio broadcaster for the Tigers, where he remained for 17 years. He was the second former player ever to become a play-by-play broadcaster when he was hired by WXYZ (now WXYT) radio in Detroit. Fans were captivated as Heilmann delivered the current action on the field to their homes while giving them a glimpse of baseball during his playing days with stories of Babe Ruth and Ty Cobb. It wasn't an easy career jump. He took public speaking classes and had to learn to read the ticker tape, since radio announcers did not broadcast from away games in those days. He used his imagination to make the game interesting and build excitement for those away games, where messages he received might simply say, "single to left." He always found time to give back, too. During World War II, he traveled to the Middle East as part of a baseball group entertaining troops.

Heilmann was a terrific broadcaster, and his voice was in homes all over Michigan and the Midwest. But tragedy struck during spring training in 1951. "He was diagnosed with lung cancer and he didn't want anyone to know it," daughter-in-law Marguerite Heilmann said. "He was a very private person. They didn't do much treatment in those days. You were mostly just sent home to die."[1]

Heilmann, who had been thrown out of the Detroit Athletic Club, along with Babe Ruth, after a wild night during his career, was given an honorary membership card in his waning days by club secretary Charles Hughes. Hughes actually brought it to Heilmann's hospital room on Grand Boulevard. He never lived long enough to use it, but appreciated the gesture. His wife used it after Harry's death and was eventually given an associate membership. The Heilmann family still has the membership card and it is one of their most prized possessions.[2]

Harry Heilmann died of lung cancer at age 56 in the Detroit suburb of Southfield, Michigan, on July 9, 1951, the day before the All-Star Game at Briggs Stadium in Detroit. The game began with a moment of silence in Heilmann's honor. Cobb, who visited his old teammate in the hospital, told Heilmann that he had earned election into the Baseball Hall of Fame, which gave him much joy. But it wasn't true. Heilmann wasn't elected until the following year. It was a notable moment of selflessness for Cobb, who knew his teammate deserved the honor and would eventually get it.

His legacy lives on through the memories of his family and stories passed down from grandfather to father to son about his ferocious hitting in Detroit. Harry Heilmann, Jr., passed away in 2002, leaving grandsons, Harry III and John, who live in Colorado, and Dan, who lives in Michigan, with the family name. His daughter, Mary Ellen, eventually moved to Cleveland. It was tough maintaining strong relationships when players were on the road for so much of the year. "My father and grandfather had a good relationship but my grandfather traveled so much," grandson Dan Heilmann said. "Between spring training and school, camp and the baseball season, there wasn't that much time. The road trips in those days were long. He could be gone a month and it could have been when my father was at camp for a month in the summer."[3]

But Heilmann made the most of the time he did have with his family and with the Detroit community, both as a player and a broadcaster. "What players did for the community back then is what makes the Tigers what they are today. They are much more disciplined and professional now, but because of that,

Harry Heilmann continued to work in baseball following his retirement as a player. Heilmann became one of the voices of the Detroit Tigers. He was one of the first former players to become a broadcaster, a trend that many would follow (contributed/Heilmann family collection).

they have lost the community feel," Dan Heilmann said. His grandfather was one of the players who gave back to the underprivileged and identified himself as a Detroiter. "He invented the word 'class,'" daughter-in-law Marguerite Heilmann said. "The man was outstanding when it came to, not only his professional persona, but his personal behavior was that of a true gentleman."[4]

Harry Heilmann III remembers little bits of listening to his grandfather.

When I was a kid, I remember my grandmother. They had one of the first TVs in Detroit. It must have been a 9 by 8 screen. Grandma tried to convince me that it was grandpa broadcasting out of that TV. I had none of it because I didn't think he could fit in there. He put a tie in his pocket and brought it home so I knew it was him. Then I thought everyone's grandfather was on TV. I remember him giving me silver dollars and sitting on his lap. I didn't remember his voice as bass as it was when he was on the radio. His voice was a rumble in those recordings.[5]

Other Detroit Tigers legendary broadcasters have been fans of Heilmann's work in the booth. "I heard some of his tapes. They were very good. He had a nice voice and they did a lot of recreations," Ernie Harwell said.

He did it at a theater in downtown Detroit. He was quite a barnstormer after the season and would go around Michigan and they'd play in Lansing or Saginaw. They would sign autographs, then go out and eat. I regret that I never did get to know him. He broadcast the Tigers games for 17 years. When they started broadcasting in Detroit, Ty Tyson was there in the 1920s because the Midwest was far ahead of New York. They had two networks, the in state and out of state. In 1934 Heilmann was the out of state voice. Then Tyson quit and

Harry did it on both networks from about 1936 on. He had a great career. People still talk about how great he was. It was great to be in the line of succession with him because he was such an outstanding broadcaster.[6]

Heilmann was one of the first former players to become a broadcaster following his career. In later generations, former star players like Phil Rizzuto, Bill White, Tony Kubek, Tim McCarver, Jim Kaat, Bert Blyleven and Ron Santo went to the booth. In fact, now, just about every team has a former player as their color man on radio or television, if not both.

George Kell went on to have one of the best combination careers in the field and in the booth. The third baseman was elected to the Hall of Fame as a player and went on to broadcast Detroit Tigers games for many years. He gave credit for making that transition to Heilmann, whom he saw make the transition himself and who also suggested Kell do the same. "We did a show every afternoon after the game," Kell said just before his own death. "People would call in and ask questions about spring training. I had never broadcast before. Lo and behold, he had cancer and I had to keep the show going the rest of the year. He thought I had a good voice and a good mind for it. It was good for me when I ended my baseball career."[7]

Kell learned a lot from working with the easy-going and consummate professional, Heilmann.

He was great. Nothing bothered Harry Heilmann. Nothing. If something would go wrong, I would get upset and he would laugh. I really admired the man. It started when I came to Detroit. I was a 22-year-old kid and got off to a good start. Harry was in the booth and sort of took me under his arm. We were friends till the day he died. We were such good friends.

He taught me a lot about broadcasting. He knew I could do it if I kept pumping away at it. He was one of a kind. He did the broadcasts of Tigers games and did not travel with the ball club. Harry had a downtown studio right on the street and broadcast from a ticker. They organized a George Kell club. They would come down to the station and come down to the studio and watch Heilmann broadcast.... He is one of the all-time great ballplayers. If he had not played in Detroit with Ty Cobb it would have been Heilmann's town. He was an outstanding outfielder with a good arm. He was just such a calm man nothing bothered him. He carried the broadcast like he was having a dinner conversation. He taught me so much about broadcasting. When I went to Detroit to broadcast and I did all the play by play. I would tell myself I wanted to do it like Harry Heilmann did it. He's just a great human being. He was like a father to me. His stats are unbelievable. He was up there at .370 all the time. He was a tremendous hitter. I was scared to death when I first went on there. First thing I knew I was listening to Harry and watching Harry, not imitating but taking it from him and I took it with me the next 30 years I was a broadcaster.[8]

21. FORGOTTEN LEGACY: HARRY HEILMANN

Of the three players in this book, Harry Heilmann is the one whose loss in Detroit fans' memory has been most difficult to believe. Why don't people remember him? He was a generation younger than Sam Crawford, who also was extremely private. He didn't bounce around from team to team like Heinie Manush, making later Detroit fans forget about him. He won four batting titles and was one of the few players in the game's history to bat .400 in a season. He also was the first player to hit a home run in every ball park. Could Ty Cobb's shadow have been that great—even in the second half of his career? George Kell said, "If he had not played in Detroit with Ty Cobb, it would have been Heilmann's town."

Other factors come into play, of course. Few players are remembered from pre–World War II, and just about every player that is generally remembered reached 3,000 hits or 500 home runs. Rogers Hornsby seems to be the one exception. He finished fewer than 100 hits short of 3,000 but had seven batting titles, with six coming in consecutive seasons. He batted .400 three times and won two Triple Crowns. It is easy to see why Hornsby is remembered. But Heilmann, a fellow right-handed hitter, should be too. Heilmann's name only seems to come up in discussions when talking about the greatest right-handed hitters of all time. Ted Williams had him ranked in the top 20 hitters of all time, at No. 17. The only right-handers ahead of him are Al Simmons (another player too easily forgotten), Hank Greenberg, Willie Mays, Hank Aaron, Joe DiMaggio, Hornsby and Jimmie Foxx. The only pre–World War II players are Hornsby, Heilmann and Simmons, who would have been remembered a little better had he reached 3,000 hits (he had 2,927). Of course there are some tremendous right-handed hitters in the game today who would be considered, like Albert Pujols and Miguel Cabrera. Williams' list omitted Honus Wagner and Napoleon Lajoie because he never saw them play. It also didn't factor in then-current players like Frank Thomas. No matter how you rank them, Heilmann is one of the top right-handed hitters of all time and one of five dominant ones in the first 75 years of baseball. That is someone who should be remembered. He came within a handful of hits of batting .400 four different seasons, something no one in baseball history has done. He batted .403 in 1923 and also had seasons of .394 in 1921, .393 in 1925 and .398 in 1927, each a batting title. Four more hits in 1921, five more in 1925 and one more in 1927 would have done it. He would have made it easily if he hadn't been nipped on grounders. He was a big fellow who didn't break away from the plate as rapidly as others, with the added disadvantage of having to take an extra stride on account of being a right-handed hitter.[1]

"It's incredible, remarkable," Harry Heilmann III said. "It was a game of inches. A right-handed hitter has an extra 25 inches to cover on the way to first base and their momentum is going the wrong way. It's remarkable that he could put together a .342 average. The fact that he was so slow. He would have an even higher average if he was able to beat out a couple more singles. He managed to maintain a relationship with both Cobb and Ruth. Not too many people could say that."[2]

It would be one thing if Heilmann was a quiet player who didn't talk to the media and disappeared after his career like Crawford. But Heilmann, who once apologized to Detroit writers for a slump, though he was hitting .328, was friends with Babe Ruth and went out on the town with his buddy. He had a good relationship with Cobb, for the most part, but he was quiet in comparison. He also was a tremendous broadcaster for many years after his career. This brought him into the homes of Detroit Tigers fans all across Michigan.

A .342 lifetime batting average, four batting crowns, a .400 season and a longtime broadcaster all adds up to someone who deserves a statue at Comerica Park.

22. TUSCUMBIA

Nestled in the northwest corner of Alabama on the shoals of the Tennessee River, Tuscumbia is rich with history. It was founded in 1820 and was a key part of America's first railroad west of the Allegheny Mountains. It was a key shipping town that used the railroad to move goods around the rapid-filled shoals and back to tame water on the Tennessee.

French traders were the first non-American Indians to visit the area, and between 1815 and 1817, permanent settlers began arriving. In 1820, future president Andrew Jackson, then a general in the army, oversaw completion of a military road connecting Tennessee with Louisiana, passing through Tuscumbia along the way. It became the area's major overland transportation route. The Tennessee River provided the area with another potential transportation route, but a 43-mile stretch of shoals made the river nearly impassable.[1]

The 1820s and 1830s saw an increase in the number of businesses that opened in Tuscumbia. Town business leaders established a steamboat landing and lobbied for creation of a railroad line to bypass the shoals. The line, on the Tuscumbia, Courtland and Decatur (TC&D) Railroad, was completed in 1832; the TC&D Railroad experimented with the use of dry sand as a way to provide traction between the track and the engine's wheels, and this practice remains in use around the world today. Tuscumbia was also an important postal routing center between Nashville and New Orleans. By the 1840s, the town had six stores, three hotels, three cabinet makers, two doctors, a wagon maker, a blacksmith, a horse-powered mill, and a public school. By 1850, Tuscumbia was a major railroad hub for train traffic throughout the South. During the Civil War, this made the town a major target of the Union Army, which destroyed Tuscumbia Landing and other parts of the town. After the war, Tuscumbia experienced renewed growth.[2]

It was there that baseball legend Heinie Manush was born the same year the American League became a major league on July 20, 1901, in Tuscumbia. Manush would grow up to be one of the league's and team's greatest stars, but everything, including baseball, came as a challenge. Manush was the youngest of eight children and faced an uphill battle playing baseball with older kids his whole childhood. Once he became a skilled enough player to think about playing baseball as a career, the challenge was getting out of the South. But Heinie Manush never backed away from a challenge, whether it come from an older brother, an opposing player or even an umpire.

It started in Tuscumbia, which is part of the greater shoals, in a four-city area that includes Muscle Shoals, Sheffield and Florence in the heart of Colbert County. But Tuscumbia is the oldest and most pivotal of the four. Helen Keller was born in Tuscumbia in 1880, five years before the Manush family built their home on East Third Street—a home

The train station in Tuscumbia, Alabama, doesn't look very different from when Heinie Manush grew up there at the turn of the century. The town has a rich history. Manush is the second most famous person to come from there, after Helen Keller (author's collection).

that still houses the name Manush. Walking through Tuscumbia today, there are many similarities to when Heinie Manush walked around his hometown as a child. The population is just 8,423. There is a perfect balance of city, farm land and woodlands. The railroad station is still in the middle of town, just a block away from Keller's home. Both are restored as museums, giving the town that classical and historical feel. Many of the buildings downtown are still standing. Some are refurbished, some aren't. The Southern, elegant houses make it difficult to remember what decade you are in while driving through the tree-canopied streets. White picket fences, porches decorated with ornate fencing and unique windows flood the town. Meanwhile, century-old trees are frequent, providing shade from the Southern sun as well as providing nature's way of showing visitors how old the town is.

Born Henry Emmett Manush at his home on East Third Street in Tuscumbia, Alabama, on July 20, 1901, he picked up the nickname "Heinie" as many Henrys of German descent did in those days. Like many German families, the Manush family began producing baseball players. His father, George Bernard Manush, was born on July 8, 1859, in Germany, according to family sources. He married Catherine Carls, who was born November 1, 1862, and a large and loving family with eight children was in their future. Most of the children were born about two years apart. Frank Benjamin Manush was first, born September 18, 1883. Then came George Herman Manush, born April 5, 1885. The only Manush daughter was Katie Mae Manush, born October 10, 1887. John William Manush was the fourth, born April 11, 1890. Charles Edward Manush was born September 8, 1892. Ernest Matthew joined the ranks on October 8, 1895, then came Harry H. Manush, whose birth date is unknown.

Finally Henry Emmett "Heinie" Manush became the last-born child of the family, and the only one born in the 20th century.[3] Each child was born at the family home at 1005 East Third Street, a home built by their father, George Manush, which has been home just to Manushes. "We lived and grew up in the same house," said Heinie's niece Norma Manush, who lives in the house currently. "His parents built the house. My father and mother moved back in. There have always been Manushes living here."[4]

It wasn't long before all of the Manush boys were playing baseball. It was, after all, the national pastime, and immigrant families were generally quick to migrate to baseball, hoping it would make them feel American. To other ethnicities, it showed that they belong in the United States. There is no documentation of when Heinie Manush fell in love with baseball, or even started playing it, but with six older brothers playing the game, it seems likely he grew up playing baseball from a very young age. Education was very important to immigrant families, and the Manush family was no different. Heinie went to school in Tuscumbia until the eighth grade, when school stopped for boys in Alabama at that time. Since education was seen as very valuable, Heinie, like many boys of the time, went north to attend the Massey Military Academy in Cornersville, Tennessee. "Boys could not go further than eighth grade at the time in Tuscumbia," Norma Manush said. "They went out to work. He went to the military school in Tennessee where a lot of boys went."[5] Like many boys during that time period, Heinie would rather be doing almost anything but going to school. His brother George had a job waiting for him. "He left school and went with his older brother, who had a plumbing business," Norma Manush said. "They ended up at a

Though it has been touched up in recent years, this is the home Heinie Manush was born in and raised in as a child. His niece and nephew still live in the house, which has always housed Manushes (author's collection).

baseball tryout. He was always interested in baseball. He thought his best chance of making the majors was to go out west and get out of the south."

Frank Manush was a third baseman by trade and played for many different town and semi-pro teams before reaching the major leagues with the Philadelphia Athletics in 1908. He played at the big-league level for one season and got into 23 games, batting .156. Ernest played in the minor leagues before becoming a coach in the minors in Columbus, Georgia. "Harry wore glasses, which stopped his career," Norma Manush said. "They were really thick glass at that time." Charlie Manush played on town teams. George, who went on Heinie's first tryout with him, was killed in a car crash in 1923.

"My family (was) athletic," Manush told F. C. Lane of *Baseball Magazine*. "I was one of a group of brothers, all ball players. I had a good build for a batter, I am told. Others no doubt were just as well off or better off. My eyes were always good. Perhaps I can take a little credit for that, for I have always used them well. I have been careful to avoid eye strain. I do not read much, particularly in the evening."[6] Heinie even played in a game against one of his brothers, Harry, according to the family. It was a minor league game with the family in attendance and loud cheering for both from their mother. "She cheered for both teams," Norma Manush said. "People in the stands were saying, 'That woman doesn't know what she is doing,' so she said, 'See that man? That's my son. And see that man? That's my son.' By the end of the game, everybody was rooting for both teams."[7]

Heinie Manush played well enough to get his wish and head west. He started his minor league career the same place that Harry Heilmann did—in Portland, Oregon. Manush played six games in 1920 for Portland of the Pacific Coast League, going 0-for-9. In 1921, he was down to Edmonton of the Western Canada League, a Class B league. Manush got his minor league career rolling by batting .321 in 83 games. His performance merited a trip to the next level in 1922, when he played for Omaha in the Western League, a Class A team (the highest at the time, equivalent to today's AAA). In the first complete season of his professional career, Manush showed everyone a glimpse of what was to come. In 167 games, he batted .376 with 245 hits. He slugged 44 doubles, 20 triples, 20 home runs, good for 389 total bases, and slugged a whopping .597. It was only a matter of time before he would head north.

23. Major League Debut

After a successful season in the minors, Heinie Manush was headed to the big leagues in 1923. He would join one of the strongest hitting teams in the game: Detroit. The Tigers had Ty Cobb coming off a .400 season and Harry Heilmann, two years removed from his first batting title, who finished the 1922 season at .356. Plus three-time RBI champ Bobby Veach was coming off a season in which he batted .327 with 126 RBI.

"Ty Cobb wouldn't even let me bat," Manush recalled of batting practice as a rookie. "Every time I'd go to the plate, Cobb would yell, 'Get outta there, kid.' Finally, Harry Heilmann felt sorry for me and said, 'You can take my turn at bat.'"[1] It was the beginning of a friendship Manush shared with Heilmann and the beginning of Manush's career in the big leagues. It didn't look like Manush was going to see much action in the outfield in 1923 with three legitimate stars roaming the Detroit outfield. All Manush could do was make the most of his opportunities—and he did beginning with his first at-bat. On April 20, 1923, Manush pinch-hit against St. Louis and promptly singled, earning the first hit of his career. Unfortunately, the Tigers lost 5–3 to the Browns.

The Tigers opened at home on April 26 with a new look to Navin Field. The stadium was remodeled with a steel upper deck that stretched from first base around home plate to third base. A crowd of 35,000 was in attendance but went home disappointed after Browns pitcher Urban Shocker beat the Tigers, 4–3. Four days later, the Tigers played with a historic lineup, though no one knew it at the time. It was the first game in which Heilmann, Cobb and Manush started in the outfield together. All three would eventually make the Hall of Fame, and it was similar to when Heilmann first came up and joined Cobb and Sam Crawford. But Manush wasn't yet a regular. The next day (May 1), he didn't play. Bob Fothergill was in left field and hit a game-winning single. He singled in the winning run again the following day and earned some more playing time over Bobby Veach and Manush. All of the outfielders would get plenty of chances the following week thanks to Heilmann, who was suspended by American League President Ban Johnson after an argument with an umpire on May 2. Heilmann, who was hitting an even .500 at the time of the suspension, returned to the lineup on May 8 and was 1-for-2 in an 8–2 loss to Washington. The Tigers desperately needed him back in the lineup after dropping the first four games during his suspension, salvaging the last game behind three hits from Manush and a home run by Cobb.

Heilmann, Cobb and Manush all started for the second time on June 16 in Fenway Park. All three managed a hit for the first time starting together, but the Tigers lost, 9–1. Nevertheless, Manush started in left field much of the rest of the season, with Veach and

Fothergill getting less playing time. The problem was pitching and Cobb was sticking with this lineup as long as he was able. The Tigers were 25–28 and buried in sixth place when Manush joined the lineup. The Tigers were starting to come around, but it was a slow process. The outfield, however, was not the problem and the future Hall of Fame trio continued to bring the big sticks. Heilmann was 3-for-4 with a home run, Manush homered and Cobb added three hits off future Hall of Famer Herb Pennock on June 20 to beat the Yankees, 9–7. Next in town was Chicago. The White Sox used five pitchers and beat the Tigers, 9–8. Strangely, the Tigers scored eight runs without much help from the outfield. Heilmann and Cobb went hitless and Manush managed one hit and scored a run.

Heilmann proved that the game was a fluke as he slammed home runs in the next three games. In the first game, unfortunately, Heilmann's solo shot was the only run scored off future Hall of Famer Red Faber in a 7–1 loss. He and Manush belted homers the next day in a 7–6 win.

Cobb took himself out of the lineup for a couple of games to focus on his managing and give himself a break, inserting Veach back into the lineup. The Tigers won the next two games to move into fifth place. On July 7, the Tigers swept the Athletics in a doubleheader, 9–6 and 5–3, to move into a third-place tie at 34–26. Heilmann homered in the second game.

Bobby Veach was hitting well for the Tigers and Cobb wanted to keep

Heinie Manush joined the Detroit Tigers in 1923 and immediately made an impact, batting .334. With Ty Cobb and Harry Heilmann already in the outfield, Manush needed to make this kind of first impression to break in to the all-Hall of Fame outfield (National Baseball Hall of Fame Library, Cooperstown, New York).

him in the lineup. He moved Heilmann to first base, so Veach, Cobb and Manush could all be in the lineup in the outfield. The first game was disastrous. For the first time, Heilmann, Manush and Cobb all went hitless and the Tigers lost to Philadelphia, 7–5. All three managed hits the next game and Heilmann homered, but the Tigers lost again, 6–5. Heilmann homered again the next day and the Tigers finally won, 7–3, against the Red Sox, then took the second game of the doubleheader, 5–1.

Detroit split the next four games before Cobb had enough of the lineup. He took himself back out of the lineup, moved Heilmann back to right field and kept Veach in center.

Heilmann struggled while at first base and his average dropped from .416 to .392. The Tigers crawled back to .500 (44–44) on July 25 for the first time since June 6 (22–22). Heilmann pinch-hit again the next day—the last day of the season—and helped the Tigers win 7–6 and hang on to second place. They edged Cleveland by a half-game, 83–71 to 82–71. It was Manush who won the game for Detroit, slamming a double and a homer and scoring twice.

Heilmann won his second batting crown with a .403 average, ten points ahead of Babe Ruth. Manush proved he deserved a place in the lineup with a .334 mark. It was a sign of big things to come.

Ty Cobb saw something in Heinie Manush during his rookie season. He saw a Southerner with a fiery temper and a great presence at the plate. It reminded him of himself almost 20 years earlier. Detroit management saw Manush's potential, too, and with Harry Heilmann and Ty Cobb continuing to win batting titles in the outfield, the Tigers traded Bobby Veach to the Boston Red Sox to make room for Manush to play regularly. It was a decision with mixed reviews since Veach was a fan favorite in Detroit who had led the league in RBI three times and batted .321 in 1923, albeit in a more limited role. Manush was the future, and after 12 strong years in Detroit, Veach was the past.

The Tigers opened the 1924 season on April 15 against Cleveland. Heilmann picked up right where he left off and went 2-for-3 with a walk and a run scored as Hooks Dauss pitched Detroit to a 4–3 victory. The Tigers beat future Hall of Famer Stan Coveleski, 5–1, the next day behind a home run and three RBI by Heilmann. For the first month of the season, Heilmann was the only one hitting. Manush was batting under .200 and no one else was steadily driving runs in for Detroit. Winning enough to hang in the race, Detroit was back in third place after a loss to Philadelphia June 10. The Yankees traveled to Navin Field for the first time of the season and Earl Whitehill outdueled Joe Bush, 7–2, as the Tigers jumped from third to first with one victory (28–22). Detroit lost the next three to the Yankees to plummet back to third place, but swept Boston in four games and was back in first place on June 18.

The Tigers remained close all season but finished 86–68, six games behind the pennant-winning Senators. Detroit had the hard luck of facing either the Yankees or Senators every time they reached first place or got on a roll in 1924. Instead of rising to the occasion, the Tigers folded and watched as Washington won the pennant and the World Series—the only championship the nation's capital has ever seen.

Manush's average dropped from .334 to .289 in 1924 with 24 doubles and 68 RBI, and with Bobby Veach batting .295 with 99 RBI for the Red Sox, Tigers fans were wondering if the team made the right move.

The Tigers were a little disappointed in what they saw from Heinie Manush in his sophomore season. His average had dropped 45 points to .289 and meanwhile, the man they traded to make outfield room for Manush—Bobby Veach—batted .295 with 99 RBI for Boston.

Manush was eager to get to spring training and show the Tigers they made the right move by keeping him. Even though Detroit had made room for Manush, he did not have a solidified starting position in 1925, unlike Harry Heilmann and Ty Cobb. Manush would have to win a starting spot over Bob Fothergill, who had also been a part-time outfielder for Detroit and batted over .300 his first three years. Manush did his part as a starting outfielder at the beginning of the 1925 season, getting at least one hit in his first seven games (13 total) to bat .433 during the stretch. His pace fell back into the .300s, but never below. He slapped two doubles and a single on August 4, scoring two runs in a 3–2 victory over Washington, his best game of the season. He finished with a .302 average for the season, but played in just 99 games, thanks to a .353 performance by Bob Fothergill and another batting title for Harry Heilmann.

Unfortunately for the Tigers, their pitching was not at the same level as their hitting. Detroit batted .302 as a team but finished a distant fourth, 16½ games behind the pennant-winning Senators. Washington advanced to its second consecutive World Series, but this time did not claim the championship. It was the last time the Senators would reach the World Series until 1933, when Manush would play an integral role.

24. ANOTHER BATTING CHAMPION

The 1926 season was an odd one for the Tigers. They continued to hit—highlighted by their carousel of outfielders—and returned to an above-.500 finish at 79–75. Astonishingly, that mark was good for just sixth place, as the American League was full of sluggers, giving every team a chance to score at will. The Tigers were one of those teams, scoring 793 runs, but the pitching staff allowed 830. Despite coming off a .300 season the year before, Heinie Manush started the season on the bench, giving way to player/manager Ty Cobb, Harry Heilmann and Bob Fothergill in the outfield. Manush did chip in immediately as a pinch-hitter, connecting for three hits in his first five at-bats of the season, all off the bench. Manush was used as a pinch-hitter in 16 of his first 32 games. But Cobb was slowing down and knew the best thing for the team was to split up more of the outfield playing time. "I can still hit over .300 and my legs aren't stiff yet," Cobb told the *Birmingham News*. "But the outfielders I have are set for a big year and should have the chance. It would be unjust to keep Manush and Fothergill on the bench much of the time."[1]

Manush got his first start on April 26 and connected for his first home run of the season, but it was Detroit's lone run in a 5–1 loss to the Chicago White Sox. Manush went hitless the next four days and his average plummeted to .222. He remained in the .200s for a month, getting just 18 hits in his next 25 games. "You had to get your hits to stay there," Manush remembered. "Two hitless games in a row and you were on the bench."[2] But in June, the weather got hot and so did Manush. Beginning June 13, Manush went 16-for-33 to surge past the .300 plateau at .311. On June 13, he laced a pair of hits against the Boston Red Sox, then duplicated the feat the following day. Manush finished the series with three hits at home against the Sox, and he was up to .282.

The Philadelphia Athletics came to town next and Manush picked up right where he left off against Boston, slamming three hits in the opener, including a home run. He drove in three runs and his average was finally approaching .300 at .296. A hit in each of the following two games brought him to .301, but he was just getting started. He pounded two hits in the series finale with Philadelphia, then had a pair of hits in both games of a two-game set against the St. Louis Browns. It capped a 13-game hitting streak, which pushed Manush's average all the way up to .317.

Unlike his previous streaks, however, this one didn't end for Manush. He had four multi-hit games in his next seven, then leapt into the batting race with two consecutive four-hit games on July 1–2. On July 1, he slammed a homer, two triples and a double with three runs scored and three RBI, but the Tigers lost to Cleveland, 11–6. The following day, Manush slapped three singles and a double to lead the Tigers to a 9–3 win over the Indians.

Unlike a lot of sluggers of the day, Manush choked up on the bat, holding it further from the handle. "I do that," he told F. C. Lane in *Baseball Magazine* following the season.

> Because if I swing from the handle, I'm inclined to pull the ball too much into right field. That's not a bad stunt either, if you can drive it to the bleachers. But I'm not that kind of hitter. I hit more line drives and I get better results by driving the ball straight out than I do pulling it into right field.... Real batting is meeting the ball on the nose and driving it straight and hard. It isn't fancy foot work or lucky breaks. But those things all play a heavy part in averages. I believe some sport writer might open up a new field if he kept track of the number of balls that a batter hit hard, right on the nose, whether or not they went safe. That would give a better report of a player's batting ability than any other system of records.[3]

Wherever the ball was going, Manush was hitting it a ton this summer, earning the playing time despite a strong year from Al Wingo, who batted .370 with 104 runs in the Detroit outfield. With a three-hit game on the Fourth of July, his average soared to .347—and he was just getting started. Beginning on July 16, Manush had his best two weeks of the season. He started a 12-game hitting streak with a stunning ten multi-hit games. On that first day, he had two hits and two RBI against the New York Yankees. Detroit then traveled to Philadelphia, where Manush's bat got hotter with nine hits in the four-game series, including a home run in the finale.

The Tigers then moved to the nation's capital for six games. Manush was just warming up. He had five hits in the July 21 doubleheader, four hits the next game, three in the fourth game against future Hall of Famer Stan Coveleski, one in the fifth game and two in the finale to total 15 hits in the six games. He finished the 12-game hitting streak with a single back at home against Boston. When it was all said and done, he was 27-for-56 and his average was a shocking .370. In a month, his average had soared 56 points—130 points in a two-month span. Not bad for someone who wasn't even in the starting lineup on Opening Day.

With the Tigers well out of the American League race by August, the only question that remained was: Could Manush keep up the hitting and hold off Babe Ruth for the batting title? His teammate Harry Heilmann held off Ruth four years before to win, but then Ruth beat him out the following year. Ty Cobb had 12 batting titles to his name. Heilmann returned to the top in 1925, but could Manush become the third Detroit Tigers outfielder to capture the crown?

Manush rattled off seven straight multi-hit games from August 6–12 to push his league-leading mark to .381. He pounded three hits against Washington, driving in three, before New York came to town. Offensive numbers were climbing in the 1920s, but there were still some dominant pitchers in the American League. Two of them were on the Yankees. Manush greeted future Hall of Fame lefty Herb Pennock with three hits and an RBI, then pounded two hits off of future Hall of Famer Waite Hoyt on August 8. After another two-hit performance, Manush clubbed a home run and a single off Urban Shocker. He hit another home run against Tom Zachary in the first game in St. Louis. It was his high point of the season. Manush dipped a little, but remained in the .370s the rest of the way. But Ruth remained hot on his trail.

The race came down to the final three games with Manush and Ruth still batting. Manush was coming off a hitless game on September 21 and was at .370. Ruth, who had been as high as .396 in late June, entered the final three games at .368. Manush, playing at home, slapped three hits against Philadelphia to move to .372 while Ruth, playing in St. Louis, had two hits to move up to .369. The Babe connected again with a 3-for-4 performance, including two home runs, the following day and was at .372. But Manush responded with his best game of the season—a 4-for-5 performance with four runs scored as the Tigers rolled to an 11–2 win over Boston. Manush jumped to .377 to lock up the title. He had two more hits in the season finale and finished at .378, six points ahead of Ruth.

Although he got only one at-bat in 17 different games, mostly at the beginning of the season, Manush had an astonishing 62 multi-hit games. He totaled just 188 hits for the season and had 14 home runs and 86 RBI. He scored 95 runs and finished fifth in the Most Valuable Player voting. Cleveland's George Burns won the award. Chicago's Johnny Mostil finished second, followed by Pennock and Washington outfielder Sam Rice. Manush's teammate Harry Heilmann finished tied for fifth with him, each garnering 16 votes. His bursts of power were enough to make up for his lack of playing time in April and May, giving him the batting title in September.

As fiery as Manush was on the field, he preferred to stay out of the limelight off of it—even in his hometown. As Tuscumbia prepared a hero's welcome for the new batting champion, Manush found out and made other plans. "The town went to the depot to meet him after he won the batting title and he was coming home. He got wind of it and got off the train early," niece Norma Manush said.[4]

Heilmann and Fothergill tied for fourth place in the American League at .367. Meanwhile, Cobb's eyes began to bother him, and he was out with other injuries; he took part in only 79 games and hit .339. It was one of the most disappointing seasons for Cobb, after which he left the Tigers. He joined the Athletics to finish his career with two seasons in Philadelphia.

But for Manush, it was just the beginning. At age 25, he had arrived. He was a batting champion and had a long career ahead of him. "One thing, the big thing that I gained, was confidence," Manush told F. C. Lane of *Baseball Magazine*.

> No one ever won a Batting Championship without confidence in his ability to hit. In fact, I'll say that once you lose confidence in yourself, you're not hitting. There's something wrong. It may be some little peculiarity of swing or stance that you've unconsciously fallen into. Or it may be purely mental, like the fear of a certain pitcher, a dread that he has something on you, that he'll cross you up. There are a lot of good hitters in this League. Anybody who beats out the field, no matter how lucky he may be, must be hitting about right. There is a fine edge to your work that you can feel but can't describe. You're swinging true, you're timing your swing, you're meeting the ball on the nose. When you lose that fine edge, things begin to happen. You start hitting a little late or a little too soon. Almost anything will cut down a batting average when you're up there in the .370s.[5]

Manush continued to break down his season, with his ability to hit lefties being key.

> Some people have claimed that last year I hit above my proper form. Perhaps I did. I don't know. Naturally I hope not. And it would be peculiar, to say the least, if a fellow at 25 reached a point in batting that he could never hope to equal again. It doesn't seem probable, for I always was classed as a good hitter. In the Minors I certainly hit over .300. Only once in the four years I have been with Detroit have I slumped under .300.... I always felt I was a good hitter. Of course I didn't expect to be a Champion.... I thought that was beyond me. Last year, I discovered that it wasn't beyond me.... Last year was my first full season in this League. By that I mean it was the first time I have been allowed to hit

against all kinds of pitching. I am a left handed batter and a theory developed in Major League baseball that left handed batters are to be benched when left handed pitchers are on the slab. There's a certain amount of sense to that theory. Beyond doubt port side hurlers do bother left handed batters. Even Cobb, with all his years of experience, admits they bother him now. But that never kept him from hitting against them and from breaking all the records that one fellow could break over a period of twenty years.... I do not set myself up as a leading authority on batting. I certainly wouldn't want to put my own individual judgment against the managerial experience of the two Big Leagues. But for all that, I'll make one statement and stick to it. A left handed hitter, who's naturally a good hitter, will fare better, in the long run, if they'll let him stay in there and face the pitchers just as they come. His work may slump a little at first, when the left handers are on the mound. But he'll get on to them and his all around average will improve. That's what happened to me last year and that's why I won the Batting Championship.[6]

While Harry Heilmann had won three batting titles followed by a significant drop in his average the next year, Heinie Manush was hoping to avoid the same fate in 1927 after capturing his first title. Ironically, Heilmann won his fourth batting title in 1927—all in odd years. Unfortunately for Manush, a drop was inevitable after winning a batting title. But how far would he drop? By May 9, Manush was down to .282, but he surged to .353 by May 22. The roller coaster season was on for Manush, who steadily dropped first to .320 on May 29, then .310 after going hitless the following game. On June 23, he was at an even .300 and spiraled down to .283 six days later. He returned to .300 for much of the season but finished at .298— an astonishing 80-point drop from his batting title the year before. It wasn't a horrible season by any means. Manush slapped 177 hits, scored 102 runs and knocked in 90 runs.

Heinie Manush became the third Detroit Tigers outfielder to claim a batting title in the first quarter-century of the American League. Manush batted .378 in 1926 to lead the league. His feat was sandwiched between two batting titles by teammate Harry Heilmann (National Baseball Hall of Fame Library, Cooperstown, New York).

For the Tigers, though, it wouldn't have mattered if Manush was hitting at his previous season's pace. Detroit had a strong season, finishing 82–71 but a whopping 27½ games behind the New York Yankees, whose batting lineup was dubbed "Murderer's Row" with future Hall of Famers Earle Combs, Babe Ruth, Lou Gehrig and Tony

Lazzeri punishing American League pitching. The Yankees scored a stunning 975 runs and allowed just 599.

The Tigers didn't know what to expect out of Manush. They had seen a remarkable batting performance from him in 1926, but it was bookended by two average seasons. The Tigers had plenty of hitting with Heilmann and Fothergill. With the need of pitching still at the forefront, Manush found himself expendable. He also made himself expendable by not getting along with new manager George Moriarty. Following the season, on December 13, Manush was traded with first baseman Lu Blue to the St. Louis Browns for pitcher Elam Vangilder, outfielder Harry Rice and infielder Chick Galloway.

It would turn out to be one of the most lopsided trades in Tigers history. Vangilder went 11–11 in two years in Detroit while Rice batted .300 in a part-time outfielder's role and Galloway played just 53 games and batted .264 for the Tigers.

Meanwhile, Blue would score 116 runs for the Browns in 1928 and add two more 100-run seasons before his career ended. And Manush? Well, at age 26, he was just getting started.

25. THE ST. LOUIS YEARS

Heinie Manush was reeling. Just one year after becoming the American League batting champion at age 25, the Detroit Tigers found him expendable and sent him to the St. Louis Browns. The Tigers didn't think Manush was consistent enough, and he would play the 1928 season with a huge chip on his shoulder. He wanted to show the Tigers what they would be missing and responded with perhaps the best season of his career. The season would also generate a new personal rivalry for Manush—one that would last the rest of his career.

The season got off to a rather fitting start as the Browns opened in Detroit. In fact, St. Louis would play the Tigers seven of its first ten games, giving Manush an ample and instant opportunity for some payback for the trade.

On Opening Day, April 11, Manush rapped a single and double off Josh Billings, scoring two runs in the Browns' 4–1 victory over the Tigers. St. Louis first baseman Lu Blue, who came over from Detroit with Manush, drove in two of the Browns' runs. The following day, Manush kept up his hitting with a single, a run scored and an RBI in a 7–2 win. In the third game, he doubled and scored to help the Browns win, 4–3, and sweep the Tigers at Navin Field to open the season.

The 1928 season couldn't have began any worse for Manush and the Browns and it would get better—but not right away. After losing two of three in Chicago, the Browns hosted Detroit for their home opener. Manush drove in the lone run for the Browns in his debut in front of the home crowd, but the Tigers won, 4–1, then took the next two games of the series. But Manush rallied the Browns in the series finale with two singles, a double, two runs scored and an RBI and St. Louis won, 5–2. It vaulted Manush's average back over .300 and got him back on track. Early in May, Manush fell back below .300, but on May 7, slammed four hits against the Washington Senators to jump from .297 to .318. He scored four runs and drove in another as the Browns walloped the Senators, 15–2. Manush, while showing flashes of brilliance, was starting to show those same signs of inconsistency he had in Detroit. But as in his batting championship season, Manush turned up the heat just as the summer heat turned up. He went 9-for-16 in a four-game stretch from June 2–7 to soar from .328 to .347 and put himself smack dab in the middle of the batting race.

The leader at this point was Leon "Goose" Goslin of the Washington Senators. The slugging outfielder was getting hits at a .407 clip on June 6. Manush, who had been friendly rivals with teammate Harry Heilmann in Detroit, would now have a rival in an opponent. In fact, he and Goslin would cross paths on several occasions and would forever be linked in the minds of many baseball fans. Manush needed another surge to challenge Goslin,

Heinie Manush was traded from the Detroit Tigers to the St. Louis Browns along with Lu Blue for Harry Rice and Elam Vangilder prior to the 1928 season. His first season on the Browns, Manush proved the trade a bad one for Detroit as he led the league with 241 hits and was second in batting average at .378 (National Baseball Hall of Fame Library, Cooperstown, New York).

but it would have to wait. Manush hovered in the .330–.340 range for more than a month.

After staying consistent around .340 for that long, it was only a matter of time before Manush went on a streak. On July 23, Heinie went 4-for-5 with three RBI in a 10–0 win over Cleveland. He lashed out four more hits with four RBI the next game in Washington—right in front of Goslin. It was a statement that Goslin would not run away with the batting title. But Manush had his work cut out for him, since Goslin's two hits put him at .397.

Manush still trailed by 30 points at the end of August, but two things happened to even things out. First of all, Manush was ready for another streak. Secondly, Goslin finally started to cool off after hovering around .400 most of the season.

As September began, Manush knew he had to make his move quickly since he had more than 30 points to make up. Wouldn't you know, the Browns were facing the Tigers as the month began. Manush slapped two hits in each of the next two games, beginning a streak where he would have 13 multi-hit games in a 15-game stretch—including two four-hit games. With a three-hit performance against the Yankees on September 18, Manush had boosted his average all the way to .371 and a tie for first place with Goslin, who had lost close to 20 points during the previous three weeks. On September 23, Manush went 4-for-5 against Philadelphia and surged ahead to .374—one point ahead of Goslin. But Goslin slammed three hits the next day to jump back ahead, .376 to .373, following Manush's 1-for-5 performance. It would all come down to the final series, and as fate would have it, Manush and Goslin would be going at it head-to-head as the Browns hosted the Senators for the final four games.

Goslin held a .375–.374 lead after Manush had two hits and Goslin one in the opener, a 6–5 Washington win on September 27. The next day, Manush laced three hits and Goslin managed just two to tie the race at .377 with two games to go. Goslin moved up to .379 with two hits in the third game while Manush remained at .377 after going 1-for-2. The title came down to the final game of the season. Goslin was two points ahead, which was easily in reach for Manush if he had a big day. With two points close enough to make up,

Goslin didn't have the option of sitting the last game out either. If he did, and Manush went 3-for-4, he would lose the title.

Players on both teams wanted to help their respective teammate win the title, and the umpiring crew was fully aware of the close battle, including the man who would get the assignment to work behind the plate for the final game of the season—Bill Guthrie. Goslin struck out and grounded out the first two times he came to the plate, then got hold of one and sent it over the center field fence. But in his next at bat he grounded out to fall three-tenths of a point behind. Manush, however, made an out in his last at bat to give Goslin a one-point lead. With the game headed into the top of the ninth, Goslin was due to bat. A note came to the dugout from the press box updating Goslin on the batting race, with the author including his advice to sit out the at bat, reminding him if he batted and made an out he would lose the title. Joe Judge warned him Manush might think he was yellow if a pinch hitter batted for him. The other players got involved in the conference, with everyone giving his opinion, and as the debate went on Goslin made a decision. He would bat. In no time Goslin was in trouble with two strikes, no balls, and his batting title in jeopardy. He thought of an idea to save his title: if he could make the umpire angry enough to throw him out of the game, he therefore wouldn't be charged with an out and would preserve the batting title. And what better umpire was there than Bill Guthrie, who had a short fuse, and was known to be quick to eject a player.... "Why those weren't even close," Goslin told Guthrie. "Listen, wise guy, there's no such thing as close or not close. It's either dis or dat," responded Guthrie. Goslin responded by acting mad; he yelled, stepped on Guthrie's big feet, and called him names. Guthrie waited for Goslin to finish before speaking. "OK, are you ready to bat now? You are not going to get thrown out of this ball game no matter what you do, so you might as well get up to the plate. If I wanted to throw you out, I'd throw you to Oshkosh. But you are going to bat, and you better be up there swinging. No bases on balls, do you hear me?" He heard him all right. The next pitch Goslin swung and hit a fly ball to right-center field. Browns right fielder Beauty McGowan, knowing if he made the catch Manush would win the batting title, ran hard, reached out with his glove hand, but couldn't get the ball in time, and when the ball landed on the outfield grass Goslin won the batting title.[1]

The new rivals had matched each other most of the season and would match each other on that final day. Both Manush and Goslin tallied a pair of hits, which gave Goslin the batting title by the slimmest of margins—.379 to .378. "Bucky Harris, my manager, left it up to me whether to bat or win sitting down," Goslin said later. He decided to sit down, was goaded into going to the plate, tried to get ejected from the game and finally got a "lucky hit" to beat out Manush by a fraction. "It was the closest finish in American League history, as far as I know, and there was something about the two of us, in the same park on the same day, battling it out, that made it a great afternoon, even if I had to lose," Manush wrote in an article for the *Chicago Daily News* later in *Baseball Digest*. "The boys tried to cheer me up by saying the official records wouldn't be out until December and maybe I was tied or something ... but I knew Goose had made it. Goose and I played on a pennant team for Washington five years later, but neither of us ever mentioned that game in St. Louis."[2]

Manush did lead the league with 241 hits and 47 doubles. He drove in 108 runs and finished second in the American League MVP voting to Philadelphia catcher Mickey Cochrane, who batted .293 for the second-place Athletics. The Browns finished third, but it was an interesting vote since the Athletics did not win the pennant and Manush had such a dominating year. Also strange was the fact that Goslin finished sixth in the voting.

At age 27, Manush had experienced many ups and downs in the big leagues. Two years after narrowly beating Babe Ruth out for the AL batting crown, Manush was on the other end of it. But even though he didn't earn his second batting championship, he proved to the Browns, the Tigers, and most importantly, himself, that he was back and would be a contender in the batting race every year.

Entering the 1929 season, Manush was coming off the best season of his career and wanted to avoid a relapse like he had following his batting title in 1926. Manush had put his inconsistencies behind him and had another strong season, batting .355 to finish third in the league. The Browns finished fourth in the American League in 1929 and were looking for bigger things as the 1930s began. The power had shifted from the New York Yankees to the Philadelphia Athletics, who were in the middle of winning three straight AL pennants. The Browns were hoping to be the next in line.

But the opposite happened. In 1930, the Browns plummeted to sixth place. Manush was hitting .328 in June but had only 29 RBI in 49 games. St. Louis needed more punch in its lineup if it wanted to be a contender. Manush was a high-average hitter, but was more of a table-setter than an RBI man. This again made Manush expendable and on June 13, in a mid-season trade, he was sent with Alvin "General" Crowder to Washington for his rival Goose Goslin. Goslin had his off year in 1929, batting just .288 one year after his batting title. But in 1930, he was having a better season.

It turned out to be a good deal on paper for both teams. Crowder, who had gone 3–7 for St. Louis, went 15–9 the rest of the way for the Senators. For St. Louis, Goslin did exactly what they wanted—drive in runs. In 101 games with the Browns, Goslin drove in a stunning 100 runs and batted .326 to finish at .308 for the season. Meanwhile, Manush again got hotter as the temperature got hotter and batted .350 with 100 runs scored, 94 RBI, 194 hits and 49 doubles. Adding a formidable hitter and pitcher gave Washington a couple of big pieces for a pennant winner that was a couple of years away. So again, even though it didn't seem like it at the time, Manush would take advantage of being in demand by joining a contender.

26. FINALLY A CONTENDER

For the second time in his career, Heinie Manush put together a dominating season at the plate only to be traded. Always ready to shove it back in former teams' faces, Manush now had two teams on that list: Detroit and St. Louis. But the ever-aggressive Manush had something bigger going for him: He was joining a contender in 1931.

It was one of the first blockbuster trades in American League history: Manush and General Crowder for Goose Goslin. Two future Hall of Fame outfielders switching teams in their prime. That sort of deal didn't happen every day (the first big trade like this was after the 1926 season when the St. Louis Cardinals traded second baseman/manager Rogers Hornsby to the New York Giants for second baseman Frankie Frisch). So how did it happen? "The trade of Goslin, who was popular with the fans and a personal favorite of [Clark] Griffith, occasioned something of a heart wrench, but he wasn't hitting and Manush was," Shirley Povich of the *Washington Post* wrote in his book: *The Washington Senators*.

It was a well-known fact that Goslin didn't see eye to eye with manager Walter Johnson. But that still wasn't enough reason to get rid of your best player. Usually when that happens, it is the manager that is let go. But the more important question was: why were the Browns willing to give up their best hitter AND best pitcher for Goslin?

The baseball world was baffled and wondered what Phil Ball was thinking. Goslin for Manush was considered an even trade, but to get a pitcher of Crowder's caliber put another feather in the cap of the "Old Fox" (Griffith). Walter Johnson was thrilled and had a big smile when he spoke with the sportswriters. "I am very pleased with the deal. I believe Manush will prove just the man we need to hit us to the pennant. We have a good club. Its record proves it. With a little more punch we'll have a great ball club, and I look to Manush to provide us with the extra punch...." "We're going to win the pennant as sure as I'm a foot high," said Manush.[1]

> There was a new opinion of Manush, who won the admiration of the Washington fans after playing on an injured ankle, sustained against New York when rookie third baseman Ben Chapman landed on him as he slid into third base. The Big Guy had made thirty-eight hits in ninety-five at bats for a .400 batting average since joining Washington, and he continued to win the fans when they heard he made three hits, including a home run, in Washington's win at Boston. Suddenly Manush was becoming as popular as Goslin, and the old cheer of "Come on, Goose" was now "Come on, Heinie."... Red Sox manager Heinie Wagner told the press he believed he saw the best team in the league. "The addition of Manush assures them of the pennant." But as happy as he was about the deal, Manush held out for more money, much to the chagrin of Washington owner Clark Griffith....

He soon came to terms with Griffith, and the sweet-swinging outfielder arrived in Biloxi in time to practice and play the entire exhibition season. When he arrived he made a loud entrance and gave his teammates a slap on the back. Griffith cringed when he felt Manush strike his bad back, but didn't seem to mind. He was happy to see his best hitter.[2]

The Washington Senators had been a mediocre team from the beginning of the century but put it together behind legendary pitcher Walter Johnson and kid manager Bucky Harris to win back-to-back pennants in 1924–25, claiming the World Series title in 1924. Johnson had retired by 1931 but served as the team's manager. Surprisingly, it was hitting, not pitching, that led the Senators under The Big Train. Shortstop Joe Cronin would knock in 126 runs and bat .306 in 1931 while another future Hall of Famer, Sam Rice, batted over .300 in the outfield. Second baseman Buddy Myer batted .293, outfielder Sam West batted .333, and the Senators also got solid performances from third baseman Ossie Bluege with 98 RBI and first baseman Joe Kuhel with 85 RBI. Manush fit right in and batted .307—a down year for him—but was third on a team that finished 92–62 in third place in the American League.

After playing second fiddle to the New York Yankees throughout the 1920s, the Senators were now third fiddle, as the Philadelphia Athletics had captured three consecutive pennants. It was frustrating for the Senators, who had put together a solid team. After they fell behind the Yankees again in 1932, tensions rose between the two teams. Things came to a head on the Fourth of July, and hot-headed Heinie Manush ended up right in the middle of it. But it began at home plate, after Washington outfielder Carl Reynolds slid in safely after a collision with Yankees catcher Bill Dickey.

Reynolds was punched by Bill Dickey while umpires were not looking. After the collision at the plate, which Reynolds was safe on July 4, 1932 ... then ... after ducking [Johnny] Allen's knockdown pitch, Myer belted a double and later in the inning tallied the first run of the game. In the third inning Allen delivered a pitch that struck Myer in the right elbow. Myer was in pain and the game was delayed for five minutes while Walter Johnson and Mike Martin attended to him. The tough second baseman remained in the game, took his base, and the game continued. The next batter was Heinie Manush, and he hit one over the right field wall. As Myer rounded third base, he shouted [at Allen].... After three innings Washington led 6–0, and Myer wouldn't have to worry about Allen since he was removed from the game, and on his way to his second loss of the season. The Yankees, however, weren't finished with Myer, and in the fourth inning, Gehrig knocked him down with a hard slide into second base. Myer retaliated an inning later by purposely chopping one to the pitcher, and as he approached first base slid with his spikes up and ripped Gehrig's trousers. Myer quickly got up in anticipation of a fight, but the Yankees first baseman gave a good-natured smile and said nothing. An inning later Babe Ruth knocked down Myer with a hard slide. Manush, fed up with the Yankees' going after Myer, decided to retaliate, and after hitting a triple he slid into third base and sent third baseman Joe Sewell backpedaling ten feet. When the game ended, with a 12–6 Washington win to complete the double-header sweep, the question was how long Dickey would be suspended.... He was suspended 30 games and fined $1,000."[3]

True to Manush's form, in 1932 he rebounded to have another monster year, despite his frustrations on the field. He led the Senators with a .342 batting average, 214 hits, 121 runs and 116 RBI. But the Senators finished almost exactly the same as the year before, this time posting a 93–61 record under Johnson.

It was hardly a season to look down on. Thirty-two games over .500 is quite an accomplishment. But owner Clark Griffith wanted to get back to the World Series, so an identical record didn't cut it. Johnson was out as manager and just like in 1924, when Griffith hired the young Bucky Harris, he turned to his young shortstop Joe Cronin to take over the reigns in 1933. It was a good formula to stick with.

27. 1933: The Pennant

The Washington Senators made a couple of major moves to bolster the team in 1933. First of all, they fired Walter Johnson as manager and replaced him with shortstop Joe Cronin. This opened up another key piece of the puzzle as Griffith, looking to get his best player back, was able to trade for Goose Goslin, who had earlier been shipped to St. Louis because he didn't get along with Johnson. Goslin was traded with Fred Schulte and Lefty Stewart to the Senators for Lloyd Brown, Carl Reynolds and Sam West, along with $20,000. So now, for the first time, rivals Heinie Manush and Goose Goslin would be teammates in the same outfield.

It was eerily similar to Manush playing in the same outfield with Ty Cobb in Detroit. Manush and Goslin were two of the best hitters in the game and both had tempers. But just like in Detroit with Cobb, they drove each other to succeed—mostly because they wanted to be better than their counterpart. Don't forget manager Joe Cronin, who was still the shortstop and out to prove he could do both jobs at a high level. And his temper was there with the best of them.

However, Manush injured his wrist after nine games and was forced to the bench on April 23. As feisty as Manush was, he didn't last the whole game on the pine. Itching to get into the action while watching his team fall behind, Manush got his chance to pinch-hit in the bottom of the ninth inning. The move paid off as Manush lined one past Gehrig and into right field. Ruth looked all of his 38 years as he chased the ball "at a snail's pace." Cronin scored the tying run and Manush made it all the way to third base. A few batters later, Cronin called on 43-year-old Sam Rice to pinch-hit, and he came through with a single to score Manush with the winning run.[1]

Manush was back in the starting lineup the next day and laced two hits to raise his average to .341. Just as in the previous year, Manush's temper got hot, as did his hitting. It happened against his former team, the Detroit Tigers, on May 7. Manush ended up getting in the face of first baseman Hank Greenberg, who was nearly twice his size.

[Firpo] Marberry fired a three-hitter in Detroit's 7–1 win, but it did not happen without controversy. The Senators complained about Marberry using his sweat to create spitballs, and also charged that Hank Greenberg was cutting the cover of the baseball with his belt buckle. Heinie Manush retaliated by kicking Greenberg's mitt as it lay on the ground between innings. Greenberg yelled at Manush, and Washington's left fielder fired back. After the inning Cronin gave Greenberg a piece of his mind, and then Marberry took matters into his own hands by throwing one close to Manush. Washington's big left fielder walked towards the pitcher, and Marberry walked towards the plate. Before the two came to blows home plate umpire Red Ormsby stepped between the two big guys and instructed them to return to their positions.[2]

It was that kind of fire that sparked strong play by the Senators. They were hot on the heels of the Yankees. Manush continued to swing a hot bat, beginning on May 25. He slapped two hits against his former team, the St. Louis Browns, and led the team to a 7–2 victory. It was the start of a pretty impressive streak.

Manush was the hottest hitter on the team, and the American League. After going five for five in the second game against Philadelphia, his consecutive-game hitting streak increased to nineteen…. The only things hotter than the St. Louis weather were the bats of the Washington Senators. The Senators rallied for six runs in the top of the ninth in a 10–3 win, with the heart of the batting order, Goslin-Manush-Cronin (2-3-4), combining for seven hits. As legendary writer Shirley Povich viewed the Washington trio's performance from the press box, he decided they needed a nickname, and he came up with "the Old Washington Wrecking Crew." On June 19 Washington … came back to pound the St. Louis pitchers for twenty-two hits, with four leaving the yard, in a 10–4 win. Cronin, who was red hot, pounded out five hits, and Manush, who had seventeen multi-hit games in his last twenty-six contests, batting .444 during that stretch, also had five hits.[3]

Manush capped his streak with four hits, including a home run, in a 7–3 win over the White Sox at Comiskey Park on June 23. It was his 26th consecutive game with a hit, and the streak was snapped the following day, although Manush did score a run in a 7–5 victory over Chicago. Manush batted .440 with 30 runs scored during this streak.

The most staggering thing was that it would not be the longest hitting streak for Manush that season. On the Fourth of July, the Senators were ahead of the Yankees by a half-game, thanks in large part to Manush. But the season wasn't quite half over and Washington faced New York head-to-head in a holiday doubleheader at Yankee Stadium. With the first game tied, 5–5, after nine innings, Manush doubled and Cronin singled him in to give the Senators the victory in the opener. In the nightcap, Manush singled and scored to lead the Senators to a 3–2 victory to sweep the series.

The Senators swept the Yankees. Six thousand loyal fans bypassed the fireworks for the opportunity to greet their team at Union Station. Heinie Manush, who surprisingly was not among the eighteen players picked to represent the American League in Chicago, was the first to appear, and as the crowd went wild, he kissed his wife, then was led to a microphone to say a few words for the radio audience. He spoke about the pennant, and said hello to his three blonde-haired daughters.[4]

As July drew to a close, the Senators were still neck-and-neck with the Yankees, dropping a half-game behind them in the standings. Disgusted at falling out of first place, Manush took matters into his own hands, starting another hitting streak that, in the end, would be even more impressive than his first.

The streak started against one of Manush's former teams, this time the Detroit Tigers on July 22. Manush went 1-for-3 in a 4–3 win. The next day, he singled and tripled against his former mates. The streak continued into August, where on August 8, he fouled off six straight pitches before hitting a home run to extend his streak to 16 games. That performance jumpstarted his teammates too, and they went on a streak.

On August 20, Manush pounded four hits and drove in three runs against the Browns and Washington won, 4–3, to sweep a doubleheader and cap a string of 13 straight victories. The win streak had stunningly vaulted the Senators 8½ games ahead of the Yankees, who couldn't match the intensity Washington brought to the park every day. Manush was hitting against everybody, but seemed to save his best games for the Browns and Tigers, maybe a little payback for the trades. The next game, the Senators went from St. Louis to Detroit and Manush slapped another three hits. It brought his hitting streak to 29 games, just 12 away from the American League record, set by George Sisler at 41 in 1922. The major league record of 44 had been set back in 1897 by Wee Willie Keeler.

Manush tallied one hit the next day, then three in each of the next two games against Detroit, and extended his streak with a single in the final game of the series against the Tigers on August 25. The next day Manush went hitless and was called out on a close play at first base. Nevertheless, the streak was over and Manush had set the best mark of his career at 33 games. It still stands as the 19th best streak in baseball history and the 14th best in the 20th century (Joe DiMaggio set the record of 56 in 1941).

> On September 1, the Senators played in Philadelphia's Shibe Park. The game began with a long, three-run homer by Philadelphia's Jimmie Foxx, who would go on to hit 534 in his career. The pennant race was making everyone tense, including the players' wives. Mrs. Crowder and Mrs. Manush, who were guests of the *Washington Post*'s sports department, became nervous upon hearing the news, and both began to chew gum. The entire sports department chewed gum after the Athletics scored four more in the fifth inning for a 7–0 lead. The Nats went on to lose 12–3. But the nation's capital would get the third and final pennant from the Senators. Thursday afternoon, September 21, was a beautiful day in the nation's capital as a ladies' day crowd of ten thousand filed into Griffith Stadium. The sun was bright, the temperature was a comfortable sixty-eight degrees, and the Senators got ready to face the Browns, with one more victory, or one more Yankees defeat, to wrap up the pennant. The good news was the Yankees were idle, meaning the Nats had the opportunity to clinch in a winning effort. Washington got a run off Bump Hadley in the second inning. The Browns evened the scored in the seventh off Lefty Stewart.... In the bottom of the seventh Kuhel got his second hit of the game, and Bob Boken, today's starting third baseman, drew a walk. Sewell followed with a hit to deep center field, and the two base runners got tangled up in the base paths.... Kuhel recovered, rounded third, and made it home with a slide to give the Nats a 2–1 lead. Stewart handled the Browns in the eighth inning, but in the ninth, Carl Reynolds led off with a single. Bruce Campbell followed with a hard grounder, which Myer gloved, and once again he started a twin killing. With one out to go for the pennant, the crowd began to buzz, as Browns second baseman Oscar Melillo was ready at the plate. In left field, Manush needed time to adjust his sunglasses, and he frantically waved his arms to get the umpire's attention. Cronin noticed and called to Stewart, but the pitcher had already started his windup. Melillo swung and lifted a fly to left field. Manush ran to his left, his sunglasses dangling from his left hand, got under the ball, and snared it with his glove hand to clinch the 1933 American League pennant![5]

Manush did his part to bring another pennant to the nation's capital. He led the American League with 221 hits and 17 triples. He also scored 115 runs, knocked in 95 and batted .336 to finish third in the MVP voting behind Jimmie Foxx and teammate Joe Cronin. The National League MVP was New York Giants pitcher Carl Hubbell, who went 23–12 with a 1.66 earned run average behind his masterful screwball. He led the Giants to the NL pennant and was waiting for the hot-hitting Senators.

The World Series began at the Polo Grounds in New York. Hubbell struck out Buddy Myer and Goose Goslin to start Game 1. Manush was next and was eager to make good in his first World Series at-bat. He couldn't hit the screwball either and went down on strikes. Hubbell was in control, leading 4–1 heading into the ninth inning.

"The Senators did not give up. In the top of the ninth Manush reached base on an error, and Cronin hit his second single of the game.... Schulte hit a hot grounder, too hot for Travis Jackson to handle, and the Washington center fielder reached with a single to load the bases. Kuhel hit into a fielder's choice, but a run [Manush] scored to make the score 4–2.... Bluege struck out on a screwball, Sewell grounded out to Jackson to end the game."[6] The Giants took the second game of the series, 6–1, with Washington's lone run coming on a home run by Goslin. The Senators were eager to get back to Washington and play in their home park. Even more exciting was the fact that President Franklin Delano Roosevelt would throw out the first pitch. The tradition of a special guest throwing the ceremonial first pitch was not yet commonplace, so Roosevelt threw from his box seat. "All right, here it goes," he warned, then threw the ball. Manush leaped and made the catch. The Washington left fielder wanted the president to sign it, but he was bashful about approaching his box, so he asked a policeman to do it for him.[7]

Manush was still struggling at the plate with only one hit in the Series through three games but caught the last out of third game off the bat of Gus Mancuso to preserve a 4–0 lead for the Senators and pitcher Earl Whitehill. Whitehill did not seem to be bothered by his injured elbow, which was now the size of a baseball. The pitching hero of the day received a couple of gifts, one from Manush, who gave him his signed baseball, perhaps to start a tradition of giving out the game ball. Another gift was handed to Whitehill, this one a telegram sent by his proud father back in Cedar Rapids, Iowa, who wired, "I'm the happiest man in Iowa—Dad."[8]

The next game was pivotal for the Senators. Win and the Series would be even 2–2, but lose and they would be in a tough place to come back from. The tension was there, especially for Manush, who was struggling to hit. Hubbell was again on the mound, which made the task even more daunting.

In the fourth inning, Hubbell's streak of retiring ten in a row came to an end when Goslin hit a sharp grounder down the first base line that Bill Terry was unable to handle. Manush followed with a walk, and suddenly the Nats were threatening. But Hubbell got out of the inning when Cronin flew out and Schulte grounded out. In the sixth inning Myer beat out a ground ball for an infield hit. Goslin moved him into scoring position with a sacrifice. Manush, who had just one hit in twelve at bats for the series, hit a sharp grounder, ticketed for a hit to right field. Terry ranged to his right and extended his right arm, but the ball was out of reach. Second baseman Hughie Critz, who was having a great series in the field, got the ball by making a great glove-hand stop, then threw to Hubbell, who had hustled off the mound to cover first base. Hubbell caught the ball after Manush had crossed the base, or that was what Manush and 26,762 fans believed. Manush turned around and walked back to the base, believing he was safe, then learned that Charlie Moran had called him out. Angry and frustrated, Manush stomped towards the umpire, slapped him across the chest with his left hand, and brushed the umpire's bow tie, knocking it loose. Realizing his mistake, Manush acted as if his actions were accidental, and immediately apologized. Umpire Moran raised his right arm, pointed his thumb, and yelled, "You're outta here!" Reserve infielder Johnny Kerr, who was coaching first base, began to argue, and Cronin ran over from the on deck circle to partake in the debate, as did Sewell and Myer. As the crowd booed, a pop bottle was thrown from the stands, and it landed close to the umpire. When Moran walked away from the debaters, two more bottles landed at his feet. Cronin peacefully followed the umpire, hoping to at least get him to reinstate his slugger. Myer also followed, but not as peacefully. Moriarty, the second base umpire, came over to warn Myer to cool it. Order was restored. Myer was on third base, with two outs, and Cronin, apparently distracted by the events, struck out to end the inning. Manush grabbed his glove and headed to the outfield for the start of the seventh. He said something as he passed by

Moran. "And you're out of the game," the umpire reminded him. After Manush took his position in left field, Moran shouted to home plate umpire Red Ormsby, to inform him that he ejected Manush. Ormsby looked into left field, and motioned to the outfielder to get off the field. Manush responded with a sarcastic wave that the crowd found humorous, and some began to cheer. Third base umpire Charles Pfirman jogged into left field to speak to Manush, and was able to persuade him to leave the field, but the angry outfielder warned that he was going to punch Moran on his way back to the clubhouse. As he approached the infield, Cronin and Myer, both aware they could not afford to lose Manush to a suspension, surrounded Manush and escorted him from the field. Moriarty followed, and whispered something into the outfielder's ear that appeared to have a calming effect. In the bottom of the seventh the Senators finally broke through against Hubbell to tie the score at 1–1…. Blondy Ryan singled in Travis Jackson in the top of the 11th. Hubbell pitched out of a bases loaded jam in the bottom of the 11th, getting pinch hitter Cliff Bolton to ground into a double play to end the game.[9]

It wasn't the first time the fiery Manush had a run-in with an umpire. He was famous for them, but they weren't always what they seemed.

"Boy, he's sure giving him what for," fans used to say as they watched Heinie blaze away at a man in blue. Heinie gave every indication of being at his best one afternoon in a game at Washington. He had tried to steal second and had been called out on a close play, with Bill McGowan as the umpire who made the decision. Heinie leaped to his feet and jumped toward Bill as though he had springs in his legs. He shoved his face within inches of Bill's fine, honest phiz, at the same time spreading his hands, apparently to show how far the infielder has missed him in trying to make the tag. That went on until the spectators began wondering why McGowan didn't tell him to take the rest of the afternoon off and just go look at the exhibits in the National Museum, or something. Just didn't seem possible that a veteran umpire would take what appeared to be a terrific tongue lashing without putting a stop to it. Heinie eventually looked and acted though he was running out of steam. And he finally walked away from McGowan and headed toward the bench, saying something extra over his shoulder as he departed. Fact of the matter was that Manush had been doing a swell job of covering up for having been thrown out on his attempt to steal. He had put up a piece of acting which would have made even the likes of John Drew or Richard Mansfield envious. All the while he was pawing at the earth and flailing around with his arms, Heinie had been making statements like this: "Bill, you're about the most capable umpire in baseball and I really don't remember seeing you make a bum decision." Looking as though he wanted to rend the umpire limb from lung, he actually had been paying him compliments, right and left. That evening, McGowan was asked how come he didn't put Heinie out of the game. "I never heard of an umpire giving the thumb to a player who told him to his face that he was efficient and a fine fellow," Bill explained, "and I certainly wasn't going to set a precedent."[10]

But no incident matched the bow tie. It was the World Series and every newspaper in the country ran the story.

In Game 5, Washington's 1933 season appeared to be finished after they fell behind **3–0**, as game five headed into the bottom of the sixth. The Giants had taken care of Crowder in 5⅓ innings. Jack Russell entered the game and ended the Giants' sixth by striking out Ryan and Hal Schumacher. Schumacher had allowed only three hits through five innings, and appeared to be heading for an easy sixth inning after disposing of Myer and Goslin. Manush, who got the OK from Landis to play today following his game ejection the day before, kept the inning alive with a hit, only his second of the Series. Cronin followed with a single…. Fred Schulte followed with a home run to tie the game. Mel Ott hit a home run in the top of the 10th that tipped off Schulte's mitt and into the stands as he was just out of reach. He fell over the stands into the crowd. The good news for the Senators was that in the bottom of the 10th the Old Washington Wrecking Crew was due up. Goslin led off, and grounded to Terry. The New York manager flipped the ball to Dolf Luque, who stepped on first base for one out. Manush, having a tough time in the Series, hit one right on the nose, but right at Critz for the second out. Cronin came through with a single, his seventh hit of the Series, to keep his team's hopes alive. Schulte followed by taking four straight balls, and the Nats had two men on base for Joe Kuhel. Luque settled down and threw three straight past the Washington first baseman to end the 1933 World Series.[11]

The Senators had finally returned to the World Series and, with a strong team returning, the nation's capital hoped for another pennant. Manush continued to play well for the Senators. He batted .349 in 1934, earning a spot on the American League All-Star team. It was only the second year of the Midsummer Classic, and Manush had been snubbed the previous season when he batted .336 and finished third in the MVP voting. The All-Star Game would see an interesting rematch between Manush and Hubbell, who had dominated the World Series for the Giants the previous fall. But Hubbell would be the only one remembered for his All-Star heroics. In the first inning, Detroit second baseman Charlie Gehringer led off with a single and moved to second on Wally Berger's error. Manush was next up and drew a walk to put the first two hitters on base with the heart of the American League lineup—Babe Ruth, Lou Gehrig and Jimmie Foxx—coming to the plate. The three were perhaps the greatest hitters in baseball history to combine phenomenal power and a high batting average. Hubbell struck them out in order to end the inning, then struck out Al Simmons and Joe Cronin to lead off the second inning. The screwball king fanned five future Hall of Famers in a row. He had two strikes on the next hitter, also a future Hall of Famer, but Bill Dickey singled to left. Hubbell then fanned future Hall of Fame pitcher Lefty Gomez. He struck out six of the nine batters in the all-Hall of Fame lineup.

Unfortunately, since the game had only been instituted in 1933 and Manush was near the end of his prime, it would be in the only All-Star Game appearance for him. Despite having the same dominating lineup, the Senators dropped to seventh.

Manush was ready for another season in Washington, but unfortunately could not keep up his hitting forever. In 1935, after seven straight years of batting over .300, Manush dipped to .273. The Senators moved up one spot to sixth in the American League, but after winning the pennant two years before, the franchise needed to turn things around again. Manush knew his name would be on the chopping block since he struggled in 1935. It had happened to him twice before, so it probably would again. Manush was also on the chopping block because the Senators knew they could get something for the star, since many teams would invest on the chance that he would return to his old form. On December 17, he was traded to the Boston Red Sox for Roy Johnson and former Senators outfielder Carl Reynolds.

28. Bouncing Around
Till the End

Heinie Manush wasn't prepared for such a drop-off in his hitting from 1934 to 1935. Not only had he failed to reach the .300 mark, but his .273 average was by far the lowest of his career. He was looking for a fresh start with the Boston Red Sox in 1936. Manush played 82 games for the Red Sox and upped his average to .291 with just 91 hits— three years after leading the league with 221. The Red Sox were hoping Manush was just having a solitary off-year like he had a couple of times earlier in his career. Unfortunately, it was a sign of Manush slowing down.

The Red Sox released him on September 27 after finishing a disappointing sixth (74–80). Manush waited for weeks for someone else to give him a chance. He knew he could get in there and continue to contribute. He definitely didn't want to end his career on a low note. Finally, on December 8, Manush was signed by the Brooklyn Dodgers and, for the first time, would move to the National League. At age 35, Manush was mainly looking to prove he could still hit. He joined a team managed by former spitball pitcher Burleigh Grimes, who, like Manush, was a competitor till the end. Manush, batting cleanup, slammed eight hits in his first five games and was hitting .364, before his average dipped below .300. Like always, Manush got hot with the weather and put together a 17-game hitting streak from May 25 to June 13, ten of which were multi-hit games. Manush's average surged to .354 and no matter what happened the rest of the season, he had proven to be the force he once was.

Manush cooled off a bit in September but still finished at .333. He was ninth in the National League in hitting (41 points behind Triple Crown winner Joe Medwick) and finished 21st in the MVP voting. He also smashed the 2,500th hit of his career during the last week of the season, putting him in a select group of hitters. It wasn't enough to challenge for the batting title, but it was enough for Manush to reserve a job for the following season.

Manush still could hit and used his reputation and mentality as much as his physical ability. "He was at bat against Johnny Vander Meer, who pitched two consecutive no-hitters," nephew George Manush said. "The catcher told Heinie he would never even see the ball. The first pitch was so fast he didn't see it either. But Heinie turned around and told the catcher that it was fast, but that it wasn't as fast as Walter Johnson's changeup. The catcher was so burned up that he called for another fast ball. Heinie, of course, knew it was coming and he hit it for a home run."[1]

For Manush, 1937 was his last hurrah as a full-timer. "Brooklyn hasn't got very far ... but we certainly wouldn't have done as well without Manush's fine hitting. I think we were lucky to get him," manager Burleigh Grimes told John J. Ward.[2] He played in 17 games for the Dodgers in 1938 before being claimed off waivers by the Pittsburgh Pirates after hitting just .235. He pinch-hit 15 times for the Pirates, meanwhile batting .310 in 81 games with Toronto of the International League to finish the 1938 season. It was a role Manush was perfect for, and he would end up making some of the best friends of his life in Pittsburgh. Manush connected for four hits, good for a .308 average.

"They miscalculated a bit, when they thought I was all through," Manush told John J. Ward of *Baseball Magazine*.

> They were a little too early with their estimates; one year too early, anyway, several years too early, I hope. For I think I have demonstrated to the satisfaction of everybody by my work this past season that I am not through as a Big Leaguer. And I am encouraged to believe that I have two or three more years before I have to join the Old Men's Club and take my exercise in golf.... I have trained down pretty well and weigh 195 pounds. At that figure I am not carrying any excess fat. I realize all too well that a ballplayer goes bad in his legs. Carrying extra weight doesn't help him. Keeping in condition with me is largely exercise for my legs. Last winter, I went to Florida resolved to get in shape for another baseball season. Every day I played eighteen holes of golf, sometimes twenty-seven. I walked at least four or five miles every day, sometimes twice that distance. Golf from an exercise standpoint is mostly walking. But the swing is also to be considered. It keeps your shoulders loosened up and helps to reduce your waist line.... I am one of the worst, but whatever my score, I get just as much exercise as the other fellows.[3]

The Pirates led the National League standings until the final month of the season, when they began to waiver and the Chicago Cubs surged. It set up perhaps the second-most famous home run of the first half of the century (after Babe Ruth's called shot in the 1932 World Series).

But unfortunately for the Pirates, it would come against them at the critical point of the season. The "Homer in the Gloamin'" would dash Pittsburgh's hope for a pennant and Manush's chance at winning a World Series.

It happened in the bottom of the ninth of a tie game on September 28 at Wrigley Field.

> But as the ninth inning got under way, darkness was settling over the Friendly Confines, and the umpires, after conferring, decided to play just one more inning. A tie would necessitate playing a doubleheader the next day, a prospect that was unappetizing to manager Hartnett, whose pitching staff was decimated, and whose team would be decided underdogs if they had to play two games in one day, needing victories in both games to claim first place. Charlie Root, a 39-year-old grizzled veteran, took the ball in the top of the ninth and shackled the Bucs with an assist from his 37-year-old catcher, Gabby Hartnett. With Paul Waner on first after lacing a single to left, and two men out, the Pirates right fielder tested the old man's arm and came out second best, as Gabby gunned him down on an attempted steal....[4] Now it was the Cubs' turn to bat, with a tie game looming before them. Mace Brown, the Pirates' premier reliever, started his second inning on the mound, quickly disposed of Phil Cavaretta on a fly ball to center field and Carl Reynolds on a bouncer to second base. The fate of the Cubs now rested squarely on the shoulders of their aging manager, Gabby Hartnett. The ruddy-faced Irishman knocked the clay from his spikes and stepped in to face the flamethrowing right-hander. Brown threw Gabby a blazer. The man from Millville swung and missed. Brown threw another one and Gabby barely

got a piece of it, fouling it off. Now, with the count 0–2 and the visibility almost zero, Brown inexplicably threw Hartnett a high curveball, and Gabby sent it screaming on a line to left field. Most fans were unable to follow the flight of the ball in the darkness, but when it settled into the left field seats for a walk-off home run, Wrigley Field erupted with a deafening roar that could be heard for blocks.... As Gabby remembered it: "I swung with everything I had, and then I got that feeling, the kind of a feeling you get when the blood rushes out of your head and you get dizzy. A lot of people have told me they didn't know the ball was in the bleachers. Well, I did. Maybe I was the only one in the park who did. I knew it the moment I hit it." On his way to second base, he was mobbed by his teammates, the fans, the venders, the ushers, even the cops.[5]

Manush and the Pirates were disappointed and he didn't want to end his career on a devastating loss like that, so he was back with the Pirates in 1939. He got into ten games, primarily as a pinch-hitter, but did not connect for a single hit. He reached base only once on a walk and tallied one RBI. The Pirates released Manush on June 7. He hoped someone would give him one last chance to end his career on a high note, but it never came.

At the time of his "retirement," the brand new National Baseball Hall of Fame in Cooperstown, New York, had just opened its doors. That door would eventually keep Heinie Manush's legacy alive for good. It would just be a long wait.

Meanwhile, Manush couldn't stay away from the game. He was still hopeful of getting one more shot in the majors. In 1940, he batted .280 for Rocky Mount, a Class B Red Sox affiliate in the Piedmont League. Then, when it was clear his days in the majors were over, he continued to play wherever he could. In 1941, Manush played 12 games for Greensboro, North Carolina, the Red Sox' new affiliate of the Piedmont League, batting .313. In 1942, he got in one game for Greensboro without a hit.

In 1943, Manush remained in the Piedmont League, following the Red Sox from Greensboro to Roanoke, Virginia. He played in ten games, mostly as a pinch-hitter. In 1944, he moved up to Class A with Scranton, Pennsylvania, of the Eastern League—still a Red Sox affiliate—and went 0-for-3 in his short stint.

Manush finished his career for good in 1945 with Martinsville of the Carolina League, a Class C affiliate of the Philadelphia Athletics. He had one at-bat and laced a hit to finish his career on his terms. In 11 minor league seasons (including the three prior to reaching the majors), Manush batted .323 in 464 games. He continued to stay in the game as a scout and became a coach of the Washington Senators in the 1950s. He recalled how much the game had changed in three decades since he broke into the majors.

"I've been back only a few days," he told the *Associated Press*, "but I've already noticed some changes since I was up here. Take this park for instance. It's quite different from the one on which I played back in 1936. There was no right field wing in the grandstand then. Many were the times I had my back to those bleacher walls and stood helplessly watching those golf shots of Ruth's sail over my head."[6]

After returning home for good, following his retirement, Manush got to spend a lot of time with his wife, Betty. It turns out he was very fortunate to have those years because Betty died of cancer in 1949 at age 44. "My mother died very young," said Manush's daughter Sue McCaw in 2010. "He never remarried. Daddy didn't even really date after that. He played golf every day."[7]

To keep his mind off his pain, Manush played golf almost constantly. He played with former teammates Paul and Lloyd Waner as well as former pitcher Paul Derringer. "Pound for pound, Paul was the greatest," Manush said. "We had been friends since 1927, and what a guy he was. Day in and day out, Waner could beat me anytime he wanted to. He was a real good putter. I called him 'One Putt' and that's all he ever took. He still had that beautiful swing. But he couldn't hit the ball more than about 150 yards. I usually saw him about once a week."[8] Manush finished second to Roy Cullenbine in the Bill Cody Golf Tournament, one that was geared for former ballplayers. He shot a 76 to Cullenbine's 74. Manush played in the annual players tournament in Miami with Paul Waner and Dick Bartell.

Unfortunately for the Manush family—especially the women—dying young seemed to be a family tradition that continued with the next generation. Manush's daughter, Shirley, died in 1987 of emphysema. His second-oldest daughter, Lillis, also died in 1987 of cancer. "They were young too," McCaw said. "Lillis was 56, and Shirley was 58."[9]

Manush continued to scout and returned to his childhood home when he could. "We'd see him every year or so when he would stop by on the way to Sarasota," niece Norma Manush told the *Times Daily*, the local newspaper serving the Tuscumbia, Florence and Muscle Shoals area. "He always came by here because this was his home. He came here more often after he retired.... He was a quiet person. When he'd come here, he didn't want to go anywhere, just sit and relax."[10]

The biggest thrill of his career came when Manush was inducted into the National Baseball Hall of Fame in 1964 by the Veterans Committee. Manush entered the Hall of Fame with his former manager in Brooklyn, Burleigh Grimes, as well as former Chicago White Sox greats Luke Appling and Red Faber, former Yankees manager Miller Huggins and 19th Century stars Tim Keefe and Monte Ward.

Here are the words he shared with the Cooperstown crowd:

Mr. Commissioner, ladies and gentlemen, and fellow ex-ballplayers. I'll never forget February the 2nd, about 4 o'clock in the afternoon, there at my house in Sarasota, Florida. I'd just left the golf course and I was watching the Olympics and thinking about some of those two-foot putts that cost me some money. I saw these two fellows walk up the steps there and I went out there, didn't know who they were, I was going to invite them in and before I could say anything, they said, "Congratulations, you're in the Hall of Fame." I says, "Are you lying?" They said, "No, here it is," and showed me the evidence. So it's hard to express the feelings that came over me when they told me that. I think I got ten years younger. And another thrill that I'd like to mention, the fact when I broke in with the Detroit Tigers back in 1923, I was going to high school, reading about Ty Cobb, Harry Heilmann, and Bob Veach. I made the ball club and playing alongside of those fellows, I thought that was the biggest thrill. But up to now, that's nothing compared to being in the Hall of Fame.

I happened to see Harry Heilmann lead the American League in hitting in 1923 for an average of .403. I says, well, if he can do it, so can I. So I set a couple goals: that I wanted to lead the American League in hitting and play in the World Series. In 1926, I led the league and in 1933 I was lucky enough to get into the World Series. Speaking of the World Series, I'd like to tell you a little story that happened. We were playing the Giants in the fourth game, the score is tied 1 to 1 in the eighth inning and Goose Goslin's on second base and I'm the hitter. I hit a ball by Bill Terry which looked like a sure base hit, so did Hubbell who was pitching. Hughie Critz came up with the ball, and here goes Hubbell for first base and here goes Manush to first base. I thought I was safe, but umpire Moran says, "you're out." So I was arguing with him and he had a little bow tie on. So, I grabbed that thing back as far as I could and let it go. He gulped a couple times and says, "you're out of the game." So the next day, all the words in the papers were "Is Manush going to be allowed to play, is Judge Landis going to his World Series sack, is he going to be suspended?" So about ten minutes before the game started, in walked Judge Landis. He says, "Everybody out except Manush." Gee, I said, well, I'm going to have to lie a little bit. So he walked over to me and he says, "Now Henry, tell me just what happened." I said, "Well, Judge," I says, "you've seen me play ball quite a few times." I said, "You know when I run, my arms and legs are flying." I said, "I could see the play was going to be close," and I said, "I actually brushed Umpire Moran." He give me a look. He says, "Henry, hereafter, when you see those plays are going to be close," he says, "keep your hands to yourself."

I have somebody else over here I'm very proud of. I'd just like for them to stand up. My three daughters, six grandchildren, and two son-in-laws. And before I back away from here, I just want the honor of thanking the fellows who are responsible for me being in Cooperstown today. Thank you.[11]

Manush still had his humor late in life. At his Hall of Fame induction in 1964, he encountered Bill Terry, the Giants first baseman in 1933 when Manush was ejected from the Series game.

"Hey Bill," Manush said, "wasn't I safe?"

"It was very close," replied Terry.

"You haven't been telling the truth for 31 years," snorted Heinie.[12]

He lost his voice after a cancer operation and was forced to answer questions with notes. While being interviewed in July of 1970, he and a reporter were watching a game on television. A player was ejected and Manush promptly grabbed his pad. "They give the umpires too much authority these days," he wrote. "You saw it there. I wish I could tell you about the 1933 World Series," itching to speak of his own ejection incident once more.[13]

Manush was just 69 when he died May 12, 1971, in Sarasota, Florida, where he and his wife had settled after his career. He had cancer and had lost the power of speech for a number of months. But he did as much as he could to remember the good old days and keep up with former teammates as he could. "He went to games and he always went to Cooperstown every year and old timers games," daughter Sue McCaw said. "He went to everything he was invited to. He loved it because it was his life."[14]

He was inducted into the Alabama Sports Hall of Fame in 1972 and was part of the inaugural Colbert County Hall of Fame in 2000—three years after the Tuscumbia City Council declared October 25 to be "Heinie Manush Day." The Deshler High School baseball field in his hometown is named for him. That was an important day for the Manush family. "There was nothing to indicate he was from here," Norma Manush said. "A lot of people who live in town didn't know he was born here."[15] It is fitting considering his great career has been forgotten everywhere else.

29. FORGOTTEN LEGACY:
HEINIE MANUSH

How does a lifetime .330 hitter become forgotten? It is an interesting question since just 30 players in the history of the game can say they retired with that high a mark. Heinie Manush's own teammate Harry Heilmann batted .342 for his career and would have faded to total obscurity if not for being a radio announcer for the Tigers following his playing career. Over the years, both players would remain legendary names to fans who had little knowledge of what they actually accomplished. Unlike Heilmann, Manush was fiery, just like his former manager and teammate Ty Cobb. Manush got in arguments with umpires, opposing players, even his own teammates. So he wasn't overlooked because he was quiet.

Several factors contribute to why Manush has faded from public knowledge. The first is that Manush played for a lot of teams—six in fact. He didn't play for any of them longer than 5½ years, which was rare in those days for a player of his caliber. There was no free agency back then, so you could only change teams if you were traded or released. Manush was traded several times and became a bat that was in demand. He began his career with Detroit and played five years with the Tigers. He spent 2½ seasons in St. Louis with the Browns, then moved to Washington for 5½ with the Senators. Manush then played one season for the Boston Red Sox, 1½ for the Brooklyn Dodgers and 1½ for the Pittsburgh Pirates.

So there was no one team that really had a claim to his career. He played well everywhere he went and had one of his dominant seasons in Detroit, two in St. Louis and the other two in Washington.

The second factor contributing to Manush's obscurity is the fact that most of the teams he played for no longer exist. He led the American League in doubles both of his full seasons with the St. Louis Browns (and led the league in hits one of those years), then helped lead the Washington Senators to the 1933 pennant. When you add two years in Brooklyn, he played 9½ years for teams that are no longer around. That heavily contributes to Manush's legendary play being forgotten. If the St. Louis Browns were still around, there would be some tribute to his stellar play there at the stadium. If the Senators hadn't left Washington, Manush may have had a statue in the nation's capital. He was only there 5½ years, but he helped them win their third and final pennant and was one of the best players in franchise history, behind Walter Johnson, Goose Goslin, Sam Rice and Joe Cronin. He may have been better than Rice, too, but Rice played 19 seasons in Washington.

A third factor is that the All-Star Game didn't start until 1933. Manush made the team

This historical marker stands in front of the home of Heinie Manush. Norma and Frank Manush, niece and nephew of Heinie Manush, still live in the home and have worked hard to give historical recognition to their uncle and the home (author's collection).

in 1934, but it was his tenth year in the league and his career was on the way down. Had the game started at the turn of the century, Manush could have made between five and eight more appearances at the Midsummer Classic. The first game in 1933 was originally looked at as a one-time thing, so many of the players made the team on their career laurels, not just performance in 1933. That left Manush off the team even though he went on to bat .336, lead the league in hits and triples, and finish third in the MVP voting.

Another factor is that Manush never reached an elite milestone club. He finished more than 400 hits away from 3,000 and hit only 110 home runs in his career. He also finished nine doubles short of 500, which isn't a club that gets a lot of headlines, but is still a tremendous feat. One could make the point that having just 30 members in the .330 club is pretty exclusive.

The next factor is that it took so long for Manush to reach the Hall of Fame. He retired in 1939 but didn't make the Hall until 1964 by way of the Veterans' Committee. Had he made the Hall of Fame in the 1940s, he would have been part of a select group of players to reach at that point and would have been talked about as a legend of the game from an earlier standpoint. The last factor is that Manush went in the Hall of Fame as a Tiger. Fitting since he won his batting title in Detroit, but he played there under the constant shadow of Ty Cobb and Harry Heilmann.

Making the Hall of Fame was a huge deal to Manush, especially after his wife died, and to his family. "Actually, I didn't realize how good he was until I finished high school," Manush's daughter Sue McCaw said. "We never knew how important he was to the team. We really understood it when he got into the Hall of Fame, and we were so glad that happened."[1]

So I guess that leaves Tigers fans off the hook for not knowing how great Heinie Manush was. If his own children weren't aware he was one of the best players in the league, how could anyone else?

His family has grown to appreciate the tremendous player he was. There is a historical trolley in town that stops at Manush's house, where his niece Norma Manush still lives. "I always get in on the trolley and talk about him," she said. "I say he hit .330 for his career and people kind of gasp. He never pushed for publicity."[2]

Manush's statistics are phenomenal but he won't be getting a statue at Comerica Park in Detroit, since he played only five years in the Motor City. His name is on the brick wall in the outfield, but it takes more than just a name to remember a legend. Manush was a batting champion, Hall of Famer, and was part of perhaps the greatest outfield in baseball history along with Harry Heilmann and Ty Cobb—who overshadowed them all.

CHAPTER NOTES

Chapter 1

1. Wahoo historical society.
2. Lawrence Ritter, *The Glory of Their Times* (New York: Macmillan, 1966; reprinted 2002), 66–68.
3. Ibid.
4. *Lincoln Sunday Journal*, undated.
5. Ritter, *The Glory of Their Times*, 66–68.
6. Ibid., 67.
7. F.C. Lane, "The King of Sluggers," *Baseball Magazine* 16.4 (February 1916): 55–68.
8. Ritter, *The Glory of Their Times*, 67–68.
9. Ibid., 45–51.
10. Alan H. Levy, *Rube Waddell: The Zany, Brilliant Life of a Strikeout Artist* (Jefferson, NC: McFarland, 2000), 38.
11. Ibid., 41.

Chapter 2

1. Benjamin Rader, *Baseball: A History of America's Game* (Chicago: University of Illinois Press, 1992), 92.
2. Lane, "The King of Sluggers," 55–61.
3. *Detroit Free Press*, April 24, 1903.
4. *Detroit Free Press*, June 1, 1903.
5. Al Stump, *Cobb: A Biography* (Chapel Hill: Algonquin, 1994), 58–60.
6. Reed Browning, *Cy Young: A Baseball Life* (Amherst: University of Massachusetts Press, 2000), 144–145.

Chapter 3

1. *Detroit Free Press*, May 19, 1905.
2. *Detroit Free Press*, June 17, 1905.
3. *Detroit Free Press*, August 19, 1905.
4. *Detroit Free Press*, August 31, 1905.
5. Ritter, *The Glory of Their Times*, 62.
6. Fred Lieb, undated article in Crawford's Hall of Fame file.
7. *Detroit Free Press*, September 19, 1905.
8. Stump, *Cobb*, 123.

9. Ibid., 144.
10. Ritter, *The Glory of Their Times*, 40–41.
11. *Detroit Free Press*, September 2, 1905.
12. Charles C. Alexander, *Ty Cobb* (New York: Oxford University Press, 1984), 51.

Chapter 4

1. Jack Smiles, *"Ee-Yah": The Life and Times of Hughie Jennings, Baseball Hall of Famer* (Jefferson, NC: McFarland, 2005), 111–113.
2. Ibid.
3. *Detroit Free Press*, April 5, 1907.
4. *Detroit Free Press*, April 7, 1907.
5. Stump, *Cobb*, 53.
6. *Detroit Free Press*, May 7, 1907.
7. *Detroit Free Press*, June 2, 1907.
8. *Detroit Free Press*, June 30, 1907.
9. *Detroit Free Press*, August 3, 1907.
10. Alexander, *Ty Cobb*, 55–56.
11. Ritter, *The Glory of Their Times*, 57–58.
12. *Detroit Free Press*, August 3, 1907.
13. *Detroit Free Press*, September 6, 1907.
14. *Detroit Free Press*, September 23, 1907.
15. *Detroit Free Press*, September 28, 1907.
16. *Philadelphia Inquirer*, September 30, 1907.
17. Letter in Crawford's Hall of Fame file.
18. Alexander, *Ty Cobb*, 61.
19. Smiles, *"Ee-Yah,"* 142.

Chapter 5

1. Frederick G. Lieb, *The Detroit Tigers* (Kent, OH: Kent State University Press, 2008; originally published New York: G.P Putnam's Sons, 1946), 107
2. *Detroit Free Press*, April 26, 1908.
3. *Detroit Free Press*, May 2, 1908.
4. Stump, *Cobb*, 160.
5. *Detroit Free Press*, June 24, 1908.
6. Ibid.
7. *Detroit Free Press*, August 2, 1908.
8. Stump, *Cobb*, 161–162.
9. *Detroit Free Press*, August 9, 1908.
10. *Detroit Free Press*, September 3, 1908.

11. *Detroit Free Press*, September 4, 1908.

12. *Detroit Free Press*, September 6, 1908.

13. Jack Smiles, *Big Ed Walsh: The Life and Times of a Spitball Hall of Famer* (Jefferson, NC: McFarland, 2008).

14. Levy, "Rube Waddell," 248–249.

15. David W. Anderson, *More Than Merkle: A History of the Best and Most Exciting Baseball Season in Human History* (Lincoln: University of Nebraska, 2000), 184.

16. Ibid., 46.

17. Undated story from the *Chicago News*, printed in *Baseball Digest*, from Crawford's Hall of Fame file.

18. Alexander, *Ty Cobb*, 71–72.

19. Anderson, *More Than Merkle*, 172.

20. Ibid., 39–40.

21. *Detroit Free Press*, October 11, 1908.

22. Ibid.

23. Anderson, *More Than Merkle*, 114–116.

24. *Detroit Free Press*, October 14, 1908.

25. Smiles, *"Ee-Yah,"* 150.

Chapter 6

1. *Detroit Free Press*, June 5, 1909.

2. Alexander, *Ty Cobb*, 78–79.

3. Smiles, *"Ee-Yah,"* 155.

4. Ritter, *The Glory of Their Times*, 59–61.

5. Alexander, *Ty Cobb*, 82.

6. *Detroit Free Press*, October 10, 1909.

7. *Detroit Free Press*, October 11, 1909.

8. Lieb, *The Detroit Tigers*, 131.

9. *Detroit Free Press*, October 14, 1909.

10. Smiles, *"Ee-Yah,"* 158.

11. Alexander, *Ty Cobb*, 85.

12. *Detroit Free Press*, October 17, 1909.

13. Smiles, *"Ee-Yah,"* 150.

Chapter 7

1. *Detroit Free Press*, May 5, 1910.

2. *Detroit Free Press*, October 2, 1910.

3. Robert Charles Cottrell, *The Best Pitcher in Baseball: The Life of Rube Foster, Negro League Giant* (New York: New York University, 2001), 59–60.

4. *Detroit Free Press*, April 14, 1911.

5. *Detroit Free Press*, April 17, 1911.

6. Reed Browning, *Cy Young: A Baseball Life* (Amherst: University of Massachusetts Press, 2000), 190.

Chapter 8

1. *Detroit Free Press*, April 21, 1912.

2. Ibid.

3. *Detroit Free Press*, May 1, 1912.

4. Sowell, *The Pitch That Killed*, 68.

5. *Detroit Free Press*, May 16, 1912.

6. *Detroit Free Press*, May 19–20, 1912.

7. *Detroit Free Press*, July 31, 1912.

8. *Detroit Free Press*, August 8–9, 1912.

9. Paul J. Zingg, *Harry Hooper: An American Baseball Life* (Urbana: University of Illinois Press, 1993), 147.

10. *Detroit Free Press*, April 14, 1913.

11. *Detroit Free Press*, April 17, 1913.

12. *Detroit Free Press*, April 30, 1913.

13. *Detroit Free Press*, May 7, 1913.

14. David L. Fleitz, *Shoeless: The Life and Times of Joe Jackson* (Jefferson, NC: McFarland, 2001), 80.

15. Timothy M. Gay, *Tris Speaker: The Rough-and-Tumble Life of a Baseball Legend* (Lincoln: University of Nebraska, 2005), 131.

16. Lieb, *The Detroit Tigers*, 149–150.

17. Gay, *Tris Speaker*, 131.

18. Undated article from *Baseball Digest*.

19. *Baseball Magazine*, November 1914, p. 78. Gay, *Tris Speaker*, 142–143.

20. Brian E. Cooper, *Red Faber: A Biography of the Hall of Fame Spitball Pitcher* (Jefferson, NC: McFarland, 2007), 44–47.

21. Gay, *Tris Speaker*, 143.

22. Lieb, *The Detroit Tigers*, 148–150.

23. Ibid., 148.

24. Ibid.

25. *Detroit Free Press*, June 2, 1914.

26. *Detroit Free Press*, June 7, 1914.

27. Robert W. Creamer, *Babe: The Legend Comes to Life* (New York: Fireside, 1974), 88.

Chapter 9

1. Lieb, *The Detroit Tigers*, 152–153.

2. *Detroit Free Press*, July 1, 1915.

3. *Detroit Free Press*, July 3, 1915.

4. *Detroit Free Press*, July 12, 1915.

5. *Detroit Free Press*, September 17, 1915.

6. Ibid.

7. Lieb, *The Detroit Tigers*, 152–155.

8. Lane, "The King of Sluggers," 64–65.

Chapter 10

1. Alexander, *Ty Cobb*, 156.

2. *Detroit Free Press*, undated.

3. *Detroit Free Press*, May 22, 1916.

4. *Detroit Free Press*, June 18, 1916.

5. Ibid.

6. *Detroit Free Press*, September 2, 1916.

7. Lieb, *The Detroit Tigers*, 155–156.

8. *Detroit Free Press*, August 26, 1917.

9. Crawford, "My 3,000th Hit," *Baseball Magazine* 19.4 (August 1917): 457.

10. Fred Lieb, undated article from Crawford's Hall of Fame file.

11. Lane, "The King of Sluggers," 63.
12. Stump, *Cobb*, 283.
13. Ibid., 189–190.
14. Ira L. Smith, *Baseball's Famous Outfielders* (New York: A.S. Barnes, 1954), 75–77.
15. Undated article from the *Lincoln Star*.
16. Ritter, *The Glory of Their Times*, 55–56.
17. Article on Crawford's Hall of Fame induction, unknown publication, from Crawford's file in the Hall of Fame Library.
18. *The Detroit News*, undated.
19. Article on Crawford's Hall of Fame induction, unknown publication, from Crawford's file in the Hall of Fame Library.

Chapter 11

1. Crawford, "My 3,000th Hit," 420, 457–458.
2. Undated *Baseball Digest* article, 1947, vol. 6, no. 1, 9–10.
3. Alexander, *Ty Cobb*, 225.
4. Arthur Daley, "A Double Bullseye," Sports of the Times, *New York Times*, February 5, 1957: 28.

Chapter 12

1. Saint Mary's College publication, undated.
2. Undated *Baseball Magazine* article.
3. Saint Mary's College publication, undated.
4. Terry Foster, *100 Things Tigers Fans Should Know Before They Die* (Chicago: Triumph, 2009), 44–46.

Chapter 13

1. *Detroit Free Press*, July 26, 1916.
2. Smith, *Baseball's Famous Outfielders*, 132–133.
3. *Detroit Free Press*, May 24, 1918.
4. *Detroit Free Press*, June 3, 1918.
5. Author interviews with Dan Heilmann and Marguerite Heilmann.

Chapter 14

1. *Detroit Free Press*, August 2, 1919.
2. *Detroit Free Press*, August 17, 1919.

Chapter 15

1. *Detroit Free Press*, August 15, 1921.
2. *Detroit Free Press*, August 11, 1921.
3. *Detroit Free Press*, May 5, 1922.

Chapter 16

1. *Detroit Free Press*, May 3, 1923.
2. Ibid.
3. *Detroit Free Press*, June 15, 1923.

Chapter 17

1. Lieb, *The Detroit Tigers*, 176.
2. Lieb, *The Detroit Tigers*, 177.
3. Ibid.
4. Ibid., 178.
5. Ibid., 178–179.

Chapter 18

1. Lieb, *The Detroit Tigers*, 185–186.

Chapter 20

1. Author interview with Marguerite Heilmann.
2. Author interview with Marguerite and Dan Heilmann.
3. Author interview with Dan Heilmann.
4. Author interview with Marguerite Heilmann.
5. Author interview with Harry Heilmann III.
6. Author interview with Ernie Harwell.
7. Author interview with George Kell.
8. Ibid.

Chapter 21

1. Smith, *Baseball's Famous Outfielders*, 135–136.
2. Author interview with Harry Heilmann III.

Chapter 22

1. Tuscumbia information provided by Colbert County Tourism & Convention Bureau.
2. Ibid.
3. Manush family records.
4. Author interview with Norma Manush.
5. Ibid.
6. *Baseball Magazine* article by F.C. Lane, 1927 vol. 39, no. 5.
7. Author interview with Norma Manush.

Chapter 23

1. Undated article from Manush's Hall of Fame file.

Chapter 24

1. Undated *Birmingham News* article from Cobb's Hall of Fame file.
2. Undated article from Manush's Hall of Fame file.
3. F.C. Lane, *Baseball Magazine* article, 1927, vol. 39, no. 5.
4. Author interview with Norma Manush.
5. Lane, *Baseball Magazine* article, 1927, vol. 39, no. 5.
6. Lane, F.C., *Baseball Magazine* article, undated, vol. 39, no. 5.

Chapter 25

1. Gary A. Sarnoff, *The Wrecking Crew of '33* (Jefferson, NC: McFarland, 2009), 46–47.
2. "Goslin vs. Manush: Face to Face for the Bat Title," *Baseball Magazine*, 1946.

Chapter 26

1. *Washington Post*, July 12, 1930.
2. Sarnoff, The *Wrecking Crew of '33*, 62–66.
3. Ibid., 88–89.

Chapter 27

1. Ibid., 109–119.
2. Ibid., 120–121.
3. Ibid., 126–127.
4. Ibid., 125–126.
5. Ibid., 165–167.
6. Ibid., 177.
7. Ibid., 183.
8. Ibid., 184.
9. Ibid., 187–191.

10. Smith, *Baseball's Famous Outfielders*, 168–174.
11. Sarnoff, *The Wrecking Crew of '33*, 191–193.

Chapter 28

1. Author interview with George Manush.
2. John J. Ward, "Burleigh Grimes, Star of Baseball's Greatest Pitching Staff," *Baseball Magazine* 25.5 (October 1920): 528–530.
3. *Baseball Magazine* article. December 1937, vol. 60, no. 1, 29.
4. *Chicago Tribune*, September 27–30, 1938. Cited in McNeil, *Gabby Hartnett*, 256.
5. Gold and Ahrens, *The Golden Era Cubs, 1876–1940*, 133. Cited in McNeil, *Gabby Hartnett*, 256.
6. Undated Associated Press story.
7. Author interview with Sue McCaw.
8. Clifton Blue Parker, *Big and Little Poison: Paul and Lloyd Waner, Baseball Brothers* (Jefferson, NC: McFarland, 2003), 268
9. Author interview with Sue McCaw.
10. Bernie Delinski, "Manush Family Fondly Recalls Tuscumbia Baseball Legend," *The Times Daily*, April 15, 2011, www.timesdaily.com/archives, accessed September 4, 2014.
11. Heinie Manush induction speech, National Baseball Hall of Fame and Museum.
12. Undated article from Manush's Hall of Fame file.
13. Ibid.
14. Author interview with Sue McCaw.
15. Author interview with Norma Manush.

Chapter 29

1. Author interview with Sue McCaw.
2. Author interview with Norma Manush.

BIBLIOGRAPHY

Alexander, Charles C. *Ty Cobb*. New York: Oxford University Press, 1984.

Anderson, David W. *More Than Merkle: A History of the Best and Most Exciting Baseball Season in Human History*. Lincoln: University of Nebraska, 2000.

Barthel, Thomas. *The Fierce Fun of Ducky Medwick*. Lanham, MD: Scarecrow Press, 2003.

Brashler, William. *Josh Gibson: A Life in the Negro Leagues*. Chicago: Ivan R. Dee, 2000.

Browning, Reed. *Cy Young: A Baseball Life*. Amherst: University of Massachusetts Press, 2000.

Cook, William A. *Waite Hoyt: A Biography of the Yankees' Schoolboy Wonder*. Jefferson, NC: McFarland, 2004.

Cooper, Brian E. *Red Faber: A Biography of the Hall of Fame Spitball Pitcher*. Jefferson, NC: McFarland, 2007.

Cottrell, Robert Charles. *The Best Pitcher in Baseball: The Life of Rube Foster, Negro League Giant*. New York: New York University, 2001.

Creamer, Robert W. *Babe: The Legend Comes to Life*. New York: Fireside, 1974.

Finoli, David, and Bill Rainer. *When Cobb Met Wagner: The Seven-Game World Series of 1909*. Jefferson, NC: McFarland, 2011.

Fleitz, David L. *Shoeless: The Life and Times of Joe Jackson*. Jefferson, NC: McFarland, 2001.

Foster, Terry. *100 Things Tigers Fans Should Know Before They Die*. Chicago: Triumph, 2009.

Gay, Timothy M. *Tris Speaker: The Rough-and-Tumble Life of a Baseball Legend*. Lincoln: University of Nebraska, 2005.

Gorman, Bob. *In Your Face–In Your Heart: The Joe Cronin Story*. Baldwin, NY: Baldwin Books, 2007.

Greenberg, Hank, with Ira Berkow. *Hank Greenberg: The Story of My Life*. Chicago: Triumph, 2001.

Harwell, Ernie. *Breaking 90*. Detroit: *Detroit Free Press*, 2007.

Huhn, Rick. *Eddie Collins: A Baseball Biography*. Jefferson, NC: McFarland, 2008.

James, Bill. *The New Bill James Historical Baseball Abstract*. New York: Free Press, 2003.

Levy, Alan H. *Rube Waddell: The Zany, Brilliant Life of a Strikeout Artist*. Jefferson, NC: McFarland, 2000.

Lieb, Frederick G. *The Detroit Tigers*. Kent, OH: Kent State University Press, 2008. Originally published New York: G.P Putnam's Sons, 1946.

Lowenfish, Lee. *Branch Rickey: Baseball's Ferocious Gentleman*. Lincoln: University of Nebraska Press, 2007.

Luke, Bob. *Dean of Umpires: Bill McGowan*. Jefferson, NC: McFarland, 2005.

McNeil, William F. *Gabby Hartnett: The Life and Times of the Cubs' Greatest Catcher*. Jefferson, NC: McFarland, 2004.

McWilliams, John L. *Tuscumbia: America's First Frontier Railroad Town*. Tuscumbia, AL: Tuscumbia Main Street Project and Preservation Incentive Project, 1989.

Parker, Clifton Blue. *Big and Little Poison: Paul and Lloyd Waner, Baseball Brothers*. Jefferson, NC: McFarland, 2003.

Povich, Shirley. *The Washington Senators*. New York: Putnam, 1954.

Ritter, Lawrence. *The Glory of Their Times*. New York: Macmillan, 1966. Republished 2002.

Sarnoff, Gary A. *The Wrecking Crew of '33*: Jefferson, NC: McFarland, 2009.

Smiles, Jack. *Big Ed Walsh: The Life and Times of a Spitball Hall of Famer*. Jefferson, NC: McFarland, 2008.

Smith, Ira L. *Baseball's Famous Outfielders*. New York: A.S. Barnes, 1954.

Smiles, Jack. *"Ee-Yah": The Life and Times of Hughie Jennings, Baseball Hall of Famer*. Jefferson, NC: McFarland, 2005.

Sparks, Barry. *Frank "Home Run" Baker: Hall of Famer and World Series Hero*. Jefferson, NC: McFarland, 2006.

Stump, Al. *Cobb: A Biography*. Chapel Hill: Algonquin Books, 1994.

Thomas, Henry W. *Walter Johnson: Baseball's Big Train*. Lincoln: University of Nebraska, 1995.

Ward, Geoffrey C., and Ken Burns. *Baseball: An Illustrated History*. New York: Knopf, 1994.

Zingg, Paul J. *Harry Hooper: An American Baseball Life*. Urbana: University of Illinois Press, 1993.

Newspapers and Publications

Baseball Digest
Baseball Magazine
Chicago Daily News
Chicago Tribune
Detroit Free Press
Detroit News
Philadelphia Inquirer
The Sporting News

Interviews

Dan Heilmann, Harry Heilmann III, Marguerite Heilmann, Ernie Harwell, George Kell, Susan (Manush) McCaw, Howard Stitzel, Norma Manush, Frank Manush

Other Sources

The files at the National Baseball Hall of Fame Library in the A. Bartlett Giamatti Research Center at the National Baseball Hall of Fame and Museum in Cooperstown, N.Y. Files include unidentified newspaper clippings in each player's file.
"Senators' Hitting Streaks and Their Contributions to Pennants in 1924 and 1933," by Steve Krevisky. A presentation at the 39th SABR National Convention, July 30–August 2, 2009, Washington, D.C.

INDEX